The Rhodesian Problem

The Author

Elaine Windrich was formerly a Professor of Political Science at Stanford University. She has been a research adviser to the Commonwealth Department of the Labour Party and a research officer in the British Information Service and Ministry of Overseas Development. At present she is a Visiting Scholar at the University of California, Los Angeles.

WINDRICH, Elaine. The Rhodesian problem; a documentary record, 1923–1973. Routledge & Kegan Paul, 1975. 312p bibl (World studies series). 18.75. ISBN 0-7100-8080-8

The series is designed to illustrate specific problems in modern history by means of documents and is intended for undergraduates and senior students in British secondary schools. Windrich, a political scientist, and formerly a research officer for the Labour party, has included documents from a great variety of sources — excerpts from speeches, books, newspaper articles, committee reports, broadcasts, etc. These are elucidated by a short introduction and brief comments. Political issues are stressed. The book would have benefited had the author provided more details with regard to military and economic questions. As she sees it, "what has kept the white power structure intact, in a society in which Africans outnumber Europeans by a margin of over twenty to one, is the security legislation that has been enacted particularly since the 1950's." This explanation does not, by itself, account for the Europeans' ability, up to now, to surmount the boycott, diversify their industrial and agricultural production, and make do with a relatively small military establishment. Competent index, but inadequate bibliography. For larger college libraries.

THE WORLD STUDIES SERIES

General Editor: JAMES HENDERSON, M.A., Ph.D.

Senior Lecturer in Education with special reference to Teaching of History and International Affairs, Institute of Education, University of London

Editorial Board: MOTHER MARY de SALES, M.A., Principal Lecturer in History, Coloma College

JOSEPH HUNT, M.A., Senior History Master, City of London School

JAMES JOLL, M.A., Professor of International History, London School of Economics and Politics, University of London

ESMOND WRIGHT, M.A.

VOLUMES PUBLISHED

Malaysia and its Neighbours, J. M. Gullick.

The European Common Market and Community, Uwe Kitzinger, Fellow of Nuffield College, Oxford.

The Politics of John F. Kennedy, Edmund Ions, Department of History, Columbia University, New York.

Apartheid: A Documentary Study of Modern South Africa, Edgar H. Brookes.

Israel and the Arab World, C. H. Dodd, Department of Government, University of Manchester, and M. E. Sales, Centre for Middle Eastern and Islamic Studies, University of Durham.

The Theory and Practice of Neutrality in the Twentieth Century, Roderick Ogley, Department of International Relations, University of Sussex.

The Search for Peace, D. W. Bowett, The President, Queens' College, Cambridge.

Soviet Foreign Policy since the Death of Stalin, H. Hanak, School of Slavonic and East European Studies, and University College, London.

Northern Ireland: Crisis and Conflict, John Magee, Department of History, St Joseph's College of Education, Belfast.

The Rhodesian Problem

A Documentary Record 1923–1973

Elaine Windrich

*Visiting Scholar, University of California,
Los Angeles*

LONDON AND BOSTON
ROUTLEDGE & KEGAN PAUL

First published in 1975
by Routledge & Kegan Paul Ltd
Broadway House, 68–74 Carter Lane,
London EC4V 5EL and
9 Park Street,
Boston, Mass. 02108, USA
Set in Monotype Baskerville
and printed in Great Britain by
Butler & Tanner Ltd, Frome and London

© *Elaine Windrich 1975*

ISBN 0 7100 8080 8

To Marc,
who doesn't deserve it

Contents

24. Guy Clutton-Brock, *Let Tangwena Be*, 1969   135
25. The Land Tenure Act, *Parliamentary Debates*, 15
    October 1969   142
26. Peter Gibbs, 'The New Industrial Conciliation Bill',
    Central African Examiner, 28 February 1959   148
27. P. F. Sithole, 'Labour Problems', *Rhodesian Journal
    of Economics*, December 1972   153
28. 'Rhodesia's Labour Calm', *Financial Mail* (Johan-
    nesburg), 5 April 1973   159
29. *Report of UN Commission on Human Rights*, 1971–3   165
30. *Judges' Report, Education Commission*, 1962   171
31. African Education, *Parliamentary Debates*, 20 April
    1966   174
32. 'African Education', *Zimbabwe Review*, 30 August
    1969   178
33. *UNESCO Report*, 25 January 1973   180
34. Jack Halpern, 'Polarisation in Rhodesia: State,
    Church and People', *The World Today*, January 1971   185
35A and B. *Municipal Amendment Act*, 1967, and Minis-
    terial Statement, *Parliamentary Debates*, 7 November
    1967   191
36. UN Secretariat, *Objective: Justice*, April–June 1973   194

PART VIII: THE INDEPENDENCE ISSUE

37. *Documents on the Negotiations, 1963–5*   201
38. Labour Government Statement, 27 October 1964   208
39. The Rhodesian UDI, 11 November 1965   210
40. *Proposals for a Settlement, 1966*   212
41. Leo Baron, 'The 1961 Constitution and the *Tiger*
    Proposals', *The World Today*, September 1967   220
42. *The Pearce Report on Rhodesian Opinion*, May 1972   227
43. Ian Smith, broadcast to the nation, 23 May 1972   235

PART IX: THE WORLD OUTSIDE

44. Prime Minister's address to *UN General Assembly*, 16
    December 1965   237
45. 'A Hard Look at Sanctions', *Financial Times*, 23 June
    1969   240

CONTENTS

General Editor's Preface

The World Studies Series is designed to make a new and important contribution to the study of modern history. Each volume in the Series will provide students in sixth forms, Colleges of Education and Universities with a range of contemporary material drawn from many sources, not only from official and semi-official records, but also from contemporary historical writing from reliable journals. The material is selected and introduced by a scholar who establishes the context of his subject and suggests possible lines of discussion and enquiry that can accompany a study of the documents.

Through these volumes the student can learn how to read and assess historical documents. He will see how the contemporary historian works and how historical judgments are formed. He will learn to discriminate among a number of sources and to weigh the evidence. He is confronted with recent instances of what Professor Butterfield has called 'the human predicament' revealed by history; evidence concerning the national, racial and ideological factors which at present hinder or advance man's progress towards some kind of world society.

Wherever and whenever the problem of disentangling the relationships between whites and non-whites has arisen, its nature cries out for historical interpretation. This is especially true of Rhodesia, where a minority white settler population confronts a massive black majority that until recently has been politically impotent. The attempt to keep it so by the Smith régime has been threatened by the British Government, against which it is still technically in a state of rebellion, and by United Nations sanctions (both so far ineffectively), and now, much more seriously, by the activities of the indigenous black people themselves. How all this has come about is both soberly and dramatically illustrated by Dr Windrich through the documents and comment which she provides in the following pages.

JAMES HENDERSON

Acknowledgments

The author and publishers wish to thank the following for kind permission to print in this volume extracts from the works cited:

Her Majesty's Stationery Office for Command Papers

Financial Times, for J. D. F. Jones, 'A Hard Look at Sanctions'

Collins Publishers and Sir Roy Welensky for *4,000 Days*

Moto, Mambo Press for 'Provincialization' by Rev. Canaan Banana

Pall Mall Press Ltd and Praeger Publishers Inc. for Frank Clements, *Rhodesia: The Course to Collision*

Africa Contemporary Record for memorandum to the OAU Conference from the President of Tanzania

George Allen & Unwin Ltd for Sir Robert Tredgold, *The Rhodesia That Was My Life*

A. D. Peters and Company for Lord Chandos, *The Memoirs of Lord Chandos*. Reprinted by permission

Leicester University Press and Dr James Barber for 'The Impact of the Rhodesian Crisis on the Commonwealth' in *Journal of Commonwealth Political Studies*

Editorial Board, *Rhodesian Journal of Economics*, for P. F. Sithole, 'Labour Problems in Rhodesia'

The Times for Eshmael M'lambo, 'A Measure of Civilization'. Reprinted by permission

Africa Report for Davis M'Gabe, 'Rhodesia's African Majority' and Peter Niesewand, 'What Smith Really Faces'

The Scandinavian Institute of African Studies for *Southern Africa: The UN/OAU Conference*

Africa Bureau for *Newsbrief Rhodesia*; K. E. E. Brown, *Land in Southern Rhodesia*; and Guy Arnold and Alan Baldwin, *Token Sanctions or Total Economic Warfare*

Mr Leo Baron and the Royal Institute of International Affairs (also on behalf of the late J. Halpern) for material originally published in *The World Today* (September 1967/January 1971), the monthly journal published by the Royal Institute of International Affairs, London

Professor Claire Palley and the Institute of Race Relations for 'Law and Unequal Society' in *Race*

Zimbabwe Review for 'African Education'

Financial Mail (Johannesburg) for 'Rhodesia's Labour Calm'

International Studies and Mr Anirudha Gupta for 'The Rhodesian Crisis and the Organisation of African Unity'

Macmillan, London and Basingstoke, and Mr Harold Macmillan for *Pointing the Way* and *The End of the Day*. Reprinted by permission

The Controller of the Department of Printing and Stationery, Salisbury, Rhodesia

United Nations Publication Board for UN and UNESCO Publications

J. M. Dent & Sons Ltd, Janson-Smith Ltd and Mr James Griffiths for *Pages from Memory*

Mr Guy Clutton-Brock for *Let Tangwena Be*

The author wishes to thank the Hoover Library, Stanford University, for the generous provision of research facilities extended to a Visiting Scholar.

Introduction

Rhodesia is in fact the microcosm of today.
Accidents of history have emphasised, but not created,
problems which are already common to humanity.
                                    Frank Clements, 1969

Rhodesia* remains one of the last strongholds of white supremacy on the African continent. Thus far it has managed to withstand the pressures from both internal opposition and external forces to accept the necessity for a radical transformation of the white power structure. It also remains the only British overseas territory not to have experienced colonial rule, nor to have undergone the transition from European minority to African majority control. The determination of the future status of this territory is legally retained by the Parliament at Westminster. But while Britain has continued to bear the sole responsibility for the colony, she has consistently denied that she has the power to exercise it. As a former Commonwealth Secretary defined the problem, in Rhodesia the British Government have 'responsibility without power'.

ORIGINS OF THE PROBLEM

Rhodesia's unique position today—a British 'self-governing' colony in a state of rebellion—has its origin in the manner in which the country was founded (see Document 1). Unlike other British colonial territories which were, in turn, occupied, annexed and governed by Britain, Rhodesia has never experi-

* The official name of the colony is Southern Rhodesia, but the 'Southern' was dropped from common usage after Northern Rhodesia became independent as Zambia in 1964. The United Nations maintains the legal title, Southern Rhodesia, often followed by 'Zimbabwe', the name used by the African nationalists.

enced a British military or administrative presence. The country was occupied in 1890 by a 'pioneer column' of Europeans from South Africa and administered by Rhodes's British South Africa Company on the basis of a Charter granted by the British Government. From Chartered Company rule, it made a direct transition in 1923 to Crown colony status, with 'responsible government' under the control of the European settlers. Union with South Africa was rejected as an alternative and a financial settlement with the British South Africa Company brought an end to nearly thirty-five years of Company rule. During these years that rule had been established by the conquest of the Mashona and the Matabele peoples, culminating in the suppression of the revolts in 1896. Control of the African population was exercised by the Company's Native Commissioner and the use of African labour in the mines and on the farms was enforced by the levying of taxes which could only be met from wages earned in the European economy. Safeguards for the Africans were limited to the British requirement that the Company set aside for agricultural and pastoral purposes a portion of land known as the 'Native Reserves'. Company rule also came to an end at the same time in the Northern Rhodesian territory, where direct control by the Crown was assumed over the Protectorate and the traditional pattern of British colonial administration established.

Since 1923 three main objectives have dominated Rhodesia's development as a self-governing colony: the achievement of independence from Britain (however slight the British connection remained); the creation of a 'greater Rhodesia' by the extension of European control from Salisbury to the northern territory of Rhodesia; and the preservation of the privileged position of a white society founded upon the exploitation of a black majority.

A 'GREATER RHODESIA'

Ironically, when Company rule came to an end, the Europeans in Southern Rhodesia were opposed to any link with Northern Rhodesia, because they feared that a connection with an adjacent territory under British protection and with a small white population would only delay the achievement of internal self-government, which was then their primary objective. But within a few years, with the discovery of the wealth of the Copperbelt, the movement began to persuade the British to consider an amalgamation of the two territories, in order that the Europeans in the southern territory might reap the financial benefits from the north. Thus began the pressures over a period of nearly three decades that culminated in the British Government's acquiescence to a union with the northern territories. The Central African Federation was imposed in 1953, against the almost universal opposition of the Africans, especially in the Protectorates of Northern Rhodesia and Nyasaland, and of the Labour and Liberal Parties in Britain.

However, the Southern Rhodesians soon discovered, in the course of their efforts to establish and then to preserve the Federation, that their three objectives were in fact incompatible. So long as Britain retained responsibility for the advancement of the Africans in the northern territories, independence for a Federation dominated by a European minority in Salisbury was ruled out. The result was that, when the British finally agreed to meet the African nationalist demands in the northern territories for secession and independence, Southern Rhodesia was left with neither the Federation nor her own independence.

THE DRIVE TO INDEPENDENCE

However, Southern Rhodesia did manage to obtain a major concession from the British in the form of a new Constitution in 1961, which, as a prelude to independence, abolished the reserved powers Britain had retained under the Constitutional Letters Patent of 1923 to intervene in Rhodesian affairs on behalf of 'native interests'—a power never in fact exercised in more than an occasional advisory manner. But Southern Rhodesia was still one step short of independence. Before this could be conceded the British Government were insistent that there had to be a greatly extended franchise to enable the Africans to gain access to political power, and a major reform of the discrimatory legislation enacted by the white 'Establishment'. Since no government in Southern Rhodesia was able or willing to make these concessions, and thus incur the risk of being evicted from power by a white electorate determined to retain their privileged position, the independence negotiations with the British reached deadlock and the Rhodesians resorted to an illegal declaration (UDI) in November 1965.

RHODESIAN-STYLE APARTHEID

The society which the Rhodesians were determined to preserve from British, or indeed from any outside interference, was founded on a system of racial segregation built up over the years since the foundation of the country. Unlike the South Africans, who had an ideological and a religious basis for their doctrine of apartheid, the Rhodesians never formulated any clear definition of the racial divisions upon which their society was based. Perhaps the inhibition was attributable to the fear (from which the South Africans had been freed in 1910) that to do so openly would be to court British censure, if not interference, since Britain retained the role of the final arbiter on matters affecting African interests. But in practice, the terms 'parallel development', as used by Huggins and the 'Establishment' party (in power for a generation), or 'separate development', as used by the Rhodesian Front of Mr Ian Smith, amounted to the English equivalent of the Afrikaner apartheid, although the latter, besides having the religious foundation, had also as its ultimate objective the complete (although unrealisable) partition of society into racially designated areas.

The principle of 'separate development' has been applied to every aspect of Rhodesian society. Perhaps the most significant, because on this depends the whole economic and social structure of the country, is the land division. Beginning with the designation of 'Native Reserves' under the Chartered Company rule and culminating in the Land Tenure allocations of 1969, the country has been divided and classified into racially restricted areas. The division is itself a reflection of inequality, in that an equal proportion of land is set aside for a population of over five million Africans and only some 250,000 Europeans. Furthermore, the land traditionally reserved for European occupation has been the best for farming purposes and has been located in the developed areas and along the line of rail. The exclusion of Africans from the ownership of property in the

European urban areas has also had a significant effect on their impoverishment. With political power linked to earnings and the ownership of 'immovable' property, the African has been effectively excluded by land apportionment and by the job reservation system governing urban employment.

Political power is also linked with educational attainment, particularly for the African who cannot hope to achieve the high level of income or property readily available to the Europeans. The two separate systems of education in effect throughout the colony's existence have ensured the perpetuation of a segregated society and have provided an additional barrier to political advance. Education is neither free nor compulsory for Africans and access to secondary education (required for the vote) is limited by the costs imposed and by the inadequate places provided for even those qualified to obtain them. If anything, educational policy for Africans has been retrogressive. Scarcely any other country in the world (except perhaps the Colonels' Greece) even boasted of the reduction of primary education as an educational achievement. In addition, teachers' pay has been cut and mission schools have accordingly been forced to close down. The 'new plan', hailed by the Rhodesian Front in 1966 as a great advance for the Africans, in fact amounts to providing them with an inferior (deceptively labelled 'junior', i.e. vocational) form of secondary education suitable for the type of unskilled labour required for the European industries and farms and in the Tribal Trust Lands set aside for African 'development'.

Social segregation has always been enforced, both by custom and by law. The Rhodesian Front régime maintains the doctrine of 'separate but equal', which in application is anything but equal, since the facilities available are equitable only 'according to the needs of each race', the latter being defined by the responsible 'Minister'. From swimming pools to bars, to hotels and postal facilities, segregation has been intensified since the accession to power of the Rhodesian Front régime. The whole system is regulated by the imposition upon the African population of identification and registration requirements and the application of fines and imprisonment for any violations.

REPRESSION

What has kept the white power structure intact, in a society in which Africans outnumber Europeans by a margin of over twenty to one, is the security legislation that has been enacted, particularly since the 1950s, to cover any eventuality of political protest, peaceful or otherwise. In addition, an effective police and military organisation has been built up over the years since Federation to deter and to destroy any threats to the Rhodesian concept of 'law and order'. The result has been to render the Africans powerless, by the detention of their leaders and the terrorisation of their supporters. Even the small segment of white 'liberal' opinion, which at least opposed the more blatant police state measures and the intensification of segregation, has been silenced, and its efforts to revive a political opposition frustrated by the increasing tendency of the European electorate to maintain a 'white laager' mentality.

THE RESORT TO CONFRONTATION

African nationalists, who in the late 1950s began to organise a political movement along the same lines as those of their counterparts in other British colonial territories, soon experienced the full rigours of the security legislation enacted to prevent such opposition. And unlike their counterparts elsewhere in Africa, they had not the ultimate safeguard of British protection or even the assurance of British mediation in any conflict between the two races, since no British presence ever existed inside the country. Three African nationalist parties, which were successively founded to operate within the prevailing political system, were in turn banned, and their organisations destroyed. In these circumstances, and in the absence of British intervention, a peaceful transition to African majority rule was never a real possibility under a constitutional system that could be made to operate to impede African advance and to ensure European domination.

The result has been that the Africans, deprived of any constitutional means of opposing the white minority régime, or of any British support in doing so, have chosen the path of confrontation. Since the Unilateral Declaration of Independence in 1965, increasing numbers of Africans have gone into exile—in Zambia, in Tanzania, in Britain and elsewhere—to carry on the political struggle or to join the military wing of the liberation movement. What at first amounted to a token resistance, easily detectable and suppressed, has now become a major force to be reckoned with. This is evident from the panic security measures enacted by the rebel régime—including the extension of the call-up to age groups hitherto exempt, and the importation of South African troops into a British colony to bolster the relatively small forces available to the European population.

EXTERNAL FACTORS

Until the 1960s Rhodesia was a relatively unknown factor to the world outside. But at the beginning of that decade, in which most of the African colonial territories advanced to independence, Southern Rhodesia was defined by the United Nations as a dependent territory to which its Declaration on the Granting of Independence to Colonial Countries and Peoples should apply. Consequently, since 1961 there have been annual debates and a series of resolutions on the issue of self-determination for the people of 'Zimbabwe', in an effort to convince the administering power, namely Britain, to take all measures, including force, to achieve this objective. United Nations action was intensified after the illegal declaration of independence by the decision that the situation in Southern Rhodesia constituted a threat to international peace and security and therefore subject to action under Chapter VII of the Charter. Economic sanctions were imposed, in varying degrees of stringency, escalating to mandatory and then to comprehensive. On all occasions when the issue of Rhodesia came before the United Nations, British policy was to restrain any action (in particular the use of military force) that went beyond the imposition of economic sanctions, even if this meant resorting to the veto in the Security Council, which it did, in fact, on nine occasions.

Similar pressures—to bring about the downfall of the white minority régime and to ensure that majority rule prevailed before independence was legally conceded—came from the overwhelming majority of the members of the Commonwealth and from the Organisation of African Unity, the latter comprising the independent African states who joined together in 1963 to work towards continental unity and the liberation of the remnants of colonialism. As pressure groups on behalf of the liberation of Zimbabwe, they also operated through the various agencies of the United Nations in concert with other sympathetic member states. Although no tangible results in the way of liberation have followed from resolutions emanating from the OAU or the UN, or from communiqués from the Commonwealth Prime Ministers conferences, they have served to keep alive the plight of the majority of the Rhodesian people and focused world attention on the possible means of alleviating those conditions. Certainly the United Nations sanctions programme has had the effect of at least eroding the basis of the Rhodesian economy in terms of withholding international investment for expansion and of making 'sanctions busting' an increasingly expensive and difficult task. Diplomatic isolation has also had its effect. It does matter—certainly to the Europeans in Rhodesia, in spite of what they may profess—that no country in the world has recognised their illegal independence, not even South Africa, who continues to supply them with material assistance. It also matters to the Africans in Rhodesia that world opinion is on their side, that they have not yet been 'sold out' by the British (although the 1971 Home-Smith deal was a close call) and that their case will not be allowed to be lost through default. As the Pearce Commission described the African response in 1972, 'if people genuinely prefer hope to present realities they are entitled to do so'.

FUTURE PROSPECTS?

Any consideration of the Rhodesian issue must of necessity leave a number of questions unanswered. In historical perspective it is possible to see how and when the initial errors were made. But it is less easy to predict the future, because the situation in that country cannot remain static but must be resolved in one way or another.

1   Many of the problems that exist today might have been avoided had Rhodesia followed the same pattern as other

British colonial territories that are now independent and ruled by the majority of the indigenous inhabitants. Is the present situation the result of Britain's reluctance to assume responsibility for the political advance and the economic development of the majority of the population, namely the Africans, and decision to surrender control over these matters to a white minority régime?

2   After the achievement of 'responsible government' in 1923, the European settler governments steadily built up a racially segregated society in which white minority rule and privilege were entrenched. Could Britain have prevented, or even modified, this development by exercising her 'reserved powers' on behalf of the African majority?

3   In view of the Europeans' determination to maintain at all costs the control of political power, was an independence agreement with the British ever a real possibility, so long as Britain insisted upon evidence of progress towards African majority rule and an end to measures of racial segregation?

4   When it became evident that the Rhodesians would not get independence on their own terms, was a Unilateral Declaration of Independence inevitable? The British Government, before the event, announced that they would never use force either to prevent it or to impose African majority rule. Was this a tactical error that encouraged the Rhodesians to go ahead and take the risk of no retaliation?

5   The main question regarding force is no longer whether it will be used to resolve the conflict, but whose force will be decisive. Will the African liberation movement be able to mount sufficient strength to challenge successfully a formidable European defence? Can the guerrillas enlist the aid of other African States in their struggle? With South African forces already stationed inside Rhodesia, a racial conflict in southern Africa would seem to be inevitable. The Zambian President, Dr Kaunda, has already warned of the dangers of a 'race war', and of the even wider implications of an ideological or 'hot war', in which the liberation forces, armed and trained to a large extent by the Russians and the Chinese, would confront a European alliance deriving its military support mainly from NATO and other Western sources.

6   Britain's role in a conflict situation will inevitably be an

uneasy one. Thus far she has relied upon United Nations assistance for the implementation of the sanctions programme which she initiated. She has been committed to intervention in Rhodesia only on the occasion of 'a breakdown of law and order' in her own colony. But on whose side is she to intervene should this eventuality occur? There is no 'legal' government in Rhodesia which could evoke British or any other outside support (except South Africa) against African violence, either in the form of an internal rebellion or an external invasion, or even both. Britain has never been committed to 'impose' African majority rule by the use of force. On the contrary, she has repeatedly denied the intention of any such action. Nor is there an African government-in-exile which could appeal for British assistance or recognition, even if Britain were willing to provide the one or concede the other.

PART I

A 'Self-Governing Colony'

Since its foundation by the pioneer column of Europeans, encouraged by the imperial expansionist aims of Cecil Rhodes and the British South Africa Company, Southern Rhodesia had been governed by the Company under the provisions of the Charter granted by the British Government in 1889, for a period of not less than twenty-five years. During this period, the Chartered Company met the costs of administering the country, thus saving the British Treasury from the burden of expenditure. The British presence, as well as responsibility for the preservation of 'native interests', was vested in the person of the High Commissioner, who was also the Governor-General of the Union of South Africa.

As the number of European settlers increased and as they gained a majority over the Company's representatives on the Legislative Council, pressure was exerted on the British Government for the grant of 'responsible government' (in the sense of control of domestic affairs) and the termination of Company rule. Since the British Government were concerned about the ability of a small white community to finance the costs of administering a large territory, with a sizeable 'native' population, and not wishing to incur the burden themselves, they had envisaged the future of the territory as an additional province of the Union of South Africa. However, while the European settlers had firmly rejected suggestions for incorporation into the Union, the British Government had either to administer the territory themselves, thus incurring a large financial liability at a time of post-war economic recession, or accede to the request

I

of the overwhelming majority of the Europeans for the establishment of 'responsible government' under the control of the local white population.

It was in these circumstances that the then Colonial Secretary, Winston Churchill, appointed a Royal Commission under the chairmanship of Lord Buxton (Governor-General of the Union of South Africa and High Commissioner until 1920) to advise on 'when and with what limitations (if any) responsible government should be granted to Southern Rhodesia'.

The Committee's recommendations were in favour of the immediate grant of responsible government, provided that the approval of the electorate was obtained in a referendum on the issue, and subject to the reservation of certain matters—such as 'native interests' and unaliented land—to the Imperial Government.

The following document provides the historical background for the foundation of the colony and its transition from Company rule to responsible government.

DOCUMENT 1. *First Report of a Committee Appointed by the Secretary of State for the Colonies to Consider Certain Questions Relating to Rhodesia* (APRIL 1921, CMD 1273), THE BUXTON REPORT

The Right Honourable Winston S. Churchill, M.P.

4. Our Terms of Reference as regards Southern Rhodesia were as follows:

(1) When and with what limitations (if any) Responsible Government should be granted to Southern Rhodesia.

(2) What procedure should be adopted with a view to working out the future constitution.

(3) Pending the coming into effect of Responsible Government what measures will be required to enable the British South Africa Company to carry on the administration.

5. We think it may be well to preface the Report with a short historical account of Southern Rhodesia as far as the present position is concerned.

6. The Administration of Southern Rhodesia is at present in the hands of the British South Africa Company under the Charter granted in 1889. The Charter reserved to the Crown

the power at the end of twenty-five years from the date of the Charter, and at the end of every succeeding period of ten years, to add to, or repeal any of the provisions of the Charter relating to administrative and public matters.

7. In 1894 the first Matabeleland Order in Council was passed, and in 1898, after the Jameson Raid and the Matabele and Mashona revolts, a further Order in Council was issued. Under the provisions of the latter Order the Imperial Government took definite powers to exercise control over the administration of the country. They appointed a Resident Commissioner to represent locally the High Commissioner, and an Imperial Commandant General to be the head of the Police and armed forces. At the same time the Legislative Council was established to which, in the first instance, the settlers were to be entitled to elect a minority of the members. Since then the elected element on the Council has been greatly developed; and the Council now consists of thirteen Elected Members and six Members nominated by the British South Africa Company.

8. In 1914, when the period of twenty-five years expired, His Majesty's Government decided, with the concurrence of the newly elected Legislative Council of Southern Rhodesia, which had adopted a Resolution asking that there might be no change in the form of Administration, to continue the administrative provisions of the Charter.

9. It was felt, however, that the circumstances of Southern Rhodesia were changing, and that His Majesty's Government would not be justified in binding themselves to a continuance of the Company's Administration for a full period of ten years. They accordingly obtained the consent of the Company to a modification of the Charter. Under a Supplemental Charter it was provided that if, at any time after the 29th October, 1914, the Legislative Council of Southern Rhodesia should by the absolute majority of the whole number of the members of the Council, as then constituted, pass a resolution praying the Crown to establish in Southern Rhodesia the form of Government known as 'Responsible Government' and should support such resolution with evidence, showing that the condition of the Territory—financially and in other respects—was such as to justify the establishment of Responsible Government, it would be lawful for the Crown to accede to the prayer of such resolution

and to modify the Charter accordingly. There is no power, however, to institute any other form of government (except with the consent of the British South Africa Company) before the end of the period of ten years, which expires in October, 1924.

10. The main question on which the Election of April, 1914, of the Legislative Council took place, was whether the Administration of the Company should continue for the present. The Members who advocated this course were returned in a large majority.

11. In May, 1919, when a further election was in prospect, the Elected Members of the Legislative Council passed a Resolution to the effect that, as the issues which would arise at the election would turn on the desirability of terminating the administration of the British South Africa Company and of replacing it by some other form of government more suited to the needs and requirements of the Country, the Secretary of State should be requested to state for public information, what proof of fitness, financially and in other respects, would be considered sufficient to justify the grant of Responsible Government to Southern Rhodesia.

12. Lord Milner, in his reply, of 12th August, 1919, stated that apart from the important question arising out of the small number of the white, as compared to the native population, he could not regard the Territory as equal, at its present stage of development, to the financial burden of Responsible Government; that it would have to meet onerous charges in connexion with capital and other expenditure, while the result of the findings of the Judicial Committee would adversely affect its financial position. He went on to mention possible alternatives: Incorporation in the Union, Representative Government, and a continuance, for the present, of the Company's Administration. He stated that he was personally inclined to the view that it would be best, in the interests of all concerned, to carry on under the present system until the situation became somewhat clearer; but that this would not necessarily involve the maintenance of that system for five years.

13. The election took place in April 1920. Out of the thirteen Elected Members twelve were returned pledged to the introduction, at an early date, of Responsible Government.

The other Member, Mr. Fletcher, was in favour of a scheme of Representative Government, and did not advocate the continuance of Chartered rule.

The voting, as analysed by the Resident Commissioner, was as follows:

For Responsible Government, including Labour vote	4,663
For Representative Government under the Crown	420
For Union with South Africa	814
For continuation of the British South Africa Company's Administration	868
	6,765

The total number of registered voters (not including one Constituency in which there was no poll) was 11,098. It will be seen that, out of the 6,765 voters who polled not more than 868 voted in favour of the continuance of Chartered Company administration.

14. At the first meeting of the new Legislative Council, in May, 1920, a Resolution was passed praying that Responsible Government should be established forthwith in Southern Rhodesia. This resolution was supported by all the Elected Members, with the exception of Mr. Fletcher, and also received the support of one of the Nominated Members.

15. The Resolution sought to prove to the Secretary of State that Southern Rhodesia was, financially and in other respects, in a position to undertake the obligations of Responsible Government. . . .

17. After some further communication with the Elected Members and with the British South Africa Company, Lord Milner, on 22nd December, 1920, replied in a Memorandum to the representations of the Elected Members.

18. The substance of the Memorandum was as follows:

The Secretary of State stated that he appreciated the desire of the majority of the Elected Members to take over the Administration, and the willingness of the British South Africa Company to be relieved of its responsibilities, and that 'in principle he was entirely disposed to give effect to that desire.' His difficulty, however, was as to the moment when this could be done. Various reasons for delay were detailed; and he proposed that the present administration should continue until after the next General Election, which, in the ordinary course, would take place early in 1923. If, as a result of that election, there should be another expression of opinion by the new Council in favour of Responsible Government, then His Majesty's Government would take the necessary steps for bringing Responsible Government into force not later than October, 1924. . . .

19. In January, 1921, the Elected Members replied at considerable length to this Memorandum. They traversed some of the arguments of the Secretary of State in favour of delay, and especially urged that Responsible Government should be brought into force at a very much earlier date than that proposed by him. They emphasized that the mandate given at the recent election was clear and unmistakable, and had proved that the Country was practically unanimously in favour of Responsible Government; and argued that as the question of the fitness of the Country, financially and in other respects, was no longer in question, that it was unreasonable to insist that the grant of Self-Government must be preceded by another election. . . .

20. This, then, was the political position in Southern Rhodesia when the Committee were asked to undertake their duties.

21. It is necessary, before proceeding further, to deal shortly with another aspect of the question.

Until the year 1914, the British South Africa Company believed that, in view of certain concessions which the Company had obtained from Lobengula, and of other circumstances, the unalienated land in Southern Rhodesia belonged to the Company absolutely. . . .

22. In April, 1914, the Elected Members passed a resolution asserting that the British South Africa Company were not owners of the land, but that it belonged to the Government which would sometime or other supersede the Company. This view was stoutly disputed by the Company; and, in July, 1914, the question at issue was referred to the Judicial Committee.

23. From time to time, previously to 1914, the Elected Members had raised the question whether the Company did actually own the land. His Majesty's Government for long

declined to intervene; but at the end of 1913, in view of the approaching expiration of the twenty-five years' term of the Charter, decided that the question ought to be referred to the Judicial Committee of the Privy Council.

24. The Judicial Committee reported in July, 1918. They stated that the unalienated land belonged to the Crown and not to the British South Africa Company; but that, until the administration of the Company should be determined by the Crown, the Company were entitled to dispose of the unalienated lands in the due course of administration, and to apply the monies or revenues derived therefrom in duly reimbursing all proper outlays on administrative account in the current or in past years. . . .

94. But government by a Chartered Company of an organized and civilized Territory, which Southern Rhodesia has become, is an obvious anomaly and anachronism; and it is natural that its citizens should desire a system of government more in accordance with the present position of the Country. This desire the Company have, we think, fully recognized. . . .

97. The people of Southern Rhodesia have themselves a record of loyalty and patriotism second to none within the Possessions and Protectorates of the Crown; and they have proved themselves, in times of war and in times of peace, worthy of the confidence of His Majesty's Government.

98. We have, as already stated, proposed that there should be somewhat strict reservations on behalf of the natives of Southern Rhodesia.

These we consider necessary in present circumstances, and, indeed, the Elected Members themselves volunteered to agree to them. But we would like to say that this offer is in keeping with the general attitude of the white population towards the natives in Southern Rhodesia, and the administration of native affairs in the Territory which, so far as we can ascertain, are quite satisfactory.

Conclusions

99. We now proceed to sum up our Recommendations in regard to Southern Rhodesia, on all of which the Committee are unanimous.

We recommend:

(1) That in the interest of Southern Rhodesia, and of all concerned, the question whether Southern Rhodesia is or is not prepared to adopt Responsible Government should be decided one way or the other at the earliest possible moment.

(2) That before Responsible Government is actually granted, the electors of Southern Rhodesia should be given a definite opportunity of expressing their opinion for or against its adoption.

(3) That as the electors have so recently expressed their views on the abstract proposition for or against Responsible Government no advantage would be gained by another vote on this abstract question. A scheme for Responsible Government should, therefore, be drawn up in detail and placed before the electors for their acceptance or rejection. The scheme should be put before them in such a way that they will be able to realize exactly the obligations—Constitutional, Administrative, and Financial—that Responsible Government will actually involve, and the limitations which will accompany it.

(4) That this opinion would be better ascertained by means of a referendum rather than by a General Election. . . .

(6) That if there appeared to be general agreement in Southern Rhodesia with the Report of the Committee, the Colonial Office would draft a Constitution on the lines of the Report. . . .

(9) That if the vote on the Referendum should favour the introduction of Responsible Government, a Proclamation or Order in Council should be issued annexing Southern Rhodesia to the King's Dominions.

(10) That annexation should be followed by Letters Patent setting up Responsible Government in Southern Rhodesia.

(11) That the main lines on which a scheme for Responsible Government to be applied to Southern Rhodesia should be based, should (with certain necessary differences and reservations) be such as to place the Colony of Rhodesia in the same position in regard to internal affairs as the Colony of Natal when the latter was granted Responsible Government in 1893.

(12) That certain Limitations or Reservations should be made if, and when, Responsible Government is granted to Southern Rhodesia, i.e.,

(a) That the Natives should be secured in their existing position, and ensured against discriminating disabilities or restrictions.

(b) That special provisions must be made for dealing with the unalienated Land of Southern Rhodesia.

(13) That with regard to the natives, the existing authority and control of the High Commissioner under the Southern Rhodesia Order in Council of 1898 should be substantially maintained.

(14) That as regards the Land, a Land Board should be created, and the control of the unalienated land should be exercised through the High Commissioner on the advice of the Land Board. The Board to consist of three members; one to be nominated by the High Commissioner, one by the Company, and one by the Governor-in-Council. There would, under certain circumstances, be an appeal to the Secretary of State.

(17) That the High Commissionership should continue as at present to be held by the Governor-General of the Union.

BUXTON.
HENRY LAMBERT.
E. W. M. GRIGG.
WALTER WARING.

12TH APRIL, 1921   R. M. GREENWOOD.

THE CONSTITUTIONAL SETTLEMENT

The approval of the European settlers for the grant of responsible government was obtained in the referendum held in October 1922. In a 79 per cent poll, the results were 8,774 for responsible government and 5,989 for union with South Africa. Once agreement had been reached with the Chartered Company on a financial settlement (see Document 3), the new Constitution was brought into operation.

The territory was annexed by Order in Council on 30 July 1923, becoming the Colony of Southern Rhodesia, and by Letters Patent of 1 September it obtained a Constitution conferring responsible government, which came into effect the following month, 1 October 1923.

The Constitution of 1923, while conferring internal self-government, reserved to the British Government significant powers of intervention. It was to provide the constitutional framework of the Colony for a period of nearly forty years. During this time, the British Government never once exercised its power to veto legislation of a discriminatory nature, although advice was sought by the Rhodesian Government in advance of enacting such legislation.

The Constitution provided for a Parliamentary system of government on the 'Westminster model'. The following document contains those sections of the Constitution—on legislation and native administration—which relate to the powers reserved to the British Government. Such powers were retained until the negotiation of alternative guarantees in the 1961 Constitution.

DOCUMENT 2. *Southern Rhodesia: Despatch to the High Commissioner for South Africa Transmitting Draft Letters Patent providing for the Constitution of Responsible Government in the Colony of Southern Rhodesia* (JANUARY 1923, CMD 1573)

Legislation

26. **Power to make Laws.**—(1) It shall be lawful for Us and Our successors, by and with the advice and consent of the Legislature, subject to the provisions of these Our Letters Patent, to make all Laws, to be entitled 'Acts,' which shall be required for the peace, order, and good government of the Colony.

(2) A Law passed by the Legislature may repeal or alter any of the provisions of these Our Letters Patent, save those contained in this section, and those contained in Section 28 (relating to the reservation of Bills), Sections 39–47 (relating to Native Administration), Section 48 (relating to the Crown Land Agent), and Section 55 (relating to the Salary of the Governor), and may likewise repeal or alter any of the provisions of any Order in Our Privy Council extending to Southern Rhodesia other than provisions affecting any matter mentioned in this sub-section.

Provided however that no proposed Law for the constitution of a Legislative Council in pursuance of Section 2 of these Our Letters Patent shall repeal or alter any of the provisions relating to the Legislative Council contained in these Our Letters

Patent, and such provisions shall not be repealed or altered save by a Law passed by both Houses of the Legislature, after the constitution of a Legislative Council as aforesaid.

Provided further that no proposed Law for the repeal or alteration of any such provisions of these Our Letters Patent as may be repealed or altered by the Legislature as aforesaid shall be valid unless it shall be affirmed by not less than two-thirds of the total number of Members of each House of the Legislature, or, pending the constitution of a Legislative Council, of the Legislative Assembly.

(3) Any Law made in contravention of the limitations imposed by Sub-section 2 of this section shall to the extent of such contravention but not otherwise be and remain absolutely void and inoperative.

27. Presentation of Laws for Governor's assent.—When any Law has been passed by the Legislature it shall be presented for Our assent to the Governor, who shall declare according to his discretion, but subject to this Constitution and any instructions in that behalf given him, under Our Sign Manual and Signet, or through a Secretary of State, that he assents in Our name, or that he withholds assent, or that he reserves the Law for the signification of Our pleasure.

28. Description of Bills to be reserved.—Unless he shall have previously obtained Our instructions upon such Law through a Secretary of State, or unless such Law shall contain a clause suspending the operation thereof until the signification in the Colony of Our pleasure thereupon, the Governor shall reserve:

(a) Any Law, save in respect of the supply of arms, ammunition, or liquor to natives, whereby natives may be subjected or made liable to any conditions, disabilities or restrictions to which persons of European descent are not also subjected or made liable.

(b) Any Law which may repeal alter or amend, or is in any way repugnant to or inconsistent with such provisions of these Our Letters Patent, as may under these Our Letters Patent be repealed or altered by the Legislature.

(c) Any Law constituting the Legislative Council passed in pursuance of Section 2 of these Our Letters Patent.

(d) Any Law altering or amending the arrangements relating to the collection and allocation of mining revenues in force at the commencement of these Our Letters Patent under any existing Law of the Colony or otherwise, or any Law imposing any special rate tax or duty on minerals in or under land within the Colony.

(e) Until legislation shall have come into force in Southern Rhodesia adopting, so far as may be applicable, the provisions of the law in force in Our United Kingdom relating to the Railway and Canal Commissioners and to the Rates Tribunal provided for by the Railways Act, 1921, any law dealing with railways within the Colony.

29. Return of Bills by Governor to the Legislature.—The Governor may return to the Legislative Council and Legislative Assembly any proposed Law so presented to him, and may transmit therewith any amendments which he may recommend and the Legislative Council and Legislative Assembly may deal with the recommendation.

30. Assent to Laws and time from which they take effect.— No Law passed by the Legislature shall take effect until either the Governor shall have assented thereto in Our name and on Our behalf, and shall have signed the same in token of such assent, or until We shall have given Our assent thereto by Our Order in Our Privy Council.

Native Administration

39. Native Department and Appointment, etc., of officers of Department.—(1) There shall be a Native Department, the permanent head of which shall be appointed by the Governor in Council with the approval of the High Commissioner, and all Chief Native Commissioners, Superintendents of Natives, Native Commissioners and Assistant Native Commissioners, or any officers appointed to exercise the functions now exercised by the aforesaid officers or any of them shall be appointed in the like manner and subject to the like approval, and the said officers shall continue to perform the duties at present assigned to them subject to any alterations or additions which the Governor in Council may from time to time, with the approval of the High Commissioner, prescribe by notice in the Gazette.

(2) The salaries of the officers mentioned in the preceding sub-section shall be fixed by the Governor in Council with the

approval of the High Commissioner, and shall not be increased or diminished without his approval.

(3) The officers mentioned in this section may at any time be removed from office by the Governor in Council, with the approval of the High Commissioner, but not otherwise.

41. Restrictive Regulations, etc., as regards natives.—No conditions, disabilities or restrictions which do not equally apply to persons of European descent shall, without the previous consent of the High Commissioner, be imposed upon natives (save in respect of the supply of arms, ammunition and liquor), by any Proclamation, Regulation or other instrument issued under the provisions of any Law, unless such conditions, disabilities, or restrictions shall have been explicitly prescribed, defined and limited in such law.

42. Native Reserves.—The Southern Rhodesia Order in Council, 1920, whereby the lands known as the Native Reserves were vested in the High Commissioner and set apart for the sole and exclusive use of the native inhabitants of Southern Rhodesia, shall continue in full force and effect as if it formed part of these Our Letters Patent, and no portion of the land comprised within the said Reserves shall be alienated except for the purposes authorized by the said Order, and then only in exchange for other suitable land.

43. Acquisition of land by natives.—A native may acquire, hold, encumber and dispose of land on the same conditions as a person who is not a native, but no contract for encumbering or alienating land the property of a native shall be valid unless the contract is made in the presence of a Magistrate, is attested by him, and bears a certificate signed by him stating that the consideration for the contract is fair and reasonable, and that he has satisfied himself that the native understands the transaction.

44. Information as to native affairs to be given to High Commissioner.—The Governor shall furnish to the High Commissioner any information relating to native affairs which the High Commissioner may request.

45. Reference of questions relating to natives to a Judge.— The Governor in Council shall, if so requested by the High Commissioner, refer any question relating to natives for report to any Judge of the High Court, and the Judge shall thereupon make such enquiry as he thinks fit, and shall report to the

Governor in Council the result of such enquiry. The Governor shall transmit such report to the High Commissioner with a statement of the action which the Governor in Council proposes to take in the matter.

46. Offences by chiefs or tribes.—In case of a revolt against the Government, or other misconduct committed by a native chief or tribe, the Governor in Council may, with the approval of the High Commissioner, impose a reasonable fine upon the offender.

47. Native Councils.—(1) It shall be lawful for the Governor in Council, subject to the approval of the High Commissioner, at any time after the commencement of these Our Letters Patent, to establish by Proclamation in any Native Reserve or Reserves such Council or Councils of indigenous natives representative of the local chiefs and other native residents as may seem to him expedient, for the discussion from time to time of any matters upon which, as being of direct interest or concern to the native population generally or to any portion thereof, he may desire to ascertain, or they may desire to submit, their views; and, subject to the like approval, to make regulations for the constitution of such Council or Councils, for the appointment of the places and times of meeting, for the manner of conducting the proceedings, and for all other matters incidental or properly appertaining to the establishment and periodical meetings of such Council or Councils, including, if he think fit, the occasional or regular meeting of any two or greater number of such Councils in joint session.

(2) It shall also be lawful for the Governor in Council, subject to the like approval, to make regulations conferring on any such Council such powers of management in connection with local matters affecting the indigenous natives as can in his opinion be safely and satisfactorily undertaken by them, and by such regulations or by any subsequent regulations to make all such provisions as may be necessary in order to give effect to such powers.

THE END OF COMPANY RULE

Before responsible government could be established, a financial settlement had to be reached between the British Government and the British South Africa Company on the termination of the Company's administration. The settlement was to be based on the award of the Cave Commission, appointed in 1919 to report on the sums outstanding to the Company.

The following document contains the correspondence relating to the settlement. The first letter, from the Colonial Office to the British South Africa Company, contains the British terms offered to the Company. The following letter, from Sir Francis Newton (the Southern Rhodesian delegate in London and a previous Treasurer of the Company) to the Colonial Office sets out the offer of the Elected Members of the Southern Rhodesian Legislative Council to meet the payments towards the administrative deficits, and their intention of acquiring certain lands and property formerly held by the Company. The 'Devonshire Agreement', between the British Government and the Company was finally concluded on 29 September 1923.

DOCUMENT 3. *Rhodesia: Correspondence Regarding a Proposed Settlement of Various Outstanding Questions Relating to the British South Africa Company's Position in Southern and Northern Rhodesia* (JULY 1923, CMD 1914)

Colonial Office to British South Africa Company.

Downing Street,
10th July, 1923.
[Without Prejudice.]

Sir,

I am directed by the Duke of Devonshire to refer to the discussions which have taken place with your Directors with a view to considering the possibility of a settlement of the various outstanding questions relating to the Company's position in Southern and Northern Rhodesia. His Majesty's Government have been desirous of arriving at an arrangement which would enable them to vest the unalienated lands in Southern Rhodesia in the new Government, and, in view of the assistance towards this end which has been promised on behalf of the Elected Members of the Legislative Council, they are glad to think that such an arrangement may be possible.

2. After full consideration, His Majesty's Government are now prepared, subject to Parliamentary approval being obtained, to agree to a general settlement on the following basis:

On 1st October, 1923, the date on which Responsible Government is to be established in Southern Rhodesia, His Majesty's Government will pay to the Company the sum of £3,750,000.

His Majesty's Government will make no claim against the Company for the reimbursement of any part of the advances made to the Company in respect of the extraordinary war expenditure incurred by the Company in connection with the late war.

His Majesty's Government and the Company agree to the following arrangements:

A Southern Rhodesia

(1) (a) The Company will accept the above payment of £3,750,000 as including a full discharge of its claims, under the terms of the judgment of the Judicial Committee of the Privy Council, in respect of the administrative deficits incurred by the Company in Southern Rhodesia up to the termination of its administration. The Company will accordingly withdraw the Petition of Right now pending and will forgo all rights and interests in the lands in Southern Rhodesia except in the estates, farms and ranches which the Company is developing and working on commercial lines as they exist at the date of this letter. Suitable steps will be taken to vest such estates, farms and ranches in the Company, subject to payment of quit rent. The Crown will make no demand upon the Company in respect of the matters referred to in paragraph 7 of the Report of Lord Cave's Commission (Parly. Paper Cmd. 1129).

(b) The Crown recognises the Company as the owner of the mineral rights throughout Southern Rhodesia subject to the provisions of the law in force in the territory.

(2) The Company will cede to the Crown, without further payment, all public works and buildings used exclusively or mainly for the administrative or public purposes of Southern Rhodesia together with the movable assets and excess of debtor balances over creditor balances of the Southern Rhodesia administration and all net assets represented by the item 'Capital Expenditure, &c., in connection with Land Settlement' appearing in the Company's published accounts.

The public works and buildings, assets, and balances above

referred to will be those shown in schedules to be prepared by the Administration or by the Land Settlement Department in the same manner as the annual schedules of works and buildings and of those assets and balances hitherto prepared for the purposes of the Company's published accounts, and to be certified in the same manner.

(3) The Company will transfer to the new Administration all separate funds connected with its administration and in particular the pension funds, the guardian's fund, the public service guarantee fund and the Post Office Savings Bank funds.

(4) The arrangements set out in (1), (2) and (3) above will take effect from the 1st October, 1923, but the Company will undertake, as from the date of this letter, not to deal otherwise than in accordance with its previous policy and practice with the lands in Southern Rhodesia, the public works and buildings, the movable assets, the debtor and creditor balances, the land settlement assets and the separate funds connected with its administration. . . .

Sir Francis Newton, K.C.M.G., to Colonial Office.
22, Ryder Street, S.W.1.
7 July, 1923.

Sir,

I have the honour to intimate, for the information of the Secretary of State for the Colonies, that the Elected Members of the Legislative Council of Southern Rhodesia would be glad to do anything in their power to facilitate an all-round settlement between His Majesty's Government and the British South Africa Company in relation to Rhodesia, which would place the new Government of Southern Rhodesia to be set up on the 1st October, 1923, in possession of the unalienated lands, the land revenues, the public works and buildings, the movable assets and the surplus of debtor over creditor balances.

They have now authorised me to state that with this object in view they are prepared, on being requested to do so by the Secretary of State, to pass a formal Resolution pledging themselves to take all necessary steps to secure—

(1) the payment to His Majesty's Government not later than the 1st January, 1924, of a sum of £2,000,000, with interest at

the rate of 5 per cent. per annum, for the period from the 1st October, 1923, to the date of payment, and

(2) the repayment to His Majesty's Government on the same date of a sum representing the two amounts of £150,000 each advanced to the administration of Southern Rhodesia by the Imperial Exchequer, in accordance with the Southern Rhodesia Loan Ordinance No. 13 of 1922, together with the accrued interest thereon.

This assurance is given on the understanding that, as a result of the settlement contemplated, the new Administration of Southern Rhodesia will acquire—

(a) All the unalienated lands in Southern Rhodesia other than the Native Reserves and the lands referred to in the Cave Commission's Report of 15th January, 1921, as appropriated by the British South Africa Company for its commercial purposes.

(b) All the rights and interests of the Crown in the alienated lands in Southern Rhodesia and the quit rents payable by the Company in respect of the lands appropriated for its commercial purposes.

(c) All public works and buildings used by the Company exclusively or mainly for the administrative or public purposes of Southern Rhodesia.

(d) The movable assets of the administration of Southern Rhodesia.

(e) The excess of debtor balances over creditor balances of the administration of Southern Rhodesia.

(f) All separate funds connected with the Company's administration, and in particular the Pension Funds, the Guardian's Fund, the Public Service Guarantee Fund, and the Post Office Savings Bank Funds.

I am instructed to add that the Elected Members are prepared to agree that the British South Africa Company shall be relieved of financial responsibility for the administration of Southern Rhodesia in respect of the whole of the financial year 1923–24 as soon as they learn that His Majesty's Government have arranged with the Company that the new Government will be placed in possession of the Company's net receipts from land for the period 1st April to 30th September, 1923.

I have, etc.,

F. J. Newton.

PART II

White Settler 'Imperialism' v. British Trusteeship

THE MOVEMENT FOR A 'GREATER RHODESIA'

Schemes for uniting the territories of Southern Rhodesia and Northern Rhodesia can be traced back to the period of Company rule and to the imperialist ambitions of Rhodes and his successors to create a white-dominated British dominion in central Africa. However, the scheme was not seriously revived by the European settlers in Southern Rhodesia until after they had obtained their first priority, namely, responsible government for their own territory. Prior to that it was feared that a union with a territory still under Colonial Office tutelage would only have delayed their own progress to self-government.

An additional impetus to union with the north was the discovery in the mid-1920s of the wealth of the Northern Rhodesian Copperbelt. For the European in Southern Rhodesia, whose economy was already burdened by debts, the lure of the added wealth of the Copperbelt was irresistible; for the European in Northern Rhodesia there was the political attraction of freeing themselves from Colonial Office control and joining a numerically larger dominant white settler community in the south.

For over two decades the British Government rejected all overtures from the white Rhodesians for the amalgamation of their territories, basing their refusal on the concept of British trusteeship for the Africans of the Northern Territories. Their only concession to the persistent European proposals was the appointment in 1937 of a Royal Commission, under the chairmanship of Lord Bledisloe, to report on whether any form of closer association between the Rhodesias (and Nyasaland) was desirable and feasible, paying due regard to the special responsibility of the British Government for the interests of the 'native' inhabitants. The Commission's rejection of immediate amalgamation or federation is based on their view of the racial policies practiced in Southern Rhodesia. The following excerpts from the Report illustrate these conclusions.

DOCUMENT 4A. THE MOVEMENT FOR UNION OF THE RHODESIAS FROM *Rhodesia-Nyasaland Royal Commission Report* (MARCH 1939, CMD 5949), THE BLEDISLOE REPORT

General Conclusions

1. *The Need for Co-operation*

473. In our view there is a need for close and continuous co-ordination of effort in many spheres of activity, including not only those public services where positive advantages in the shape of economy and increased efficiency may be plainly and immediately discernible, but in matters, such as the relations between natives and non-natives, in which joint study of the different paths which the Governments may at present appear to be pursuing should be helpful in leading to a solution based on the best interests of all concerned.

Federation Not Recommended

474. We find ourselves unable to accept this suggestion. Southern Rhodesia already enjoys responsible government. In the other two Territories ultimate control still rests with the Secretary of State for the Colonies, and in our view the stage has not yet been reached in either where self-government can be confidently introduced. Any attempt at federation between Governments enjoying such different measures of responsibility and in such different stages of social and political development would not in our opinion achieve success. The wide disparity between them constitutes a fundamental objection to any scheme of federation.

2. *The Question of Amalgamation*

Immediate Amalgamation Not Desirable

479. We have been at some pains to examine the policies of the three existing administrations in respect of their dealings

with the native population, bearing in mind that in our Terms of Reference particular mention is made of the special responsibility of Your Majesty's Government in the United Kingdom for the interests of the native inhabitants in all the territories. The native policy of the Government of Southern Rhodesia, and the principles which, under the guidance of the United Kingdom Government, the administrations in Northern Rhodesia and Nyasaland are seeking to apply, are both in the early stages of experiment, and it is too soon as yet to say which of these policies (in so far as they are different), or what blend of both, is in the long run most likely to promote the moral and material well-being of the African inhabitants. It is clear, however, that, in their present application, they do present certain well-marked differences, and that while Southern Rhodesia, along her own course, has progressed furthest in the provision of certain social and development services, that course is in some respects restrictive and will, if persisted in, limit the opportunities open to Africans, as they gradually emerge from their present backward condition. We have mentioned some instances of this restrictive tendency, such as the virtual exclusion of Africans, under the Industrial Conciliation Act, from skilled employment in certain vocations, and the limitation of opportunity for the employment of natives in clerical and other subordinate posts in the central Government service.

480. One cannot, however, overlook the fact that under any scheme of amalgamation the Government of the combined Territory must rest mainly in the hands of those who at present direct the policy of Southern Rhodesia, and it is therefore necessary to envisage a situation where that policy might be extended in greater or less degree over the Territories now known as Northern Rhodesia and Nyasaland. In these circumstances we feel that, in view of the special responsibility of Your Majesty's Government in the United Kingdom, to which we have just referred, there should, before amalgamation can be contemplated as a practical and salutary development, be a greater degree of certainty than there is at present that Southern Rhodesia's recently initiated policy of Parallel Development, will in the long run prove to be in the best interests of the natives, and will afford them full opportunity of advancement in those fields of activity for which they are fitted, and at the

same time open up the prospect of a reasonably rapid improvement in their economic and cultural status. . . .

484. So far as the European community was concerned, the general idea of those, at any rate in Southern and Northern Rhodesia, who advocated amalgamation was the application of the present constitution of Southern Rhodesia to the combined Territory. In Northern Rhodesia one of the main reasons for the advocacy of amalgamation by many Europeans was the prospect thereby opened up of speedy emancipation from 'Colonial Office control'. Insufficient consideration appears to have been given to the dominant question of the position of the native consequent upon any such changes, or to the problem of the unification or the assimilation of the divergent native policies at present being pursued.

485. Nevertheless the striking unanimity, in the northern Territories, of the native opposition to amalgamation, based mainly on dislike of some features of the native policy of Southern Rhodesia, and the anxiety of the natives in Northern Rhodesia and Nyasaland lest there should be any change in the system under which they regard themselves as enjoying the direct protection of Your Majesty, are factors which cannot in our judgment be ignored.

486. If so large a proportion of the population of the combined Territory were brought unwillingly under a unified Government, it would prejudice the prospect of co-operation in ordered development under such a Government.

BLEDISLOE

P. A. COOPER

ERNEST EVANS

T. FITZGERALD

W. H. MAINWARING

IAN ORR EWING

1ST MARCH 1939

*

Not deterred by the Bledisloe Commission's recommendations against immediate amalgamation or federation of the Central African Territories, the Europeans in the Rhodesias revived the scheme again after the end of the war. In Britain, the Labour Government then in power were reluctant to engage in negotiations on the subject, in view of the known hostility of the Africans and the opposition of members of their own party concerned with colonial affairs. The Labour Colonial Secretary (until 1950), Creech Jones, made this clear to Roy Welensky, then the leader of the Europeans in the Northern Rhodesian Legislative Council, although Welensky claimed that 'federation' was not completely ruled out as an alternative to amalgamation (see Document 4B).

Nevertheless, by 1950 the Labour Government (with Mr James Griffiths as Colonial Secretary) had agreed to the suggestion of Sir Godfrey Huggins, the Prime Minister of S. Rhodesia, that there should be a fresh examination of the problem, by a conference of officials of the Central African Government and the British Government. In making this concession, Mr Griffiths insisted first that the work of the conference would be 'purely exploratory'; second, that it would not commit any of the participating governments; and third, that full account would be taken of African opinion before any changes affecting their interests could be considered.

It was mainly the latter condition that prevented agreement between the British and Rhodesian Governments on implementing the recommendation of the conference of officials for immediate federation. In the view of the Southern Rhodesian Prime Minister, the Labour Government's consultation of African opinion had turned their Victoria Falls Conference into 'a native benefit society'.

The following extracts from the memoirs of Sir Roy Welensky and Mr James Griffiths give their versions of the responsibility for the establishment of the Central African Federation. The Conservative Government view appears in the section dealing with the imposition of the Federation. Even today, the issue of responsibility remains in dispute.

DOCUMENT 4B. SIR ROY WELENSKY (FEDERAL PRIME MINISTER, 1956–63), *4,000 Days* (COLLINS, 1964, P. 23)

'Do you really believe, Mr Welensky [asked the Labour Colonial Secretary, Creech Jones] that any Government, either Tory or Socialist, would ever consider either granting Northern Rhodesia a constitution like Southern Rhodesia's, or if there were amalgamation of the two, the kind of constitution which would place the control of several million black people in the hands of a few hundred thousand whites? No Government, irrespective of its political hue, would carry out that kind of action today. The world wouldn't put up with it.'. . .

'That is perfectly accurate', said Oliver Stanley [Conservative Colonial Secretary, 1942–5]. 'No Government in this country, Tory or Socialist, could give you what you ask.'

I went on to mention to Stanley a suggestion which Creech Jones let fall that morning: why didn't I turn my thoughts in the direction of some kind of federal system of government. . . . 'I do urge you', Creech Jones had said, 'to think about this idea and don't stick rigidly to amalgamation and only amalgamation.'

DOCUMENT 4C. JAMES GRIFFITHS (LABOUR COLONIAL SECRETARY, 1950–1), *Pages from Memory* (DENT, 1969, PP. 113–19)

In 1950 it was urged upon me [and the Commonwealth Secretary, Mr Gordon Walker] that there were new and urgent reasons for promoting the closer political association of the three countries. Representations to this effect were made by our advisers in Whitehall and many people from the Rhodesias, including the then Prime Minister of Southern Rhodesia (Huggins) and Sir Roy. . . .

It was for these reasons—that the desirability of promoting common action in the economic development of the three countries and of ensuring that their political progress was in accordance with British principles and tradition—that Gordon Walker and I agreed that the officials of our two Departments, together with officials from the territories, should prepare a draft constitution for a Central African Federation.

It was clearly understood from the outset that the proposal to amalgamate the three countries into a unitary state was ruled out, that the protectorate status of Northern Rhodesia and Nyasaland would be maintained and that all the people in the three countries would be consulted before a final decision was made. . . .

The officials' proposals were published and commended for consideration without any commitment.

Before I went out to Central Africa some of my critics had derided the idea of consulting the African people on such a complicated matter as federation. . . . At all the meetings I attended they put their case clearly, they asked penetrating questions and held their own in argument.

Our discussions [at the Victoria Falls Conference] revealed, as the communiqué published at the close makes clear, that there were differences in principle, as well as detail, on the proposals for a federation. These would call for further consideration before any binding decisions could be made. . . .

It was clear to me from the discussions at the Victoria Falls Conference that the most important of these consultations would be those with the African representatives. These were bungled from the moment Lyttleton [his successor as Conservative Colonial Secretary] made his statement [in Parliament] in November 1951. . . .

Their [the Africans'] suspicions that the affair was being rushed without consultation with them were deepened when in January 1952 Sir Godfrey Huggins and the Governors of Northern Rhodesia and Nyasaland came to London to discuss federation. No African was invited to be present. The consequence was that when the full conference was convened later that year, the African representatives refused to attend.

Notwithstanding pleas from my colleagues and myself not to proceed with the conference in the absence of the Africans, Lyttleton and the European leaders from Central Africa proceeded to prepare a constitution for the federation. They made changes in the scheme prepared by the officials, the most important of which was to drop the proposal for an African Minister, and the conversion of the African Affairs Board into a Standing Committee of the Federal Legislature—thus weakening the safeguards for Africans. From that moment they destroyed any chance of securing African agreement to federation. However, this did not deter them from carrying their plans through Parliament against the opposition of the Labour and Liberal parties, and of imposing it on the protectorates, against the unanimous opposition of the Africans. . . .

Unfortunately, he [Welensky] chose his friends among the racialists, who not only killed the Federation but were later to reject, and humiliate him and put in his place men of lesser ability like Ian Smith. In our discussions in the early fifties he had seemed aware of the danger that the country of his birth—Southern Rhodesia—might fall into the hands of the racialists and had considered federation the surest way of preventing this happening.

FEDERATION IMPOSED

The negotiations for a federation in Central Africa, begun by the Labour Government with the Rhodesians, were interrupted by the British general election of October 1951. After the Conservatives were returned to power, the new Colonial Secretary announced that a conference would be held to draft a federal scheme, which would form the basis for the unification of the Central African Territories.

The following document on the agreement reached by the London conference on federation shows the high hopes with which the federal scheme was launched by the Conservative Government in 1953. It is followed by an account of the establishment of the federation by the Conservative Colonial Secretary at that time, Oliver Lyttleton (later Lord Chandos) and by a critical commentary from the Rhodesian Chief Justice, Sir Robert Tredgold.

DOCUMENT 5A. *Report of the Conference on Federation held in London in January 1953* (CMD 8753, 1953)

The Federal Scheme: its History and Purpose

The year 1953 is one of opportunity in Central Africa. Ever since the report of the Bledisloe Commission in 1939, the desirability of closer association of the Central African Territories has been canvassed in one form or another. The importance of the objective has been generally accepted, but there were wide differences of opinion as to how it should be achieved. The realisation alike of the importance of the subject and of its increasing urgency led the late Government to embark on an intensive attempt to find a final solution. Starting with the official enquiry in 1951 there has been a succession of conferences, visits, commissions and reports over the last two years.

These have now culminated in the Conference of the Governments of the United Kingdom, Southern Rhodesia, Northern Rhodesia and Nyasaland which has been meeting in London since the 1st January and which has reached agreement on the whole matter.

Closer political association between the three Central African Territories is esential if they are to develop their resources to the full and reach their proper stature in the world. Individually the Territories are vulnerable. Their individual economies are ill-balanced and ill-equipped to withstand the strong economic pressures of a changing world. Of the three Territories only Southern Rhodesia has any significant secondary industries. Northern Rhodesia is very largely dependent on her copper industry, which provides over four-fifths of her exports. Nyasaland, an agricultural community, has to rely too much on a few primary products such as tobacco, tea and cotton and cannot develop herself unaided. The economies of the three Territories are largely complementary; their closer association is essential if they are to achieve the economic and social development of which they are together capable. . . .

Development of the largely untapped resources of this potentially wealthy area demands the combined efforts of the three Territories acting together. The right thing must be done in the right place. There are railways to be built; there are rivers to be harnessed; power must be developed to meet the needs of industry; food production must be expanded to meet the ever growing needs of a steadily increasing population. Such development requires expenditure of capital and material resources on a large scale. Only a well balanced and co-ordinated economic unit would be able to attract development capital from outside on a scale necessary to realise the full potentialities of all three Territories. All the inhabitants of the three Territories would benefit if an effective central authority could take major economic decisions in the interests of the whole area. . . .

The solution lies in a Federation on the lines set out in the Scheme which we have now prepared; in this, we believe, lies the best hope of strengthening that co-operation and partnership between the races and Territories by which alone their peoples can attain a full measure of well-being and contentment.

The preamble to the Scheme recites the fact that the Colony of Southern Rhodesia would continue to enjoy responsible government in accordance with its Constitution; Northern Rhodesia and Nyasaland would continue, under the special protection of Her Majesty, to enjoy separate Governments; the association of the three Territories would enable the Federation, when the inhabitants of the Territories so desire, to go forward with confidence towards the attainment of full membership of the Commonwealth. . . .

To give the new Federal State time to establish itself, and to build up confidence in the Federation among all the peoples of the Territories, provision has been made that, for a period of ten years after the Constitution comes into force, there shall be no change in the division of powers between the Federation and the Territories except with the consent of all three Territorial Legislatures. Towards the end of that period Her Majesty's Government in the United Kingdom, the Federal Government and the three Territorial Governments will review the Constitution. . . .

We have reached the moment for decision. We are convinced that a Federation on the lines proposed is the only practicable means by which the three Central African Territories can achieve security for the future and ensure the well-being and contentment of all their peoples. We believe that this Federal Scheme is a sound and a fair scheme which will promote the essential interests of all the inhabitants of the three Territories, and that it should be carried through.

SWINTON (COMMONWEALTH SECRETARY)
OLIVER LYTTLETON (COLONIAL SECRETARY)
SALISBURY (COMMONWEALTH SECRETARY, 1952)
G. M. HUGGINS (SOUTHERN RHODESIA PRIME
MINISTER)
G. M. RENNIE (NORTHERN RHODESIA GOVERNOR)
G. F. T. COLBY (NYASALAND GOVERNOR)

DOCUMENT 5B. OLIVER LYTTLETON (CONSERVATIVE COLONIAL SECRETARY, 1951–4), *Memoirs of Lord Chandos* (BODLEY HEAD, 1963, PP. 369–77)

'We ought not to get too much trouble in the House of Commons, because the Labour Party is already committed to federation. The present deadlock and the muted noises in Northern Rhodesia are only because they have fumbled it.' [to Colonial Minister of State.]

We had, in fact, much more trouble in the House of Commons than over the negotiations. We had to face eleven debates, in which the Labour Party attacked the policy with great bitterness.

The opposition of the Labour Party and their *volte face* was due ostensibly to the premise that federation was against the wishes of the Africans. If, in this context, the word African could be construed as a small number of political leaders, it would no doubt have some substance, but the word was used to embrace all the inhabitants of the three territories, and in that sense it had little or no foundation. Most of the peoples concerned were illiterate; there is no word for federation in any of the native languages.

On the other hand, if an African leader wished, he could fan public opinion into flame by the simple expedient of saying that federation meant the never-ending domination of the white man. In fact it meant nothing of the kind. If it had meant this then I can at least give the Labour Party the credit of believing that they would never have advocated it. Their changed attitude was in my belief as much dictated by Parliamentary expediency as by any belief that a majority of Africans were opposed to federation.

If, therefore, we were determined that to federate Northern and Southern Rhodesia and Nyasaland would advance their political stature and economic growth and promote the happiness and welfare of their inhabitants, it was our duty to propound the policy, and having negotiated a constitution with the necessary safeguards, and with the necessary checks and balances, to try to make it acceptable to the majority, even against the opposition and maybe the violence of a vocal minority. . . .

The judgment of Ministers and of the highly trained Colonial Service, both at home and overseas, may have been wrong, but at least the motives underlying the policy of federation were enlightened, liberal and unselfish. . . .

The first difficulty was to assemble a constitutional conference. . . . Opposition to the conference was fanned by the left-

wing press, as well as by Labour Party leaders; the first conference was consequently boycotted by the Africans. It has been
claimed that we should therefore have dropped the policy in
which our opponents had believed and in which we still
believe. . . .

It is now alleged (1963), and I confess that I think with some
justice, that the Europeans sat still during the seven years and
made no progressive, or at least too hesitant, moves to engage
Africans in a further share of the government.

Many of the troubles of my successors at the Colonial Office
no doubt sprang from the rigidity of the white man's attitude.

DOCUMENT 5C. SIR ROBERT TREDGOLD (CHIEF JUSTICE OF SOUTHERN
RHODESIA 1950–5 AND THE FEDERATION 1955–60), *The Rhodesia
That Was My Life* (ALLEN & UNWIN, 1968, PP. 192–201)

When self-government had been attained by Southern Rhodesia the possibility of amalgamation was periodically revived.
Conferences were held and inquiries by Commissions or otherwise made, that are now only of historical interest.

Then, in 1952, the prospect became real and immediate.
What precipitated it, it is hard to say. If the truth were known
it was most probably the financial plight of Southern Rhodesia,
where the urge to progress had demonstrated that, if this was to
come swiftly, a larger and more diversified economic unit was
essential. One thing for which I can vouch is that when, at the
time, I tried to sound to the politicians a note of warning of the
difficulties and to suggest that delay and further consideration
could do nothing but good, I was told that I did not understand 'the financial set-up'.

At this stage, the confusion of motives became clearer, as
would be apparent to anyone who studied the campaigns
conducted in the two Territories. In Northern Rhodesia the
major appeal was for the consolidation and strengthening of the
white communities; an appeal that was, in a measure, offset
by the fear that the treasure of the Copperbelt would be used
to bolster up the faltering economy of Southern Rhodesia. In
Southern Rhodesia, the Europeans had to be reassured that the
obvious economic advantages would not be outweighed by the
greatly increased disproportion between black and white,

especially if Nyasaland were included. Meanwhile, the newly-awakened political consciousness of the Africans in the Northern Territories was obsessed by the fear of the entrenchment of white settler rule. The United Kingdom Government was troubled by its responsibility in this regard, whilst alive to the material advantages that must come with the larger and more viable state.

In one of those perversions of history that have become so common of late, it has been asserted, in more than one recent publication, that Federation was 'forced upon' Southern Rhodesia by the United Kingdom Government. Nothing could be further from the truth. Though attitudes varied somewhat with successive Governments, it would be more correct to say that Federation was wrested from a reluctant United Kingdom by the white political leaders in Northern and Southern Rhodesia. (At the time it was usual to talk of the 'fight for' or the 'struggle for' some sort of union of the two countries). It is however true to say that the United Kingdom did insist on the inclusion of Nyasaland.

After long vacillation the United Kingdom did yield what was thought to be the compromise of a federation, in which the power to direct and control African advancement was left with the Territories. There could not have been a more inept solution. Indeed I would go so far as to assert that this form of association introduced a weakness that reduced, almost to vanishing point, the prospect that the unification of the three territories should succeed. . . .

At times in the past I have been inclined to blame both Huggins and Welensky, each of whom in his day was in a position to exercise commanding personal influence, for their failure to give a more positive lead in the direction of liberalism. I believed that the electorate would have responded. Now I am not so sure. I may have underrated their difficulties. I still think they exaggerated them.

In the launching of the Federation, however, they were in a desperate dilemma. If they did not convince the Africans that the purpose of the Federation was a genuine multi-racial state, the Federation must fail. They could only achieve this by speech and action that must be regarded distrustfully by the white electorate. . . . The wonder is, not that it failed, but that it survived for Welensky's four thousand days.

FEDERATION CONDEMNED

When the Central African Federation was established in 1953, it was intended that a review of its progress and future status should take place within seven to nine years of its foundation. The Federation Government, under Welensky's leadership, anxious to press their case for 'Dominion status' or independence from Britain as soon as possible, had got the British Government to agree that a review conference would be held in 1960. The British were also under pressure from the African nationalist leaders in the three territories, in their case to use the review conference as a means of bringing an immediate end to the Federation by allowing its territories the right to secede. The build-up of African hostility against what they regarded as an institution to perpetuate white domination from Southern Rhodesia, culminated in the demonstrations and consequent arrests, first in Nyasaland (where Dr Banda had returned to lead the independence movement) and then in Southern Rhodesia and Northern Rhodesia. In Southern Rhodesia alone, more than 500 African members of the African National Congress were detained and the party outlawed in the emergency declared in February 1959.

It was in these circumstances that a commission was appointed, under the chairmanship of Lord Monckton, and with a membership drawn equally from the British and Central African Governments, to consider the current attitudes and the future prospects of the Federation, in preparation for the review conference planned for the following year.

It had already been established, by the Devlin Commission of enquiry into the Nyasaland disturbances, that Federation was opposed by the overwhelming majority of Africans in the north. The Monckton Commission was to arrive at the same conclusions and, in the course of doing so, was obliged to recommend that in its existing form the Federation could no longer be preserved. The basis for the fear and hatred of Federation which the commission found among its African inhabitants was that the discriminatory racial policies existing in Southern Rhodesia would be extended to the Territories in the north, a conclusion already recorded by the Bledisloe Commission in 1939.

The excerpts from the Monckton Commission report are those dealing with Southern Rhodesian attitudes and proposed reforms of racial discrimination in that territory. If such reforms were implemented, the commission implied, Federation, perhaps under a different name, might still, at the eleventh hour, survive. But the possibilities of the Europeans in Southern Rhodesia voluntarily renouncing the safeguards to preserve their privileged position were so remote as to make the recommendations of the commission on this subject an irrelevant speculation on the prospects of preserving some sort of federation in the future.

After the Monckton Commission report, the choice for the Europeans in Southern Rhodesia was to reform their racial policies or to renounce Federation. In effect, they chose the latter: and within three years the Federation was dissolved and racial discrimination was secured.

DOCUMENT 6A. *Report of the Advisory Commission on the Review of the Constitution of Rhodesia and Nyasaland* (OCTOBER 1960, CMND 1148)
THE MONCKTON REPORT

Present Attitudes Towards Federation

27. The dislike of Federation among Africans in the two Northern Territories is widespread, sincere and of long standing. It is almost pathological. It is associated almost everywhere with a picture of Southern Rhodesia as a white man's country. This attitude, rather surprisingly, is adopted even by Africans who go frequently to Southern Rhodesia to work and enjoy the higher wages and standard of living available to them there. . . .

34. There is no doubt that racial discrimination, although it exists in some degree all through the Federation, is felt to be particularly galling in Southern Rhodesia. Sincere efforts have been made, especially in the last few years, to remove the colour bar, but it still operates, and presses hardest on those naturally most sensitive to it, namely, members of the emerging professional and middle classes. It exists in Southern Rhodesia to a degree that causes such offence as to make association with Southern Rhodesia appear insupportable to Africans in the Northern Territories. The indignities that many of them have suffered on visits to Southern Rhodesia are very vivid in their

minds, and these are felt most acutely by those who are the leaders of political thought. . . .

39. Another ground of criticism of Federation in practice lies in the siting of the Federal capital in Southern Rhodesia. This has strengthened the belief of Africans in the Northern Territories that Federation meant rule by white men, and its particular location in Salisbury, alongside the Government of Southern Rhodesia, has enhanced African fears that the laws and practices of Southern Rhodesia will be imported into Federal policy.

40. In one other matter Africans have felt that Federation has been harmful to their interests. The number of Europeans in both Southern and Northern Rhodesia has increased greatly in the last few years as a result of economic expansion. Many Africans, while recognising the need for European skill and capital to develop the country, fear that the continuation of European immigration will keep them out of the jobs for which they are now fitting themselves. They also fear that European immigration will lead to the extension of the Southern Rhodesian land policies to the Northern Territories.

41. In brief, the opposition to Federation which, as we have seen, was strong at the time that Federation was introduced, has gathered further strength by African disappointment in the manner of its operation. Partnership, in their view, has been a sham. The constitutional forms have given them a meagre part to play and have not provided sufficient protection for their interests, and rule from Salisbury is distrusted as too much influenced by European interests and by the native policies of Southern Rhodesia. The opposition to Federation, in part emotional and blind, has indeed become so strong that, however radical might be the changes in form and outlook, the retention of the name 'Federation' which has become a hated word and is associated in their minds with a policy of white domination, will cause opposition to linger on. In our view, it should be changed.

Views of Africans in Southern Rhodesia

42. Although there was no organised boycott by African political parties in Southern Rhodesia, a significant number of

34

Africans were not prepared to give formal evidence. Nevertheless, we did receive a large amount of formal evidence from Africans, and from this and from informal contacts we believe that we were able to obtain an accurate impression of their attitude towards Federation. There is a clear distinction between this attitude and that of Africans in Northern Rhodesia and Nyasaland. Many Africans in Southern Rhodesia, as in the Northern Territories, have little appreciation of what Federation means, but most of them either expressed no opposition to Federation or indeed supported it. Africans in Southern Rhodesia who favour Federation do so partly because they believe that close association with the large African majorities in the Northern Territories, will strengthen their position in relation to the Europeans. In their view the Federal Government has proved more liberal than the Southern Rhodesia Government, and they have a clearer appreciation of the economic benefits which have come from Federation since so much of the development has taken place in their Territory. In striking contrast to the position in the Northern Territories, Africans in Southern Rhodesia want more departments of government to be made Federal because it appears to them that Federal services are more liberally financed. Some fear that the break-up of Federation would force Southern Rhodesia into closer association with the Union of South Africa and lead to the introduction of *apartheid*.

43. This does not mean that Africans in Southern Rhodesia are satisfied with things as they are. Like their neighbours in the Northern Territories, many complain that Federation has failed to introduce partnership to the degree they had been led to expect, and they feel that more should be done to implement it at once. We heard, for example, frequent demands that they should cease to be treated as a separate section of the community through the medium of the Native Affairs Department. They also feel strongly that Africans should play a bigger part in public life. In particular, they want substantial representation in the Southern Rhodesia Legislature where at the moment there are no African members. We welcome the measure recently passed by that Legislature increasing the number of seats therein; this should give Africans a greater chance of being elected as members.

Views of Europeans

44. In Southern Rhodesia there is a large volume of European opinion hostile to Federation. Many believe it will bring about a too rapid increase in the political power of Africans both in the Federation and in all three Territories. The strength of this belief has made it more difficult for both Federal and Territorial Governments to move faster towards abolishing racial discrimination, particularly in the political sphere. Only a relatively small number actively want to maintain exclusive white domination indefinitely. There is an even smaller number who, rather than surrender this domination, might prefer union with South Africa.

45. Some Europeans in Southern Rhodesia feel that Federation has caused African unrest and political disturbances in the two Northern Territories to spread to the south. They do not believe that the nationalist movement in Southern Rhodesia would have been so active had it not been instigated by nationalists in the Northern Territories. Some go so far as to believe that Federation in its present form must inevitably cause increasing agitation, civil disturbance and even bloodshed. It is also frequently said that, if Federation had not been introduced, the self-governing Colony of Southern Rhodesia would long before now have been granted full status as a member of the Commonwealth. White Southern Rhodesian nationalists, like black nationalists in the north, believe that Federation has been an obstacle to their constitutional advance.

Removal of Racial Discrimination

222. The maintenance of the colour bar and the prevalence of discrimination in Southern Rhodesia has turned the Africans in the Northern Territories, and many of those in Southern Rhodesia itself, against the Europeans who control it. It follows that no new form of association is likely to succeed unless Southern Rhodesia is willing to make drastic changes in its racial policies. We recognise that much progress has lately been made in this direction. Certain hotels can now apply for multi-racial licences and several have done so.

Legislative steps have been taken to promote the establishment of non-racial trades unions and to provide for workmen's compensation and apprenticeships on a non-racial basis. The Southern Rhodesia Government recently played its part with the Federal Government, the Northern Rhodesia Government and the Railways Administration in extending the range of jobs open to Africans on the Rhodesia Railways. In addition, a number of irritations have been removed, such as certain restrictions on betting and buying alcoholic liquor. Multi-racial sport is beginning to be an accepted part of Southern Rhodesian recreations. While these are only beginnings, they do mark a trend which is accelerating and is moving in precisely the opposite direction to the trend of present government policy in the Union of South Africa. Even since we were working in the Federation, a Select Committee has recommended the radical reform of the Land Apportionment Act. But what has been done, however good, is not enough, if the fears which have bedevilled Federation are to be allayed. To say that events are moving fast in Africa is a truism. They are moving like an avalanche, and it appears only too likely that those who merely cling to their familiar positions will be swept away. We strongly urge, therefore, that if it is the genuine desire of the Europeans of Southern Rhodesia to preserve an association with their neighbours in the north, they should remove as quickly as possible from their laws and practices all instances of unfair racial discrimination.

222. The unfairly discriminatory laws and practices which we think should be removed, wherever they exist throughout the Federation, include relatively minor, if irritating, matters such as restrictions on the use by Africans of cinemas, hotels, bars, restaurants, cafés and public lavatories and on their buying certain types of liquor. They also include the following more important matters about which we have heard particular criticism.

The Pass Laws in Southern Rhodesia

223. These not only hamper an African in travel, but oblige him to carry the appropriate pass whenever he is in a town, and particularly when he goes out at night. We think that, except in so far as certificates of identity may be required for all

inhabitants irrespective of race, passes should be abolished. We understand that the Southern Rhodesia Government is at present considering legislation on this subject.

Urban Local Government

224. The present system whereby electors for municipal and other local councils are limited to ratepayers results in inadequate representation of African interests. Even where African representatives are elected, this is at present limited to special African advisory bodies. We think that Africans should be able to qualify for the vote in municipal and other local council elections. We also think that they should be directly represented on the Councils themselves and not merely on advisory bodies associated with them.

The Public Services

225. Much dissatisfaction exists among Africans because opportunities for their advancement in the public services are still so limited, and, in as much as special facilities for training in certain branches of the service are provided for Europeans and not for Africans, there is discrimination. No Africans have yet been promoted to commissioned rank in the police forces of the Territories or in any branch of the defence forces of the Federation. Although the Senior Branch (Branch I) of the Federal Civil Service is open to all races and some Africans are now employed in it, Europeans are eligible for direct entry whereas non-Europeans, other than doctors, can enter only through Branch II. There are at present no non-Europeans serving in the Southern Rhodesia Civil Service, though the Southern Rhodesia Government have announced their intention of taking early action to admit them.

Advancement in Industry

226. Discrimination exists in a number of industries, where Africans get much lower pay than Europeans even when they have the same qualifications. They are still often not admitted to apprenticeships, nor are they trained in sufficient numbers

for the more skilled posts in industry and commerce; this applies not only to private firms but also to industries directly or indirectly controlled by Governments.

The Southern Rhodesia Land Apportionment Act

227. This Act is regarded by Africans as a major discriminatory measure. It reserves for the sole use of Europeans some 48 million acres of land, and prevents Africans from occupying plots in the main towns of Southern Rhodesia. It also contains provisions which protect African land and trading rights. Without these, Africans would not have been able, in the face of direct competition from European businessmen with capital resources and wide experience, to build up businesses in African townships. And, although the 21 million acres of the Native Reserves were already secured to them under the Constitution, the additional 21 million acres of African land in the Native Purchase Areas and in the Special Native Areas would have been a fraction of what they are today if protection had not been given by the Act against European purchase. The value of these protective aspects tends to be overlooked by Africans because of the intensity of their feelings about those aspects which discriminate against them. The Act was introduced as a result of the Morris Carter Land Commission of 1925, and the thirty-five years which have elapsed since then have made many of its provisions out of date. This was recognised by the Government of Southern Rhodesia when they appointed a Select Committee two years ago to examine the resettlement of Africans and other related matters. This Committee reported on 16th August, 1960, and made a number of recommendations which, we believe, if accepted, will go a long way to remove the major causes of African dissatisfaction.

228. The Select Committee heard evidence from many people and went into this complex and difficult matter far more thoroughly than we could have done. As a result of its report, the Government of Southern Rhodesia will no doubt reconsider its whole attitude to the question of the tenure, use and occupation of land. We do not, therefore, wish ourselves to make any specific recommendations. However, evidence we heard suggested to us that African dissatisfaction would be

considerably relieved if, in the towns where new development is taking place, land could be set aside for purchase by all races; if, in the European urban areas, Africans could acquire or occupy land for trading or professional purposes; if the power of proprietors of hotels, places of entertainment and the like to refuse entry to Africans could be withdrawn; and if, in the African rural areas, freehold title to any land could be acquired by Africans.

DOCUMENT 6B. HAROLD MACMILLAN (PRIME MINISTER OF GREAT BRITAIN, 1957–63), *The End of the Day* (MACMILLAN, 1973, P. 323); *Pointing the Way* (MACMILLAN, 1972, P. 133)

The Federation *was* a good idea. But it has been wrecked by two things. (a) The 'wind of change' which has swept through Africa with unexpected force (unexpected, at least, ten years ago). (b) The policies first of Huggins—now Lord Malvern— and secondly of Welensky, which have made the Federation in the mind of Africans a symbol of white domination. . . .

Had I then realised, or had indeed any of us realised, the almost revolutionary way in which the situation would develop and the rapid growth of African nationalism through the whole African continent, I think I should have opposed the putting together of three countries so opposite in their character and so different in their history. . . . Thus both British Ministers and many others would have been spared much painful controversy and bitter recriminations.

DOCUMENT 6C. FRANK CLEMENTS (FORMER MAYOR OF SALISBURY AND PRESIDENT OF THE LOCAL GOVERNMENT ASSOCIATION), *Rhodesia: The Course to Collision* (PALL MALL PRESS, 1969, PP. 109–10)

As all articulate Africans were quick to recognize, Federation, in the eyes of the majority of whites who supported it, was an attempt to widen the boundaries and to strengthen the forces of white supremacy throughout Africa south of the Equator. . . .

Those two-thirds who voted with Lord Malvern to join the Federation were far from being as single-minded as those who opposed. Many were influenced by the economic advantages

which would accrue to Rhodesia by becoming a part of a large
Central African Common Market which would supply protected outlets for the growing industrialization of Salisbury,
Bulawayo and other southern towns. With Lord Malvern in
charge they saw the northern territories becoming extensions of
the Rhodesian social and political sphere. Far from believing
that they risked forfeiting any of their privileges, they saw their
enjoyment of them being extended to their white fellows in
Northern Rhodesia and Nyasaland. Though attempts to call it
something of the sort were frustrated, the Federation in its
advocates' eyes was to become a Greater Rhodesia. Relatively
recent immigrants, as yet with no experience of a clash with
Westminster, and already provoked by the nationalism of the
Afrikaners in South Africa, saw the Greater Rhodesia as a
patriotic goal, a powerful state where British traditions and the
English language would prevail. The Queen was newly on the
throne and there was a brief period of British confidence in the
dawn of a second Elizabethan era.

Whoever supports British traditions has a wide range from
which they can select, and those chosen by the settlers in
Rhodesia certainly included the xenophobia and the arrogance
towards coloured peoples, as conspicuous a part of the British
heritage as respect for property and the manipulation of the
law in defence of privilege. This qualified British patriotism
suited the emotions no less than the purpose of most of the
immigrants from South Africa, in number about the equal of
those from Britain. They had crossed the Limpopo not so much
in protest at the South African policy towards blacks and
Coloureds as in resentment of Afrikaner policy towards themselves. In Rhodesia they could find the privileges which the
Afrikaner was eroding, and they could hope to retain their
favoured position by building up the Rhodesian to match the
South African power.

PART III

Party Politics

Rhodesia has in effect been a one-party state since the Rhodesian Front came to power in the general election of December 1962. Although small splinter parties—such as the Centre Party and the Rhodesia Party—have appeared since then, they have had no significant following nor have they had any effect as pressure groups in altering the policies of the ruling Front. The African nationalist parties have been banned, their leaders being in detention or exile. The official Parliamentary Opposition consists of small and unrepresentative groups of Africans, elected by default on the 'B' or African Roll as a result of the boycott of elections by even the small number of Africans qualified to register as electors.

Although the Rhodesian Front's opponents—the United Federal Party—were routed in the 1962 election, and rapidly disintegrated as a party unit after disatrous defeats in the by-elections that followed, they had been the ruling party in Rhodesia for an entire generation. Under various labels (in later years, the United Party and the United Federal Party), the party had been led by Sir Godfrey Huggins (later Lord Malvern), Prime Minister for over twenty years, and by Mr Garfield Todd, Sir Edgar Whitehead, and (on the Federal level) Sir Roy Welensky. Known as the 'Establishment' (in Huggins's rule as the 'Huggins-bureau'), the party represented the community of business, commerce and finance and the larger agricultural interests. It led the movement for a federation with the Northern Territories and, in the course of convincing the British Government of the necessity for this concession, became the chief exponent of the doctrine of 'partnership'. While in the 1940s the party leader, Huggins, was envisaging a 'parallel development' of the races (see Part IV) and 'native' rule by a 'benevolent aristocracy', twenty years later Whitehead, his successor, was trying to convince the world outside that his party was working for a 'partnership' of the races.

While 'partnership' could be defined in accordance with the views of its beholders (Huggins calling it the 'horse and the rider'), its implications for African advance were sufficiently repugnant to a European electorate fearful of the loss of its land, job reservation and social status. The majority of that electorate—the small farmer, the artisan, the newly-arrived immigrant—who had most to fear from the actual implementation of that policy, therefore turned to a party—the Rhodesian Front—openly committed to the retention of European power and privilege.

In the following document, Whitehead attempted to justify before the world community the policy to which his party, the UFP, had been committed over the decade of Federation. It can be argued, with considerable justification, that for home consumption he might have chosen a more cautious approach. Nevertheless, his party manifesto for the 1962 general election did contain the pledge to abolish racial discrimination, particularly in the form of the Land Apportionment Act; and that pledge (as Malvern later said) might well have led to the end of the ruling 'Establishment' and the victory of the Rhodesian Front.

DOCUMENT 7. THE PRIME MINISTER, SIR EDGAR WHITEHEAD: ADDRESS TO THE TRUSTEESHIP COMMITTEE, 30 OCTOBER 1962 (FROM UNITED NATIONS GENERAL ASSEMBLY, 17TH SESSION, *Official Records*, FOURTH COMMITTEE, 1366TH MEETING)

Sir Edgar Whitehead (United Kingdom delegation) said that he had come to the United Nations, as the Prime Minister of Southern Rhodesia, to explain something of the background in his country and of the plans and accomplishments of his Government. . . .

7. One problem which had been mentioned during the Committee's discussions was the land problem. With the population

increase it was no longer easy for a young man to obtain land when he married. In the early days a certain amount of land had been set aside by law for the use of the Africans only and the remainder had been divided into land for African purchase and land for European purchase. That had been done because at that time the economic position of the Whites had been such that without such provisions they would have been able to buy up all the land in the country. The amount of land reserved for the use of the Africans had since been added to; at the present time about four-ninths of Southern Rhodesia's land was so reserved, about one-ninth was national land and the remainder was divided between land that might be bought by people of any race and land that was available for purchase exclusively by white people or exclusively by Africans. It was the Government's intention to do away with the latter distinction within the next year. The time had come when all available land in the country must be brought into productive use and, while the reserved tribal land would remain, all other land would become open to purchase by persons of any race.

8. While land was the first need of the Africans, the question of education was also of the greatest interest to them. He had recently toured the country, including all the remote rural areas, meeting and talking with the people, and he therefore knew what their needs and interests were. According to the last estimate, 95·1 per cent (sic) of the country's children were now receiving five years of primary education. Figures for the remaining three years of primary education were not so good, but the standard was very high and the experts at the latest UNESCO meeting in Paris had agreed that the final two years of primary education would be counted as secondary education in most African countries which had a six-year primary course. Allegations had been made to the Committee that the Government was holding back secondary education, but the fact was that during the four years that he had been Prime Minister secondary schools had increased in number from twenty-three to forty-two. The Government clearly could not be expected to expand secondary education at the expense of universal primary education; none of the parents would agree to that.

9. Against that background, the political problems in his country could be readily understood. In Southern Rhodesia

there was a white community of about 225,000 persons who had made a permanent home there. There were not, as in many other parts of Africa, expatriates living and serving in the country and then retiring to their homes elsewhere. Some of his friends were the fifth generation born in Africa. None of the Whites had ties or loyalties outside the boundaries of the country. They had fulfilled an invaluable service to the country and would continue to do so. The Africans, for their part, had only recently begun to take a keen interest in politics; as recently as 1953, when the plan for the Federation of Rhodesia and Nyasaland had been discussed, little interest had been found among the Africans. A sudden and violent political change-over would be impossible, particularly in a country where already 600,000 people were dependent for their employment and livelihood on the industries which had been built up.

10. He was aware that there was a considerable amount of suspicion among the Africans—particularly among those who participated actively in politics—that the white minority intended to cling to power for ever. That was quite untrue. He had told the predominantly white electorate that the Africans would undoubtedly have a majority within fifteen years. That might seem a long time to the Committee, but the intention was that from now on both Whites and Blacks should take part at every stage of planning and development and that gradually the African majority would predominate, while the white minority would continue to perform their indispensable role. He was absolutely satisfied that that course was the wisest one in the conditions of Southern Rhodesia and it was gaining wide acceptance.

11. Of the three alternatives which were open to his country, the first, that of maintaining white supremacy indefinitely, he had completely rejected: he had told the Southern Rhodesian Parliament that white supremacy in Southern Rhodesia was as extinct as the dodo. The second alternative was that followed in most of tropical Africa, where Europeans gradually disappeared and were replaced by Africans. In Southern Rhodesia that solution would be disastrous, for if the Europeans were driven out the economy that had taken forty years to build would collapse. The resulting situation would probably be worse than that which had arisen in the Congo. The third

alternative was the one which he was trying to follow. In the first place, every vestige of discrimination against the Africans must be eliminated and made illegal. Secondly, all separation of land between races, except for the old tribal land, must be abolished. Thirdly, people of all races must be involved in planning and decision-making. Fourthly, the Government must show by its acts during the next few years the absolute sincerity of its desire to build a new society. The attempt would be something unique in Africa but he intended to make it succeed.

12. Turning to constitutional matters, he observed that when he had taken office the Constitution that had been in force for some thirty-six years had given complete administrative power to the Southern Rhodesian Government. On the legislative side, the all-white Parliament had had complete freedom except in matters involving discrimination.

13. On examining the old Constitution, he had come to the conclusion that it was out of date. For one thing, the rate at which Africans would be likely to obtain seats in Parliament under it would be unduly slow; moreover, many of its provisions needed to be amended. He had therefore suggested to the United Kingdom Government that a new Constitution should be discussed. The United Kingdom Government had said that it would be necessary to have a full conference with all political parties represented, and he had readily agreed to that proposal. . . .

15. He knew that many people still felt that African representation in Parliament would be inadequate. There was now, however, a certainty that African voters would control at least seventeen seats in the first election, and nothing could prevent that number from increasing. He did not think that that rate of progress was as unreasonable as it would be in a country where Africans made up 98 per cent of the population. All his Government asked was limited time to build a non-racial State.

16. Problems with regard to law and order had been mentioned in the Committee. In Southern Rhodesia any one could hold whatever opinions he wished and could join a political party holding any principles he chose; at one time there had been about twelve political parties in the country. The one thing he had taken action against was the refusal of a particular party

to allow those who disagreed with it to lead a normal political life. The meeting of other political parties had been broken up; those who belonged openly to another political party had been ostracized or subjected to violence; one man had even been beaten to death for attending a football match instead of a political meeting which the man had been ordered to attend. It was for such action, and not for their opinions, that political parties had been banned. Parties which were prepared to argue their case peacefully could do so without fear, but he would continue to take action against parties which refused to tolerate their opponents. . . .

18. He believed that if the new Constitution was carried through in the spirit in which it had been drafted, it would be possible to build up a nation in Southern Rhodesia of people of every race, to remove all barriers between races and to create a society in which both human and natural resources were used to the greatest benefit of all the people. Those who knew him realised that he had risked his political future, with a pre-dominantly white electorate, in preaching that ideal. He believed that something could be created in Southern Rhodesia which would be of real value to the world as a whole.

THE RHODESIAN FRONT'S CHALLENGE

The Rhodesian Front was formed in 1962, as a successor to the right-wing Dominion Party, but also incorporating other racialist associations and even some dissident members of the United Federal Party, including Mr Ian Smith. The basis of its original membership included the small farmer and tobacco grower, and the skilled and the semi-skilled industrial worker. On a policy of 'separate development' and Rhodesian inde-pendence, the party came to power in the 1962 election and brought an end to a generation of 'Establishment' rule by the United Federal Party and its predecessors.

Document 8 contains the principles and policies to which the Front is committed. The case for the implementation of these policies is provided in the statement of the Party leader (see Document 21) and those of other Rhodesian Front Ministers in the following sections of this volume.

DOCUMENT 8. THE RHODESIAN FRONT, *Principles and Policies,*
SALISBURY, SEPTEMBER 1973

Principles

1. The Party affirms its loyalty to the Independent Country of
Rhodesia.
2. The Party views the National Flag as the only and exclusive
symbol of our independent Rhodesian Nation.
3. The Party will ensure that the Government of Rhodesia
remains permanently in responsible hands.
4. English will remain the official language of the Country.
5. The Party will preserve a strong and prosperous State based
upon the fundamental principles which affect a sound society,
including:

    (i) recognition of the family as the basis of society;

    (ii) the right of all individuals, within the framework of the
law, to private ownership, freedom of worship, freedom of
speech, freedom of the association and opportunity to develop
their abilities to the full and to receive reward and recognition
entirely on merit.

    (iii) total opposition to Communism and Communistic
Ideologies.

6. The Party will ensure the permanent establishment of the
European in Rhodesia and to this end will encourage to the
utmost European immigration.
7. The Party will uphold the principle of the Land Tenure
Act.
8. The Party will uphold the principle of the preservation of
the Tribal Trust Lands and will promote their development.
9. The Party opposes compulsory integration and believes that
the peaceful co-existence of people can only be achieved when
communities have the right and opportunity to preserve their
own identities, traditions and customs, and, therefore, recognises the obligation of Government and respective communities
where necessary to ensure the provision of such separate
facilities as will make this possible.
10. The Party will ensure that law and order are maintained.
11. The Party will promote the full economic development of
Rhodesia and to this end will seek the co-operation of all her
people.

12. The Party will encourage and stimulate private enterprise, subject to the right of the State to intervene when necessary in the interests of the Country.

13. The Party will strive to create conditions in which all inhabitants of Rhodesia may attain reasonable standards of housing, health, social services and employment.

14. The Party will ensure that Government honours its obligations in the payment of pensions.

15. The Party will protect the standards of skilled workers against exploitation by cheap labour.

16. The Party recognises the desirability of consultation and co-operation with other States in the solution of common problems.

Party Policies: Preamble

The Rhodesian Front recognises that the members of each racial group are desirous of preserving their own identities, traditions, customs and ways of life. Respecting these differences, the Rhodesian Front introduced the 1969 Constitution and the Land Tenure Act. This legislation affords the opportunity to each race to develop to its fullest extent in its own Area and in accordance with its own social structure, without intrusion upon its privacy and rights by any other race. It will set the example to the public by providing separate facilities for the different races in State Offices and Institutions. It further aims to engender between the races the mutual confidence and respect that will encourage the fullest participation of persons in their own development, and so enable all to contribute to the overall growth of the Nation.

Traditionally, land in Rhodesia is divided into two main areas, namely, land in which European interests are paramount and land in which African interests are paramount.

The Front will introduce a system of provincialisation which will allow each race to control many of the matters which affect the daily lives of its people. National services will be maintained and expanded to meet the requirements of a rapidly developing country, controlled by a strong central Government, which will remain in responsible hands.

The Front will sustain a concerted drive by all arms of

49

Government to ensure the maximum effectiveness of a population control programme, related to a proper ecological balance.

THE AFRICAN NATIONALIST RESPONSE

African political organisations in Rhodesia have tended to
operate outside the confines of the formal party system, which
has been designed for and limited to the Europeans. Their
operation within the political system has been precluded by
the repressive security legislation which had led to their being
repeatedly banned and by the highly qualified franchise which
has excluded them from any effective voice in the electoral
process. In effect, they have tended to operate as movements
rather than as parties.

The first of these—the African National Congress—was
founded in 1957 and banned in 1959. It was succeeded by the
National Democratic Party, which survived for two years
before its banning in December 1961, and then by the Zimbabwe African People's Union, which was banned nine months
later. A breakaway group—the Zimbabwe African National
Union—was also banned, along with the surviving membership
of ZAPU, and the leadership of both groups was rounded up
and detained or restricted in August 1964.

African political leadership today is either in detention or in
exile. Both ZAPU and ZANU maintain organisations abroad,
in Lusaka, in London and in other countries where their
exiles are based. While ZAPU, led by Mr Nkomo, and ZANU,
led by the Rev. Sithole, have retained their separate organisations, they have agreed to the formation of a joint military
command to mobilise the guerrilla movement operating against
the Smith régime (see Part X).

The following article, by a former ZAPU branch chairman,
examines the origins and policies of African political organisations since the 1950s. The very moderate aims of the original
ANC have been overtaken, if not made irrelevant, by the
events that followed the bannings. The successor parties,
ZAPU and particularly ZANU, have become committed to the
ideals of socialism and pan-Africanism and to the policy of
confrontation in response to the rebel régime.

DOCUMENT 9. 'RHODESIA'S AFRICAN MAJORITY' BY DAVIS M'GABE
(FROM *Africa Report*, VOL. 12, NO. 2, FEBRUARY 1967)

In the late 1940s, protest against European rule began to take the form of party politics for the first time. The Rev. T. D. Samkange and the Rev. E. Nemepare, among others, came back from visits to South Africa with a new blueprint for organizing African resistance. Launching the African National Congress (now referred to as the old ANC), they formally set forth their demands—including repeal of specific discriminatory legislation and exemptions for educated Africans from pass laws. The settler movement ignored them, the British exerted no pressure, and the African National Congress died a quiet death in the early 1950s.

About this time, yet another concept of organization began to sweep the towns. Since Africans were largely restricted to laboring roles, they would mobilize a powerful labor movement. After Charles Mzilingeli and others successfully organized and carried off a country-wide strike in 1948, everybody went labor. Indeed, Mzilingeli's Reformed Industrial Council of Unions (RICU) soon found itself fighting a mushroom crop of dissident groups each intent on becoming the power center of the new movement. George Nyandoro, for one, built his stronghold in Harare. The Builders and Artisans Workers' Union produced Jasper Savanhu, Reuben Jamela, and later Eric Gwanzura. The Commercial and Allied Workers' Union was led by Washington Malianga, Zebediah Mapfumo, and Mark Nziramasanga. The Railway African Workers' Union, the only union with a paid secretariat, had Joshua Nkomo, Michael Mawema, Jason Moyo, John Moyo, Knight Maripe, and John Chirimbani in the front ranks. The style of the 'labor phase' was non-violent mob action, notably the strike and the sit-down demonstration. Only the African Teachers' Association (ATA) where Ndabaningi Sithole, Robert Mugabe, Edison Zvobgo, Leopold Takawira, and Josiah Chinamano held forth, challenged the labor thesis that urban organization must take priority over rural organization.

As history records, Rhodesia did not prove a fertile ground for trade union organizations to flourish. The settler government declined to acknowledge their legitimacy, and used force to make the point. Then the white liberals moved in, suffocating in the embrace of multiracialism whatever vitality trade unionism had.

By the early 1950s, the quasi-political multiracial society had become the fad. Hardwicke Holderness, Eileen Haddon, Nathan Shamuyarira, and all the other intellectuals and would-be intellectuals launched the Interracial Association in 1953. They debated, had coffee, and occasionally danced. In 1955, Colonel David Stirling brought his Capricorn Africa Society from East Africa to Rhodesia. This was another interracial association on a much bigger scale, and many of the leading nationalists of today were in its ranks. Leopold Takawira and Robert Chikerema were among them. Meanwhile, settler politics also went multiracial. In fact, some Africans almost reached the top in Godfrey Huggins' (later Lord Malvern's) United Federal Party—notably Josuha Nkomo, Jasper Savanhu, Mike Hove, Charles Mzilingeli, and Chad Chipunza. Stanlake Samkange took an active role in Garfield Todd's Central African Party, and Ndabaningi Sithole also patched up a longstanding disagreement with Todd to join the CAP. But in time, the multiracial phase also spent itself.

Two young men, dismayed by the dead end to which multiracial politics had brought the African, decided to revive the resistance movement under new guidelines. Edison Sithole and the late Dunduza Chisiza (Malawi's Minister of Finance-designate at the time of his death in 1962) joined forces with Thompson Gonese, Henry Hamadziripi, Stanley Parirewa, and Nhapi to organize Salisbury youth. They were inspired by Sukarno's youth movement which had infiltrated the Dutch colonial government in Indonesia and brought it down with a militant youth revolution unique in style. They formed the Southern Rhodesia Youth League.

The Youth League was a going concern by 1956 when it was decided to hold elections. The organizers' original concept of a clandestine organization infiltrating the various elements of the administration, in both urban and rural areas, was unfamiliar and not widely understood. With the election of Robert Chikerema of the Capricorn Society as president, and George Nyandoro, a trade unionist, as secretary-general, the Youth League evolved into another trade union organization, albeit a successful one. In early 1957, it called for a bus boycott to protest a rise in fares on buses going to the African township of Harare. The boycott was a remarkable success. The Youth League was suddenly a national movement (though all Shona) with branches in many parts of the country.

The movement still was not quite sure what it was or where it was going, however, and the executive decided to clarify the issues by dissolving the League itself and calling for a mammoth conference of all organized African groups throughout the country. Here is the story of what ensued at that meeting as Edison Sithole told it to me:

> On September 12, 1957, the 'grand conference' met in Salisbury. Everybody was represented, and a few people represented themselves. The day was auspicious. September 12 is an official holiday in Rhodesia—Occupation Day, when the settlers celebrate the occupation of Mashonaland. It was on that day that the New African National Congress was born.
>
> The two militant groups contesting for leadership at the meeting—the Youth League group, led by James Chikerema, George Nyandoro, and Paul Mushonga, and the Bulawayo branch of the Old African National Congress, led by Jason Moyo, Francis Nehwati, and Knight Maripe—could not reach agreement on the chairmanship of the meeting, and so it was that a neutral outsider, Joshua Nkomo, was asked to chair the meeting. [Nkomo was a 'neutral' in this situation on two counts: first because he was not an in-group Ndebele, and also because he had quit trade unions for the UFP.]
>
> By the end of the day, in fact, the leadership of the New African National Congress had been placed in Nkomo's hands. Some participants objected strongly to this development, citing his membership in the United Federal Party, but the desire to 'commit the minority group of the West' carried the day. James Robert Chikerema was elected deputy president, George Nyandoro secretary general, and Paul Mushonga treasurer.

Nyandoro and Mushonga returned to the techniques of B. B. Burombo, who had been the driving force in the first

Rhodesian Native Association. They went into the country and remained there, organizing resistance to the administration. The areas where they stayed longest are to this day the core of the nationalist movement—Sipolilo, Mtoko, Mrewa, and a few others. Most of the other leaders continued the labor-style meetings around the cities.

The Government Reacts: 'Operation Sunrise'

Although the city rallies were drawing good crowds by the end of 1958, these did not concern the government as much as the potential threat seen in the rural organizations being created. It was the spread of the resistance movement among the villagers that prompted 'Operation Sunrise.'

In the early hours of the morning of February 29, 1959, Prime Minister Sir Edgar Whitehead called out government troops, banned the African National Congress, and loaded every nationalist leader, from village chairman to the top ranks of the party, into army trucks. Most of the arrests were in rural branches.

Under fresh legislation, the ANC leaders were detained without trial in large camps at Marandellas, and later in prisons in various sections of the country. The hard core, including Nyandoro, Chikerema, Edison Sithole, Henry Hamadziripi, Moris Nyagumbo, Daniel Madzimbamuto and Oldman Chiota, spent almost four years in detention at Gokwe, a hot Siberia in the Zambezi valley. The only national leader who escaped was Joshua Nkomo, who was attending a meeting abroad when the party was banned.

While much politicking went on in the camps, the movement did not have an underground network capable of continuing the work of organizing the people. Unlike Malawi, where a similar ban in 1959 sparked a sustained rural resistance which led to the early triumph of the Malawi Congress Party, the Rhodesian organization was centrally powered. When that power was removed, it collapsed. Debate dragged on for almost a year about how to resuscitate the movement. One school of thought believed it should be re-established as an underground organization, while the other favored creation of a new party along the lines of the old.

On January 1, 1960, the National Democratic Party (NDP) was formed. Michael Mawema was its interim president and the secretary treasurer was Sketchley Samkange. Those who disagreed with the idea of forming a new party came into open opposition later in the year, when it became apparent that Joshua Nkomo, though in exile, was again a front-runner for the party presidency. The dissidents formed the Zimbabwe National Party (ZNP), which later became the Pan-African Socialist Union (PASU). Thompson Gonese, Edison Sithole, and later Patric Matimba, major figures in the ANC and PASU, believed that the formalities of party politics should be abandoned under the circumstances and that all energies should be put into building an underground resistance movement.

The National Democratic Party (NDP) meanwhile became ever more deeply involved in a political poker game whose rules were made in London and Salisbury. It put forward a formal demand for one man, one vote. It organized mass meetings where the law permitted, and sought opportunities to put its case before the European and African publics in a dignified manner. The time was auspicious, for 1960 was the year in which all Africa felt the full force of 'the wind of change'. Prime Minister Edgar Whitehead, sniffing this wind, decided to change his tactics.

The arrest in July 1960 of Michael Mawema, Sketchley Samkange, and Leopold Takawira (then chairman of the NDP's Harare branch) precipitated disturbances which ended in what seemed to be a major concession from Whitehead. He called for a constitutional review conference in London. Mawema and his lieutenants became heroes, and politics suddenly became a race for office. The chances of becoming Members of Parliament and of greater things ahead fired the imagination of even the comfortable educated groups, who up to now had remained interested observers.

In October 1960, the NDP held its annual conference in Salisbury. Joshua Nkomo, still abroad, was again elected to head the party and to lead the delegation to the constitutional conference scheduled to begin in January 1961. Morton Malianga was elected his deputy, George Silundika, secretary-general, Ndabaningi Sithole, treasurer, and Robert Mugabe,

55

publicity secretary. A wave of optimism permeated the movement.

The constitutional conference turned into a nightmare for the NDP delegation. The Africans could not get the counsel they wanted, were outmanoeuvered at the bargaining table on every major issue, and finally accepted a draft constitution that gave the Africans 15 seats in a parliament of 65—this in a country where 94 per cent of the population is African. When the final communiqué was released in Salisbury in March 1961. Nkomo came under heavy criticism. Several members of the executive simply would not go along with the 15 seats settlement. Nkomo then renounced the constitutional agreement. This was a blow to Whitehead, who could not win without substantial participation. The NDP's position was even worse. Having been effectively channeled away from the route of a resistance movement into British-style party politics, it was unprepared for any protest more vigorous than a boycott of the December 1962 elections.

The Problem of Style

The movement at this time had genuine grass roots support. By the middle of 1961, there were over 250,000 paid up members of the party. Branches such as Highfield and Harare were collecting as much as £500 a week in subscriptions. There were scooters for the field men, Volkswagens for the top officials, Ford Consuls for the national leaders, and even a Rambler station wagon for the president. In fact, the story might have had a happy ending if the nationalist movement had been contending with the British Colonial Office instead of a settler government that had long enjoyed the unique status of a 'self-governing colony'. We have been conditioned to be good churchmen and encouraged to carry out our politics according to British ground rules, but we are facing an entrenched adversary fervently dedicated to preserving a way of life, not a handful of itinerant British civil servants. The Rhodesian ruling group must never be confused with the authorities that have been faced by nationalist movements in other British territories in Africa.

We now had a following, but we were rudderless. Two conferences of the party held during 1961 produced nothing more than a new commitment to party politics and the existing power structure. Radical elements within the NDP organized acts of sabotage on their own, but these were disclaimed and actively discouraged by the party leadership. It was decided that there would be no unconstitutional politics. Even so, the NDP was banned in December 1961 and all the leaders within the country detained.

Nkomo, who was again out of Rhodesia when this roundup occurred, arrived back in Salisbury to find two groups working at the idea of launching still another party. The committee in Highfield indicated that it would like to see a new party established with his co-operation and participation, but under a new leader. Nkomo did not commit himself, and largely steered clear of the working group while making his political rounds in Highfield. He spent a few days in his home town, Bulawayo, and then announced on December 17 the formation of the new party—the Zimbabwe African People's Union. ZAPU was banned nine months later before any conference or election had been held.

For those nine months, ZAPU followed in the footsteps of its predecessor. It gathered thousands upon thousands of faithful supporters, who turned up at every meeting. It collected thousands of pounds in donations and subscriptions, and the confiscated scooters of the NDP were replaced by Land Rovers and better sedans. The leadership, intoxicated by the numbers who responded, confidently proclaimed that 'freedom is round the corner', though in retrospect it was never quite clear precisely how the plum was to fall into our laps. We talked all day and all night about what would come to pass when the elections were over in December 1962 and negotiations toward majority rule could get under way again. It was an exhilarating time, but we did not really undertake to develop the power potential of our mass following. I should know, for I was chairman of one of the most active branches of that time—Highfield, Salisbury. . . .

The ban of ZAPU was announced in September 1962. Sir Edgar Whitehead hoped this action would win him wavering white votes in the coming election, but the effect was the reverse. The rightist Rhodesia Front, led by Winston Field, won the election and came to power in December 1962. In a clever tactical move, Field immediately released the 1959 detainees still rusticating in the remote hot desert of Gokwe in the Zambezi Valley, and released all the detainees within the next three months. This brought everyone onstage for a power struggle. Chikerema and Nyandoro assumed they would return to their old positions in the movement, if not to even higher echelons due heroes who had suffered imprisonment for the cause. The new reform group had lost its leverage, and Sithole, Chitepo, Takawira, and the others found themselves on the fringes. With so many aspirants to secondary positions of power, the party president was in a strong position to dictate terms.

The release of the detainees was a cause of great celebration all over the country. For the next three months, the leadership was dined and wined in every town in the country. The Zimbabwe Traditional and Cultural Club of Highfield, which had started the whole circus, was the first to question the duration of the festivities. The ZTCC went even further, openly criticizing the party leadership for failing to get down to business and to endorse some acts of sabotage that had been carried out without party authorization. The party leadership then issued explicit instructions that all extra-legal activities should cease pending the launching of a 'master plan' in early 1963.

As set forth by Nkomo to the executive, the 'master plan' would be launched from outside the country. Certain assigned members of the executive committee were to set up headquarters in Dar-es-Salaam, while an anchor group headed by Nkomo was to remain inside Rhodesia. Those assigned to serve as the external branch arrived dutifully in Dar-es-Salaam, but the 'master plan' they were to implement did not materialize. To add to their embarrassment, the founding conference of the Organization of African Unity (May 1963) chided them for departing the country. Seven members of the party executive committee announced in Dar-es-Salaam on July 9, 1963, that Nkomo had been suspended as party leader by a 13–7 vote, and would be replaced on an interim basis by Reverend Sithole. Nkomo responded by announcing from Salisbury that the dissidents had been dismissed from the party executive committee. A month later, the split in the movement was formalized when the formation of the Zimbabwe African National Union was announced by Sithole in Salisbury. While ZANU had the support of most elected branch officials in all provinces except the West, Nkomo retained the loyalty of all full-time paid party workers throughout the country. Each group believed that the other had no right to exist, and the petty war continues to this day. [ZAPU and ZANU agreed to a joint military command of the liberation movement (see Part X).]

*

The African National Council (the new ANC) was set up by a group of people under Bishop Muzorewa between December 1971 and January 1972 when it became known that the British Government was sending out the Pearce Commission to Rhodesia to test the acceptibility of the proposed settlement terms (see Part VIII). It set out to inform black Rhodesians what the proposals would mean in terms of their future political prospects. The ANC is committed to non-violence and non-racialism and its Manifesto reflects the Christian principles of its president and deputy president, Bishop Muzorewa and the Rev. Canaan Banana (the latter now in exile). But the movement also includes former members of the African nationalist parties who have thus far evaded detention and whose only remaining 'legal' association remains the ANC.

DOCUMENT 10. *Manifesto of the African National Council*, HIGH-FIELD, SALISBURY, 10 MARCH 1972

Beliefs

1. This Council believes in the power of the unity of the African masses in the imperative need for the opposition of those elements or forces which seek to sow the seeds of division among our people. Divided we will remain slaves and strangers in the land of our birth. United though we may suffer, we shall toil, but with dignity, until we are free. We should, therefore, be warned that our worst enemies are those who seek to divide us and those who labour to keep us in perpetual oppression, be they black or white.

2. We believe in the invincibility of numbers of the masses of men and women of goodwill in Rhodesia and that the African

National Council is truly a grass-roots organisation in its very scope, membership and spirit.

3. We believe in a government that will establish and promote the sanctity and practice of the essential human freedoms of conscience, of expression, association, religion, assembly and movement of all the people irrespective of colour, race or creed.

4. We believe in non-racialism, the universal brotherhood of man under the fatherhood of God. This means forced segregation and forced integration violate the principle of free choice of association.

5. We believe in a non-violent, peaceful, orderly but permanent and continuing struggle to be waged within the Law and for the establishment of a constitutional government.

6. We believe that true peace and harmony among all people and economic stability of this country can only be assured for all time by the establishment of 'the government of the people, by the people, and for the people'.

7. We believe that the rights and property of the minority should be protected; we do not however believe in the minority's amassing of social, political and economic privileges at the expense of the freedom of the majority.

Declaration

The African National Council solemnly dedicates itself to strive for the realisation of those universal human rights conceded to the citizens in all democratic and just societies. This being so,

1. We shall not waver or prevaricate in our demand for the creation, in this country, of a just social order; but shall strive to achieve this justice which is long overdue;

2. We shall not deviate from our just demand for universal adult suffrage;

3. We shall never concede to the fallacy that there is any justification for racial and other forms of discrimination as between one human being against another. Thus, we shall continue to oppose racial bigotry, religious intolerance, class arrogance, the idiocy of tribalism and undeserved economic privileges. And we shall strive to create a nation where black and white can live as children of the One Almighty God.

4. We shall never compromise with the sin of greed which is the main characteristic of a minority controlled economy; but will continue to promote a fair and free participation of each and every citizen of this our motherland—rich in natural resources.

5. We shall forever abhor the continued denial, under the pretext of 'preservation of Western Christian civilisation', of the masses' demand for legitimate self-determination.

6. We shall never support nor respect a system which lays emphasis on Law and Order at the expense of charity, justice and human dignity; but will continue to call upon the conscience of this country to influence the establishment of law and order with justice.

7. We shall require and desire nothing less than self determination.

PART IV

The Constitutional System

THE 'LEGAL' CONSTITUTION

In response to the repeated demands of the European leaders for the removal of Britain's remaining reserved powers to intervene in Southern Rhodesian affairs on matters concerning 'native' interests, and from Africans for representation in the exclusively white Parliament, the British Government agreed to the convening of a constitutional conference in 1961 to discuss proposals for the amendment of the Southern Rhodesian Constitution (the Letters Patent of 1923). In exchange for the removal of the reserved powers, the British Government obtained agreement on the establishment of a Declaration of Rights, a Constitutional Council to report on the observance of those rights and a special amendment procedure by which certain basic clauses of the Constitution were to be entrenched.

In addition to the members of the governing United Federal Party, those attending the conference included delegates from the African National Democratic Party, the right-wing Opposition Dominion Party, the moderate Central Africa Party and representatives of the Chiefs and the Asian and Coloured communities.

At the conclusion of its deliberations, the conference (with the Dominion Party dissenting) agreed to a number of recommendations for a new constitution. The African NDP, however, recorded its opposition to the proposals on representation and the franchise. The final settlement, agreed between the British and Southern Rhodesian Governments, provided for an Assembly of fifty 'A' Roll (mainly European) seats and fifteen 'B' Roll (African) seats. The franchise qualifications for the 'A' and 'B' Rolls were virtually the same as those prevailing for the 'Ordinary' and the 'Lower' Rolls under the Colony's Electoral Act of 1957, with a few additions to the 'B' Roll and the removal of the limitation on the number eligible to register on the 'Lower' Roll.

The case against the qualified franchise is made by a spokesman for the African nationalists, Mr M'lambo. A criticism of the constitutional proposals as a whole, from a Rhodesian legal adviser, Mr Leo Baron, is contained in the article in Part VIII, comparing the 1961 Constitution with the *Tiger* proposals.

DOCUMENT 11. *Report of the Southern Rhodesian Constitutional Conference*, SALISBURY (FEBRUARY 1961, CMND 1291)

Declaration of Rights

5. The Conference agreed that there should be enshrined in the Constitution a Declaration of Rights to be enjoyed by the people of Southern Rhodesia.

6. This Declaration of Rights should conform with the following general principles:

(a) It should prescribe those fundamental rights and freedoms that ought to be secured to every individual of any community.

(b) Such rights should apply without distinction of race, colour or creed.

(c) The exercise of any such rights by one individual should not prejudice the exercise of similar rights by others.

(d) While the rights of the individual should be protected, the State should nevertheless be enabled to assume and exercise whatever powers may be necessary in peace and war, for the purposes of:

(i) defence and public safety;

(ii) law and order;

(iii) public health and morality.

7. Any law, regulation, bye-law, or other subsidiary legislation, passed after the enactment of the new Constitution, which contravened the provisions of the Declaration of Rights, should be invalid. It should be open to any person adversely affected by a law, which in his opinion contravened the Declaration of

Rights, to question its validity in the Courts; and there should be an ultimate appeal to the Judicial Committee of the Privy Council.

Constitutional Council

9. The Conference agreed that, as an additional safeguard for human rights, there should be created a Constitutional Council with certain advisory and delaying functions. The Council would comprise about twelve persons, chosen by an Electoral College, in accordance with procedure which has still to be worked out.

10. It would be the duty of the Constitutional Council to examine any new Bill (other than a Money Bill) passed by the Legislative Assembly, before submission for the Governor's Assent, and to report to the Assembly (within a maximum of thirty days) whether, in its opinion, the Bill was unfairly discriminatory or otherwise contravened the provisions of the Declaration of Rights.

11. In the event of an adverse report from the Constitutional Council, it was assumed that the Legislative Assembly would normally withdraw or amend the Bill. If, however, it disagreed with the opinion of the Council, the Assembly would be entitled to confirm the Bill by a two-thirds majority, or, after a delay of six months, by a simple majority. . . .

15. The above procedure would not apply to any laws or subsidiary legislation in force before the enactment of the new Constitution. However, the Council could draw the attention of the Legislative Assembly to any such laws which, in the opinion of the Council, were inconsistent with the provisions of the Declaration of Rights and should be amended or repealed.

Representation and Franchise

16. The Conference had a number of long and detailed discussions on the subject of parliamentary representation and the franchise.

17. When the Conference opened, the various groups explained their attitudes towards this problem as follows:

(a) The *United Federal Party*, while recognising that Africans must over the years play an increasing part in the affairs of the country, stressed the importance of not lowering the qualifications for the franchise.

(b) The *Dominion Party* advocated: (i) that there should be no change insofar as this would involve a lowering of existing standards; (ii) that the present Lower Roll should be eliminated; and (iii) that the monetary qualifications should be related to the value of money.

(c) The *Central Africa Party* advocated a simple franchise qualification of literacy in English and the inclusion of additional categories of persons holding responsible positions in public service who would not necessarily be literate in English.

(d) The *National Democratic Party* maintained that 'one man one vote' was the only realistic solution to the question of the franchise.

(e) The *Coloured Community* asked that two special seats in the Legislature should be reserved for them; since they considered that this was the only practical way of safeguarding their political status as a minority group.

(f) The *Asian Organisation* accepted universal adult suffrage as the ultimate objective, but considered that this should be achieved by stages.

18. Having regard to these widely varying views and aspirations, it was not surprising that no group was able to secure the agreement of the Conference to the particular system it favoured. Nevertheless, while maintaining their respective positions, all groups (with the exception of the representatives of the Dominion Party) considered that the scheme outlined below should be introduced.

19. Voters would register on two rolls—those with the higher qualifications on the 'A' Roll and those with the lower qualifications on the 'B' Roll.

20. The Legislative Assembly would be increased from 50 to 65 members. Of these, 50 would be 'A' Roll constituencies (delimited on the basis of the number of voters on the 'A' Roll). The remaining 15 would be 'B' Roll constituencies (delimited on the basis of the number of voters on the 'B' Roll).

21. One Member would be elected for each of the fifty 'A' Roll constituencies by the 'A' Roll and 'B' Roll electors, voting together. If, however, the 'B' Roll votes cast should amount to

more than 25 per cent of the 'A' Roll votes cast, the 'B' Roll votes would be proportionately reduced in value, so that the total number of 'B' Roll votes would be equivalent to 25 per cent of the total 'A' Roll votes cast in the constituency.

22. Conversely, one Member would be elected for each of the fifteen 'B' Roll constituencies by the 'B' Roll and 'A' Roll electors voting together. If, however, the 'A' Roll votes cast should amount to more than 25 per cent of the 'B' Roll votes cast, the 'A' Roll votes would be proportionately reduced in value, so that the total number of 'A' Roll votes would be equivalent to 25 per cent of the total 'B' Roll votes cast in the constituency.

23. The electoral system should provide for a single transferable vote.

24. It was agreed that every effort should be made to encourage all who are eligible for the vote to register as electors. In addition, all practicable administrative measures should be taken to facilitate registration and to eliminate practical obstacles which tend to discourage enrolment.

Amendment of the Constitution

25. The Conference agreed the procedure to be followed for effecting future amendments to the Constitution.

26. Any amendment to the Constitution would require a two-thirds majority of all the members of the Legislative Assembly.

27. For the amendment of a few basic clauses of the Constitution, it would be necessary, in addition to the two-thirds majority of the Assembly, to obtain either (a) the agreement of a majority of each of the four principal racial communities voting separately in a referendum, or alternatively (b) the approval of the United Kingdom Government. The latter would be at liberty to decline to give a decision, on the ground that they considered that the issue should go to a referendum. Those entitled to vote in a constitutional referendum should be the registered voters, subject to the proviso that, until there are 50,000 African voters, all Africans who are 21 years of age or over and who have Standard VI education should be entitled to vote.

28. The basic clauses of the Constitution to which this special procedure would apply would include those relating to the Declaration of Rights, the Constitutional Council, the Judiciary, appeals to the Privy Council, and the procedure for amending the Constitution.

30. Any amendment to the composition of the Legislative Assembly or the franchise would require a two-thirds majority of all the members of the Assembly. However, it should be specified that the franchise should not be restricted below the level prevailing at the time of the enactment of the Constitution, save by the procedure described in paragraph 27, subject to the proviso that monetary qualifications might have to be adjusted to conform with changes in the value of money.

Reserved Powers of United Kingdom

31. The Conference agreed that the decisions to enshrine a Declaration of Rights in the new Constitution, to establish a Constitutional Council and to permit appeals in this connection to the Judicial Committee of the Privy Council, would provide safeguards against discriminatory legislation as fully effective as those at present afforded by the powers reserved to the United Kingdom Government.

32. The Secretary of State for Commonwealth Relations accordingly informed the Conference that he would be prepared to recommend the elimination of the powers retained by the United Kingdom Government:

(a) to advise the Sovereign to withhold assent to Bills of the Legislative Assembly of Southern Rhodesia or to annul Acts already passed by it; and

(b) to exercise control over matters relating to the Native Department.

33. In the time available, the Conference was not able to consider the provisions of the present Constitution dealing with Native Reserves and the Land Apportionment Act. However, it was agreed in principle that the powers of the United Kingdom Government in relation to these matters should be eliminated, provided that fully effective alternative safeguards could be devised.

34. The Southern Rhodesia Government asked that the

United Kingdom Government should initiate legislation to provide that, in future, Parliament at Westminster would not

Franchise Qualifications (Appendix, Cmnd 1399)

The proposals provide for an 'A' Roll and a 'B' Roll.

2. The following requirements will be common to both Rolls:

(a) *Citizenship:* Citizen of Rhodesia and Nyasaland.

(b) *Age:* 21 years or over.

(c) *Residence:* Two years' continuous residence in the Federation and three months' residence in the constituency and electoral district concerned immediately preceding application for enrolment.

(d) *Language:* Adequate knowledge of the English language and ability to complete and sign the prescribed form for registration (except in the case of duly appointed Chiefs and Headmen).

3. The following are the different additional qualifications respectively required:

'A' Roll

(a) Income of £720 during each of two years preceding date of claim for enrolment, or ownership of immovable property of value of £1,500.

OR

(b) (i) Income of £480 during each of two years preceding date of claim for enrolment, or ownership of immovable property of value of £1,000, and (ii) completion of a course of primary education of prescribed standard.

OR

(c) (i) Income of £300 during each of two years preceding date of claim for enrolment, or ownership of immovable property of value of £500; and
(ii) four years Secondary education of prescribed standard.

OR

(d) Appointment to the office of Chief or Headman.

'B' Roll

(a) Income at the rate of £240 per annum during the 6 months preceding date of claim for enrolment, or ownership of immovable property of value of £450.

OR

(b) (i) Income at the rate of £120 per annum during the six months preceding date of claim for enrolment, or ownership of immovable property of value of £250; and
(ii) two years' secondary education.

OR

(c) Persons over 30 years of age with—
(i) Income at the rate of £120 per annum during the six months preceding date of claim for enrolment or ownership of immovable property of value of £250; and (ii) completion of a course of primary education of a prescribed standard.

OR

(d) Persons over 30 years of age with—
Income at the rate of £180 per annum during the six months preceding the date of claim for enrolment, or ownership of immovable property of value of £350.

OR

(e) All kraal heads with a following of 20 or more heads of families.

OR

(f) Ministers of Religion.

legislate for Southern Rhodesia, except at the request of the Government of Southern Rhodesia, in regard to any matter within the competence of the Legislative Assembly. The Secretary of State for Commonwealth Relations took note of this request without commitment.

*

Under the Rhodesian constitutional system, the key to political power lies in the franchise. In the following article, Mr M'lambo, chairman of the research committee of the Zimbabwe African National Union, analyses the franchise qualifications that have been devised by successive Rhodesian Governments to retain the right to vote in 'civilised' (i.e. European) hands. (On the 1961 Constitution, see Document 41.)

DOCUMENT 12. 'A MEASURE OF "CIVILIZATION" IN RHODESIA: THE RESULTS OF THE QUALIFIED FRANCHISE' BY ESHMAEL M'LAMBO (FROM *The Times*, 16 NOVEMBER 1971)

Since it was introduced in 1898 the franchise in southern Rhodesia has been based on Cecil Rhodes's formula of 'equal rights to all civilized men'.

The fact that Rhodesia is one of the few countries in the world which still retains this old qualified franchise system escapes those who support the policy. On the other hand, the Africans maintain that the qualified franchise in Rhodesia is a racial device by the minority to keep power for themselves in perpetuity.

In order to understand the arguments, it is necessary to examine the franchise qualifications of Rhodesia to see whether they embody 'civilized standards'. It is argued that the vote should be given to a responsible person who knows how to use it wisely. Responsibility is measured in terms of the income, property and education of a citizen.

The economic boom that came to Rhodesia after the war increased the income of some Africans, which led to the registration of 453 voters. Further registration was forestalled by the 1951 Electoral Act, which more than doubled the income requirements—from £100 p.a. The annual average earnings for Africans were below £70 p.a., while the white workers were getting above £800. The country at the time employed 6,812 African teachers, educated and responsible citizens, yet only 453 Africans were voters. The reason was that the average salary of teachers was miserably low. These teachers were, none the less, better educated than the thousands of white workers who earned higher salaries which in turn enabled them to vote.

Only one election, that of 1953, was conducted under the franchise qualifications of 1951. Mr Garfield Todd discovered in 1956 that the number of African voters was only 560 out of an electorate of 52,184, yet the number of Africans in responsible positions, and with education, had increased enormously after the war. It was agreed that either money was to be found to increase the salaries of the Africans to qualify for the franchise, or a method of lowering the franchise qualifications had to be devised to increase African voters.

Parliament passed the Electoral Act, 1957, after the Tredgold Commission, which recommended lowering the franchise qualifications. The Act provided for two electoral rolls, 'ordinary' and 'special', whose income requirements were: for 'ordinary', £720 p.a., or £480 p.a. and complete primary education, or £300 p.a. and four years' secondary education. The special qualification, which was restricted to only 20 per cent of the ordinary roll voters, was £240 p.a. or £120 p.a. and two years' secondary education.

The paradox was that, contrary to the talk of lowering the qualification, it had in fact been raised from a simple £240 to as much as £720 and £480 p.a. Most Europeans could qualify still because their incomes averaged £948 at this time, but Africans earned an average of £80 p.a. The average salary of African teachers was £116 p.a., of nurses £109 p.a., of government officers in agriculture £103 p.a. By the time of the general election in June, 1958, only 2,000 Africans were registered.

The 1961 franchise was introduced as a result of the constitutional changes introduced in 1961. The roll was divided into A and B categories. It was hoped to enrol altogether more than 60,000 African voters. The government of Sir Alec Douglas-Home told the UN in June, 1964, that if Africans had not been misled into boycotting the vote in 1961-62 100,000 of them could have been on the voters' roll. Like most of the previous claims, this has no basis. Only 50,000 could have registered on the B roll, and 5,500 on the A roll.

A major provision of the franchise qualifications is in property. It often provides the vote for owners of houses or farms valued between £550, with four years' secondary education, or £1,500 without education. This is superfluous. It encourages double counting and so false figures.

The third requirement for the franchise is education. Like the property requirement, this is unnecessary because most Europeans qualify without even needing the full primary education qualification. In 1961, the European average income was £1,154 p.a., while the Africans earned an average of £94 p.a. The majority of whites thus qualified under the £792 income requirement, which does not need to be supported by education.

The standard of African education is higher than that of whites if assessed by the sheer weight of numbers. Between 1928 and 1968, 304,413 Africans obtained Standard Six certificates. In the same period, 126,717 Africans obtained various secondary education certificates. This is a larger number in fact than that of the total adult European population, which is lower than 100,000. No doubt the white population has a higher number of professional men and women, but this is due to the privileges they receive from the system.

THE 'ILLEGAL' REPUBLICAN CONSTITUTION

Four years after the Unilateral Declaration of Independence the Rhodesian Front Government finally introduced a republican constitution, implementing the basic principles of government to which they were committed, but which they had hesitated to enact while the possibility of a settlement with Britain still remained. Although the Government had proclaimed a 'new' independence Constitution in 1965, it was virtually a continuation of the 1961 Constitution, with a few but significant changes, such as the abolition of the complex amendment procedure which had required the consent of all the races by means of a referendum to alter the so-called entrenched clauses, and the right of appeal to the Judicial Committee of the Privy Council in London.

The basic ideology on which the Constitution is founded is set out in the introduction to the White Paper. The key provisions are those relating to the Legislature, tribal representation and the franchise. Also significant is the provision that the Declaration of Rights is not justiciable. The Prime Minister's address to the nation justified the adoption of republican status and a separate franchise for the races. At the same time, it rejected the proposal for separate parliaments for the races, advocated by a large proportion of his own ruling party.

The most articulate statement against the Constitution was made by the only European member of the Opposition, Dr Ahrn Palley, elected to represent the African township of Highfield in Salisbury.

DOCUMENT 13. *Proposals for a New Constitution for Rhodesia*, THE RHODESIAN FRONT GOVERNMENT WHITE PAPER ON THE 1969 CONSTITUTION (C.S.R. 32–1969)

Introduction

The Government of Rhodesia believe that the present Constitution [1965] is no longer acceptable to the people of Rhodesia because it contains a number of objectionable features, the principal ones being that it provides for eventual African rule and, inevitably, the domination of one race by another and that it does not guarantee that government will be retained in responsible hands.

Therefore it is proposed that there should be a new Constitution which, while reproducing some of the provisions of the existing Constitution, will make certain major changes in order to remove these objectionable features.

The proposed new Constitution will ensure that government will be retained in responsible hands and will provide Africans with the right to play an increasing part in the government of Rhodesia as they earn it by increased contributions to the national exchequer. Moreover, the new Constitution will recognize the right of the African chiefs, as the leaders of their people, to take part in the counsels of the nation.

The existing inequality in the treatment of the land rights of the races will be remedied. Provision will be made for the same protection to be given to the European Area as that given to the African Area. New Bills governing land tenure, which will replace the Land Apportionment Act [Chapter 257] and the provisions relating to Tribal Trust Land in the present Constitution, will be introduced into Parliament at the same time as the new Constitution. The provisions of the new Bills which are designed to protect land rights of Europeans and Africans will be entrenched in the Constitution.

Power will be vested in the Legislature to delegate to provincial or regional councils or other bodies certain functions of government as and when such delegation is considered to be appropriate.

The new Declaration of Rights will not be enforceable by the courts. The rights enshrined in the Declaration will be entrenched and will be safeguarded by the creation of a Senate and the vesting in it of power to delay legislation. In this important function the Senate will be advised by a special committee. As the Senate will be entrusted with the duty of upholding the Declaration of Rights no provision will be made for a Constitutional Council. In addition, the proposed procedure for constitutional amendments will ensure that the Senate will play a significant part in protecting the Constitution and the rights conferred by it. . . .

Any reference in this paper to a European means a person who is not an African.

The Legislature

Senate

7. The Senate will consist of twenty-three senators of whom—

(a) ten will be European members elected for the whole of Rhodesia by an electoral college consisting of the European members of the House of Assembly from candidates nominated by voters on the European voters roll;

(b) ten will be African chiefs elected by the Council of Chiefs, five of whom will be from Matabeleland and five from Mashonaland;

(c) three will be persons appointed by the Head of State. . . .

House of Assembly

9. Initially there will be sixty-six members of the House of Assembly of whom—

(a) fifty will be European members elected by the Europeans registered on the rolls of voters for fifty constituencies; and

(b) sixteen will be African members—

(i) eight being elected by the Africans registered on the rolls of voters for four constituencies in Matabeleland and four constituencies in Mashonaland; and

(ii) eight being elected by four tribal electoral colleges in Matabeleland and four tribal electoral colleges in Mashonaland comprising chiefs, headmen and elected councillors of African councils in the Tribal Trust Lands.

Increase in the number of African members

10. In principle the number of African members in the House of Assembly will be in the same proportion to the total number of members as the contribution by way of assessed income tax on income of Africans is to the total contribution by way of assessed income tax on income of Europeans and Africans until the contribution by Africans amounts to one-half of the total contribution.

Until the contribution of Africans amounts to sixteen sixty-sixths of the total contribution of Europeans and Africans the principle will not be applied and the number of African members will remain at sixteen. When the contribution of Africans exceeds sixteen sixty-sixths of the total contribution of Europeans and Africans the following procedure for increasing the number of African members will come into effect.

The number of African members will be increased two at a time being one additional member for Matabeleland and one additional member for Mashonaland, until the number of African members is equal to the number of European members.

The first increase of two African members will be allocated to the African members elected by tribal electoral colleges and the number of colleges will be increased accordingly. The second increase of two African members will be allocated to the members elected by the voters on the African rolls and the

74

number of African constituencies will be increased accordingly. Subsequent increases will be made in a similar manner.

Every increase of two African members will be made in direct proportion to the increase in the contributions of Africans compared with the total contribution of Europeans and Africans in such a manner that when the contribution of Africans amounts to half of the total contribution of Europeans and Africans at that time the number of African members will be equal to the number of European members.

DOCUMENT 14. THE 1969 CONSTITUTION: ADDRESS TO THE NATION BY THE PRIME MINISTER, THE HONOURABLE IAN DOUGLAS SMITH, MP, 20 MAY 1969

As the intractable British attitude has ended our hopes of a negotiated settlement, we now have the alternative available, which we are about to place before you. This new Constitution epitomises a sincere search for a formula which will reconcile radical differences of race, culture and society of all the people who live in Rhodesia. . . .

We have aimed to create a Constitution which will enable us to develop conditions in Rhodesia under which the two main races can live in harmony without fear of dominance or subjugation. The very essence of the Constitution is the maintenance of stable and progressive government. This is offered to you in large measure for as far ahead as we can see; thereafter it will be lodged safely in the hands of future generations.

We accept the policy of offering fair and reasonable opportunity to all people, which will allow them to develop and progress for the good of Rhodesia on the principle of merit. This does not, however, include the denial of the rights of others, nor does it encourage or tolerate any measure which will be prejudicial to racial harmony.

It is an historical fallacy that a shared or common franchise is the only guarantee of individual freedom, dignity and equality. We reject this as impractical in the light of present-day realities, and point to many cases in this world where it is a proven failure.

We do subscribe, however, to the dictum that all are entitled to be heard in the councils of the State, and to this end we

75

propose a separation of the franchise, while at the same time envisaging a central Parliament of the Legislature and the Senate, in which representatives of the races may consult, work and plan together. Such Legislature will therefore be built on what we have already, but its influence will be spread to ensure a better reflection of African urban and rural interests. In other words, it will be more truly representative of African opinion. In addition there will be a Senate in which Chiefs as well as mature Europeans will play an important role.

We believe that Common Roll seats, with African contesting European for the same seat is an unsatisfactory and distasteful business. It leads to bitter and unrelenting conflict, which is a contributory cause of increased racial tension and disharmony in the struggle for power based upon common roll and common constituencies. This is something we seek to abolish completely from the parliamentary structure of the new Rhodesia. It will be supplanted by differing methods of election. The most important innovation is one which allocates racial representation in our Legislature, *pro rata* to Income Tax contributions. This surely is a reasonable yardstick for assessing worth and contribution to the common weal. We have studied this aspect of parliamentary representation very closely, and have yet to be convinced of a better system.

It opens up a vista of a new, imaginative and bold attempt to meet a problem and place the constitutional future of our country on a realistic basis, untrammelled by the political theories of other countries alien to our own.

So, let us have the courage to take the initiative and implement this new idea. After all, who else is better able to provide the answer to our problem than us, the people who live with it, who understand it. Certainly not the British, who have left a trail of disaster in the wake of their departure from so many countries. . . .

On the issue of a Republic, I have been at pains on previous occasions to point out that Rhodesia is left with no choice other than to accept a Republican form of Government. I know that there is deep and sincere sentiment towards the monarchy amongst many sections in Rhodesia. However, it is abundantly clear that even had we settled a Constitution with the British Government, we would have been a State outside the Commonwealth, for membership requires approval of all the member States and this would not have been forthcoming for Rhodesia, particularly from certain of the Afro-Asian countries, unless we had accepted and implemented majority rule. I discussed this question on more than one occasion with the British Government and they concurred with this view which I have given you. In other words, the choice has been taken out of our hands.

I believe that I should tell you that I and my colleagues in Government are satisfied that benefits will flow from the creation of a Rhodesian Republic. . . .

Let me remind you that our predecessors in Government had accepted the desirability of a hand-over to majority rule, and they were busy conditioning the Rhodesian public to accept this. The only thing over which they were not at one was the time required to complete the operation, and this varied from about 3 to 12 years.

It was this which was the very reason for the formation of the Rhodesian Front—a rallying ground for people of different political parties who realized that if the then Government were not checked, we were going to lose our country. We marshalled our forces, in order to prevent the implementation of this mad idea of a hand-over, of a sell out of the European and his civilization, indeed everything he had put into his country. That was the story then: it is the same old story today; and as far as I am concerned it will be the same old story for ever. It is a story of which we are proud, one which we have no wish to hide away. It is for this reason that we now put before you our new Rhodesian Constitution, to take the place of the present Constitution which, however innocuous it may look at the moment, leads on relentlessly to majority rule.

In all fairness to our critics, let it be conceded that they have stuck to their same old story, too—going back to the time before we came to power, they advocated a hand-over to majority rule, and today they advocate the same course. Let me warn you to take care that you don't allow these people to pull the wool over your eyes. They have powerful forces at their disposal, and these will be directed towards you ceaselessly, every day, until the referendum is over, and finally, the die has been cast.

77

I do not think that there is any doubt that some Europeans will say that this is not the ideal Constitution as far as the Europeans are concerned; on the other hand, there will be some Africans likewise, who will claim that this is not the ideal Constitution as far as the Africans are concerned. However, I and my colleagues in Government have to be realistic and responsible, for Government is responsible for both our main racial groups. . . .

Let me say to you that while our relations with the rest of the world are important—and your Government is very well aware of this—even more important are the internal relations between our two main races. We will not allow ourselves to be deviated from this fundamental belief. In all honesty, our success must be conceded—today Rhodesia is one of the most peaceful countries in the world, with our race relations the envy of many others.

That is how it must continue, and we have taken great pains to ensure that our new Constitution was designed with this end in view.

DOCUMENT 15. THE 1969 CONSTITUTION: THE OPPOSITION VIEW, FROM DR AHRN PALLEY, MEMBER FOR THE AFRICAN TOWNSHIP OF HIGHFIELD (FROM RHODESIA, *Parliamentary Debates*, VOL. 75, 8 OCTOBER 1969, COLS 1190–200)

DR. PALLEY: This Constitution is the summation of political steps that must inevitably have followed the unilateral declaration of independence. It is the summation of events that are inescapable and within this Constitution is spelt out clearly and purposefully the true reasons for the taking of U.D.I. No matter how these reasons may have been hedged in previous debates and on previous occasions, the main reason for the taking of U.D.I. was the halting of political advancement by the African population. As a corollary to that, there was that an end should be brought to the experiment of multi-racialism that had been practised in this country up to that point. I have no doubt in my mind whatsoever that those were the true basic causes and true reasons for the taking of U.D.I. The question of a republic is ancillary to that and is merely a constitutional by-issue because as long as there was any constitutional right inherent within Her Majesty's Government in the United Kingdom, those two policies which I have suggested as the true cause and true reason for U.D.I. could not, of course, become implemented.

Therefore, a republic, though a major constitutional step, is with due respect to members of the Cabinet, merely a constitutional by-product to those two primary and major reasons and basic purposes. In my opinion, everything else was secondary to those two issues and I do not believe that there is a single supporter of Government or a single member who sits in this House supporting Government who accepts the principle of political partnership, complete and absolute political partnership. I say that deliberately; I do not believe that there is a single supporter of Government or a single hon. member who sits in this House supporting Government who accepts the principle of complete and undiluted political partnership with its equivalent of the sharing of power. Political partnership means political power; politics are power. That is the whole essence of politics. Therefore, the theoretical presentation of parity as it occurs within this new proposed Constitution, in my opinion, is merely a single presentation to attempt to perhaps delude external opinion, but it has not done so. In my opinion, the sole presentation of parity, which is absolute equality, the eventual absolute equality within a Chamber in the very far future, is politically dishonest and politically deceitful, and, indeed, not meant by Government.

If any hon. member, who supports Government accepts this principle of political parity which means the sharing of political power within the state, which means the sharing of all power within the state, then I ask that hon. member this afternoon to get up and say so. Until any hon. member says that he believes in this complete and absolute sharing of political power within the state, I will say that is not meant by Government. It is not meant by the Rhodesian Front party and it is merely window-dressing and political deceit . . .—[MR. DIVARIS: Do you accept it?]— . . . because the inevitability of the sharing of political power means inescapably majority rule.—[MR. JAMES: Hear, hear.]—All hon. members know that and there is not a single hon. member supporting this Constitution who will accept the inescapable outcome of the concept of parity.—

[HON. MEMBERS: Hear, hear.]—That is why I say it is bogus and a sham.—[MR. DIVARIS: Do you accept it?]

Of course, it is a project even within the Constitution of the very distant future. Hon. members may do projections and estimates when that even theoretically might occur but it is a very far off political occasion, should it ever arise. My own personal belief is that it will never occur.

Let us look nearer at hand; let us look to the immediate position; let us see what this Constitution has to offer in the guise of power because when we talk of politics let us clear our minds of the dross and realize that we are talking basically of power.

Now, in the sense of the power structure of the state there emerges one feature from the Constitution and that is that the lower House, or the Assembly, will be dominant in every aspect; it will be dominant in every sphere. It will control the legislation completely and the Senate is a mere appendage to the Assembly or lower House, as the Senate itself will have no real power whatsoever. It will, on occasions, be able to delay a measure but on every occasion when that occurs the Assembly or lower House, will have the overriding power of being able, in most cases, by a mere resolution passed on a majority vote, to enforce the will of the Assembly. The only occasion on which the Senate will have any power whatsoever—and that will not be the power of enforcement, it will be the power of veto—is in respect of the specially entrenched clauses. Then, of course, it will have the power of veto but not the power of enforcement.

Under those circumstances, I think it is right and proper to give major attention to the composition of the Assembly because of the Senate having very minor subsidiary powers, not that that must be taken to be felt that the Senate is of no consequence, but in relationship to the Constitution it is the Assembly that should get major attention. There one must look at the composition of the lower House because within the lower House is the tell-tale key to power. As all hon. members know, the composition of the lower House is clear and explicit. It will consist initially of 50 European members elected by the European voters of the country.—[MR. JAMES: So-called European.] It will consist of 16 African members elected in a different way from those European members who are elected but elected with

80

the primary political instinct of divide and rule.—[HON. MEMBERS: Hear, hear.]—It is odd indeed that that principle should have been called upon so early in events when there is not a shadow of doubt who will rule. It is beyond doubt who will rule and yet in spite of that at this very early, initial stage the age old political principle of divide and rule is called into existence in this Constitution.—[MR. CHIGOGO: Shame.]

Of the 16 black members who will be in the future House there will be eight elected by—let me call them loosely—the urban voters, though they will not be entirely urban. They will be those Africans who enjoy the vote at the moment and they, as hon. members know, will be apportioned, four for Matabeleland and four for Mashonaland. Those eight will be the only eight African members who will sit in this House elected as direct representatives of an electorate. The other eight will appear as indirect representatives of an electoral college consisting of chiefs, headmen and certain councillors of various local African councils. There the election speaks for itself. As far as possible wedges will be driven into the African representatives to prevent a consolidation of Africans who are likely to sit in opposition, of achieving a unity of opposition.

Under those circumstances, with other aspects of the Constitution, it seems to me that in future the interests of the white community and the interests of the African community must inescapably begin to diverge and inescapably lead to conflict. Rather than producing a state of cohesion and co-operation or creating a situation when that is likely to occur, I feel that this Constitution is more likely to lead to conflict and lack of co-operation. By the nature of things I think that is inescapable. Though perhaps that may be insignificant in the early stages, it is a very dangerous situation to create because in that situation created by this Constitution can lie the seeds of tremendous trouble in the future.

Therefore, when the Minister of Justice, in introducing this Bill, suggested that the new basis for representation and the question of taking the tax position as the basis for representation would take the emotion out of politics and, in a sense, take the P out of politics, I feel he has never been more wrong. If he was not talking double talk, then he was making the most naïve statement that any representative of Government could be

81

making. But I believe that the Leader of the House understands the political situation in this country very thoroughly
indeed and very deeply. I feel that when he put forward this
suggestion he knew indeed that it could not hold water. There
again, he put it forward because he could find little sound
argument to justify it.

Hon. members know that already within the Constitution
there is an existing escape clause. Hon. members know that the
numbers within the lower House may be increased at very
early stages, providing the ratio and proportion of black and
white members does not alter. Therefore, even at this early
stage, on theoretical consideration, the European numbers
could be increased, let us say, to 150 and the black members,
say to 48. The political difference between 16 and 50 is small
compared with the political difference in power between 150
and 48. There with skill or cunning, depending how one looks
upon it, the first chink is shown for the progression of events.—
—[THE PRIME MINISTER: Your mathematics are wrong.]

If my mathematics are wrong, which may well be, my politics are not. Hon. Members know that parity will never be
reached for the simple reason that the Rhodesian Front
Government which sits in power, and in my opinion will sit a
very long time in power . . .—[HON. MEMBERS: Hear, hear.]—
[THE PRIME MINISTER: Let's hope so.]—. . . more even than the
oft-stated 40 years, and the reason that parity will never be
reached is a very simple one because no Rhodesian Front
Government will ever want it. It is as simple as that.—[MR.
MAJONGWE: As clear as crystal.]—Hon. members who sit in
Government know that. Hon. members who sit in Government
do not wish for anything else. If I am wrong I give them every
opportunity to get up and say that they wish to enjoy political
parity between black and white with the sharing of power in
this country. . . .

Let us for a moment look at the present position; the income
tax position.—[THE PRIME MINISTER: Counting of heads.]—The
total tax—that is income tax—paid for the year ended 30th
June, 1968 was £28,560,000. That paid by the African sector
was £64,744. For practical purposes, the entire amount of direct
taxation has been paid by the European community, a negligible amount by the African community. For the earlier year,

year ended 30th June, 1967, the amount of £28,720,000 was paid in direct taxation; by the African sector a mere £50,534. Again, for practical purposes, the entire amount of income tax —direct taxation—was paid by the European community; in other words the yardstick speaks for itself. There is such a gap between the tax paid by the African sector and the European sector that no matter how long a period of time is given, this method of parity will always be receding into the future. That, of course, is exactly what the Prime Minister and his colleagues want and again I am fortified in my contention by the faint little smile which once again crosses the face of the Prime Minister, and then I know I am always right. It shows for practical purposes perfectly clearly that this gap between the contribution of the African sector in direct taxation and the contribution in direct taxation by the European is for practical purposes unbridgeable and that is why it has been taken as the yardstick on which to base representation. Almost for the first time the same smile which I see periodically on the face of the Prime Minister I see now on the face of the Minister of Justice. It makes me doubly right. It is an endorsement of my analysis.— [THE PRIME MINISTER: You have not much confidence in the future of the African.]—[AN HON. MEMBER: Quite right.]—That was a very silly remark to be made by the Prime Minister, because now let us analyse an aspect of income tax.

As has been wisely pointed out by hon. members in the earlier part of this debate, income tax is purely a tax on income and to contribute tax the opportunity for income earning has to be there.—[MR. MAJONGWE: That is it.]—It is no use saying little is produced in the way of tax if the opportunity to earn income is restricted. Income in a society such as we enjoy is based on two requirements; it is based on the job one holds and the salary one is paid or the property one owns and the income one derive's from one's property. That is what income depends on in a society such as we enjoy. If one looks at the position, no one can surely deny that in respect of the job position and in respect of the salary position in this country, the European enjoys an infinitely better position than the African sector. In respect of property ownership, that also applies. Because the system that has developed in this country is such that the better jobs, the more highly paid jobs in this country are in the hands of the

European section of the community. If the proposition of Government is politically honourable and politically truthful as they wish us to accept it and if indeed they accept the principle of parity, then job opportunity must go hand in hand with this requirement of representation based on direct taxation.

I ask the Government to deal with the position and look, for instance, at the Civil Service, to look at commerce, to look at industry, to look at banking, to look at the professions, to look at the trades, to look at the apprenticeship position and ask themselves what role the African plays in all these aspects and one will find that in none of these does the African hold other than the lowest and lowest paid position and that is the position. Whether one likes it or not though job reservation is not a matter of legislation in this country, the practice and mores of the society is that such a situation for practical purposes exists. That is the condition that occurs in the whole aspect of society within the wage and salary earning structure and the composition of the state. That is a fact that anyone can ascertain on an examination of these aspects. Therefore, I say that is why this yardstick of tax has been chosen because Government knows that it is a perfectly safe yardstick to employ to keep the question and the shadow of parity so far off in the future that for practical purposes it is not an issue at all.

Now the other aspect of income is the question of property ownership and all hon. members know that property ownership in respect certainly of immovable property is very limited in so far that the African sector enjoys the right at all to acquire immovable property and own it in his own right. It exists to a very limited extent within the urban townships—to a very limited extent. Within the rural area it exists within the Native Purchase Areas also to a limited extent and that alone is where the African can enjoy the right to personal ownership of immovable property. In so far as the Tribal Trust Lands are concerned, all hon. members know that there is no ownership of property in an individual sense, there is merely the right of occupation and usage but in the society such as we know and we exist in it is the right to the ownership of property and particularly immovable property and land that produces wealth and income.—[THE PRIME MINISTER: Quite the reverse.]—That is the major source of wealth and income together with salary and wages.—[THE PRIME MINISTER: Quite the reverse.]—On that question where the African only enjoys the right of occupation and usage in the Tribal Trust Lands and the tribesmen only enjoy that right he cannot enjoy the advantages of capital availability and so forth leading to wealth and income. It is at that point, perhaps, that we come across that aspect of the Constitution which to the Prime Minister's way of thinking, and Government's way of thinking, I would say is perhaps the weakest part of the Constitution. . . .

I concede that this situation can be held and developed for a measurable length of time. It is hard to know how long.—[MR. MAJONGWE: Not very long.]—I am not suggesting that this constitutional structure will break down overnight, but we must not build constitutions, metaphorically speaking, for days; surely we must build constitutions for the years to come for the good of the country—a constitution that will be endurable and will be able to allow government within the tremendous complexities and difficulties that exist in this country. This country, by virtue of the fact that there is such a diversity in the ranges of its population, has problems and difficulties that other countries do not face.

PART V

Security and Repression

The original Law and Order (Maintenance) Act was initiated by the United Federal Party Government of Sir Edgar Whitehead in October 1960 (along with the Emergency Powers Act and the Vagrancy Act) following disturbances in the African townships arising from the arrest of a number of African leaders of the National Democratic Party under the provisions of the 1959 Unlawful Organisations Act, which banned the African National Congress. The Southern Rhodesian Prime Minister justified the 'drastic' new legislation as necessary to deal with 'hooligans, loafers and spivs'. The Chief Justice, Sir Robert Tredgold, who resigned over the measure, called it a 'savage, evil, mean and dirty' Bill. The Bill was supported by the Dominion Party Opposition, the precursor of the Rhodesian Front. After the Rhodesian Front came to power in 1962, it repeatedly amended the Act in order to extend its provisions and increase its penalties. Originally intended by the UFP Government as a deterrent against internal disorders, the Act was broadened by the RF Government to meet external threats and incursions. The Act's chief exponent in the RF Government, Mr Lardner-Burke, had no real opposition in Parliament (except for the Independent Member, Dr Ahrn Palley), to contend with, so the Act was never seriously challenged in the course of its many amendments.

DOCUMENT 16A. THE LAW AND ORDER (MAINTENANCE) BILL, 1960, INTRODUCED BY THE UNITED FEDERAL PARTY GOVERNMENT OF SIR EDGAR WHITEHEAD (FROM *Southern Rhodesia Legislative Assembly*, VOL. 46, 27 OCTOBER 1960, COLS 2515–32)

Minister of Justice and Internal Affairs [Mr Reginald Knight]:

Experience of the work of these three Acts [the Sedition Act, 1936, Subversive Activities Act, 1950, and Public Order Act, 1955] in practice has shown that for obvious reasons the existing law is inadequate to deal effectively with many of the activities of known subversive elements in this Colony. . . .

The Bill now before the House empowers a Police officer who has reasonable grounds for belief that a breach of the peace may occur, or that public disorder may be occasioned, to call upon three or more persons assembled in a public place to disperse. . . .

The Bill confers on any Police officer the power to forbid any person from addressing any gathering, and he may enter and remain on any premises, or attend at any place where three or more persons are gathered, whenever he has reasonable grounds for believing that a breach of the peace may occur or that a seditious or subversive statement may be made.

Under the Bill before hon. members, if the Minister is of the opinion that the printing, publication, dissemination or possession of any publication or series of publications may be contrary to the public interest, he may, by order published in the *Gazette*, declare that printed publication or series of publications or all publications published by any person or association of persons, to be prohibited publication; and if the order specifies by name a publication which is a periodical publication, such order shall, unless a contrary intention is expressed, have effect with regard to all subsequent issues of such publication, and not only with respect to any publication under a name, but also with respect to any publication under any other name if the publishing thereof is in any respect a continuation of or in substitution for the publication named in the order. . . .

The section of the Bill [III] has been widened to make it an offence not only to wear prohibited uniforms but also to display any banner, placard or notice bearing any slogan or words or emblem which may lead to public disorder or to any strike. It has also been made an offence to sing any song or utter any slogan which may lead to disorder. . . .

The penalty in the case of any person who threatens violence to another in his absence, or behaves in a manner which is likely to lead to acts of violence on the part of another person, has been increased to liability to imprisonment for a period not exceeding ten years instead of seven years.

Provision is also made that where a person without lawful excuse makes any statement indicating or implying that it would be incumbent or desirable to do any act or acts likely to lead to the destruction of any property, or to do any act or acts or to omit to do anything with the object or which has the effect of defeating the purpose or intention of any law, the penalty for such offence remains imprisonment for a period not exceeding seven years. . . .

Provision is also made in Part III of the Bill in connexion with inducing any person unlawfully to cease work or leave any particular piece of work unfinished or unlawfully to refrain from returning to work. The penalty in that particular instance is imprisonment not exceeding two years providing the person has not got a lawful excuse. . . .

A new offence has been created, that of any person using any opprobrious epithet or any jeer or gibe about any other person in connexion with the fact that he has remained at work or has absented himself therefrom, or has refused to work for any employer, or has undertaken any duties as a member of any Police reserve or in any Government department. . . .

Similarly, any person who does anything which is likely to expose to contempt or ridicule or to store up hatred against, or to impair the authority of any officer of the Government of this Colony or of the Federation, or any Police officer in the carrying out of his duty, will be guilty of an offence and liable to imprisonment for a period not exceeding three years. . . .

Subversive statements have been defined in the Bill and the Government is given power in determining whether or not an oral statement is subversive, to have regard to the person or persons or class or persons to whom such statement was made, to the circumstances in which it was made and to the question whether such statement was made fairly, temperately, with decency and respect and without computing any corrupt or improper motives. The Bill further implies that any statement which computes any corrupt or improper motive to the Legislature or Government of the Colony or the Federation shall be regarded, *prima facie*, as subversive. . . .

I made reference to the unprovoked attacks by stoning on motor vehicles, and in order to make these hooligans who act with such disregard for human life and property, realize that this conduct will not be tolerated in Southern Rhodesia, the Bill provides a liability to a minimum period of imprisonment of not less than five years and a maximum period of not less than 20 years.

The Government has come to the decision that it is absolutely necessary to have these minimum penalties in order to act as a deterrent in the present circumstances. . . . Provision is made in the Bill that magistrates shall have special jurisdiction to impose on summary trials, fines not exceeding £100 or imprisonment for a period not exceeding five years. . . . Another matter of importance is that the Attorney-General may bring a sentence on review before the High Court if he considers that it is grossly inadequate, and the High Court is in those circumstances empowered to impose a different sentence. . . .

I should like to indicate straight away that the Bill is absolutely non-racial, as I hope all hon. members will appreciate. It is not aimed at any section of the public. It is merely aimed to see that law and order are maintained in this country. . . .

It has been said that this is in effect an evil Act. What I would prefer to say is that it is an Act to counteract evil. It is to counteract evil which has occurred recently and there would be a tendency for that evil to become a habit. . . .

I am perfectly satisfied that the ordinary, moderate, law-abiding African will have nothing but gratitude for the fact that this Bill is about to receive the approval of this House.

Mr William Harper

[Dominion Party leader and a future Minister of Internal Affairs in the Rhodesian Front Government]:

There is a very large measure of agreement for this Bill, and I do not think the Prime Minister [Sir Edgar Whitehead] need have any qualms that there will be any attempt to reduce to a ridiculous minimum any of the penalties that Government have in this Bill. . . .

I believe that a substantial proportion of the responsibility for these problems lies with Government in that they have not dealt with the problem of breeding grounds for the ideas of Pan-Africanism in this country. They have felt that their own methods, which, as I have said, is a method of integration and appeasement, was an adequate means of dealing with the breeding grounds. I consider that Government made a very grave mistake in thinking that way. The Prime Minister's own viewpoint was clearly indicated when he went on to say that this was not a problem of black versus white. He said that in Bulawayo it was typified as being a problem of the 'haves' against the 'have-nots'. I say that the Government is fantastically wrong. It was an attack on the things associated with Europeans and European advancement. . . .

DOCUMENT 16B. LAW AND ORDER (MAINTENANCE) AMENDMENT BILL, 1968, INTRODUCED BY THE RHODESIAN FRONT GOVERNMENT (RHODESIA *Parliamentary Debates*, VOL. 72, 24 SEPTEMBER 1968, COLS 1569–81)

Minister of Law and Order [Mr Lardner-Burke]:

The mandatory death penalty was first introduced into the Law and Order (Maintenance) Act at the beginning of 1963. I do not need to remind hon. members that at that time there was a spate of petrol bomb attacks in African townships in Rhodesia. After very deep and serious consideration Government at that time decided that the mandatory death penalty should be introduced in relation to certain offences where a petrol bomb or explosives were used. Although there was much opposition to the introduction of this provision which is now contained in section 37, Government was convinced that it was necessary in order to deal with the situation. Offences of the type in question decreased considerably after the introduction of that provision, and I think that this was due in no small measure to the introduction of the mandatory death penalty.

Petrol bomb offences are now very rare and there have, in fact, been no cases of this type during 1968.

The second case where the mandatory death penalty was inserted in the Law and Order (Maintenance) Act was last year, when section 48A was introduced imposing the mandatory death penalty for persons possessing arms of war with intent to endanger the maintenance of law and order in Rhodesia or any part of Rhodesia or in a neighbouring territory. The Bill to amend the Law and Order (Maintenance) Act, which I introduced on the 19th July 1968, and have subsequently withdrawn, was intended to amend subsection (2)(b) of section 48A of the Act because it was found that terrorists usually enter Rhodesia under strict discipline and therefore those who wish to abandon their arms in order to avoid the death penalty could not do so within the limits prescribed.

The reason for the introduction of these two measures, in 1963 and 1967, respectively, was to deter extremists from using petrol bombs and terrorists from entering Rhodesia with arms of war. With regard to the use of petrol bombs, Government is satisfied that the deterrent aspect of the penalty has proved effective, and that the position is so well under control that Government can now abolish this provision.

In so far as terrorists are concerned, the organizers in countries to the north of us are careful to ensure that those terrorists waiting to be sent to Rhodesia are isolated and kept unaware of the provisions of our law. Moreover, when these terrorists do enter Rhodesia the strict discipline exercised by their communist-indoctrinated hard-core leaders and control are such that they have no chance to abandon their arms of war until after their entry. Often it is only when the security forces arrive on the scene that the terrorists have a chance to evade the vigilant control of their superiors. It appeared from a practical point of view that it was more often than not impossible for them to surrender within one mile of the border of Rhodesia or within a period of one hour from time of entry. This state of affairs led to the introduction of a Bill which had its First Reading in the House on the 19th July 1968, and which would have amended subsection (2)(b) of section 48A. That amendment was designed to make it easier for terrorists to surrender and thus avoid unnecessary bloodshed.

It must be realised that as far as Government is concerned, the prime object is to save the lives of our security forces and if we can do anything to this end, it must be done. This being so, leaflets were dropped on the terrorists earlier this year suggesting that they surrender and thus save their own lives. Immediately this was done we realised that there was a conflict with section 48A, and, therefore, it was decided to amend that section.

Interrogation of terrorists has proved to us that the communist masters in Zambia do not allow the terrorists to get any information from outside. The subsequent intention to introduce this current Bill was the reason for my recent withdrawal of the Bill introduced on the 19th July. In this section concerning terrorists, the Government is also now quite satisfied that it can abolish the provision with regard to the mandatory death penalty. Legislation can express to the judges how serious Parliament considers a crime to be by setting out the penalties, but it should be left to the judges to decide on such penalty. . . .

Government has often been accused by certain left-wing elements of using Draconian powers to maintain law and order in Rhodesia. I deny this, but if such powers which we have employed have produced the generally peaceful situation which prevails in Rhodesia today, then we must continue to use them, but never let it be said that we do not constantly review and relax our use of such powers when the situation, in our opinion, warrants such review or relaxation. . . .

The Bill is a simple one. In the two clauses mentioned provision is made for the repeal of the mandatory death sentence, but the death sentence remains, with the option of imprisonment, either of which can be imposed at the discretion of the court. The opportunity has also been taken to provide for life imprisonment as the alternative to the death sentence. . . .

There is one point, however, that I wish to make absolutely clear. Although the Government is repealing the mandatory death penalty, let there be no misunderstanding that, in respect of the two offences mentioned in the sections, the death sentence may still be imposed if the court considers it appropriate. It is the mandatory aspect of the provisions which alone is affected. . . .

DOCUMENT 17. COMMENT ON THE SECURITY LEGISLATION INTRO-
DUCED BY THE WHITEHEAD GOVERNMENT IN SOUTHERN RHODESIA
(FROM THE FORMER CHIEF JUSTICE, SIR ROBERT TREDGOLD, *The
Rhodesia That Was My Life* (ALLEN & UNWIN, 1968, PP. 228–31)

There had been a steady build-up of the security legislation.
The Unlawful Organisations Act provided for the banning of
organisations 'likely to endanger public safety, to disturb or
interfere with public order or to prejudice the tranquillity or
security of the Colony', or again if it was 'likely to . . . promote
feelings of illwill or hostility between or within different races'.
. . . The Preventive Detention Act provided for the detention
of persons concerned in activities that led to a state of emergency or that might lead to another. The Public Order Amendment Act created new offences of boycotting and intimidation.
The Firearms Act tightened up the control of such weapons to
an extraordinary degree.

The deeper motives that prompted this spate of repressive
legislation must, at this stage, be a matter for conjecture. It is
certain that the debates in Parliament afford only a clue.
There had been disturbances amongst the Africans and there
was probably reason to anticipate even greater trouble, but
nothing to justify these drastic curtailments of ordinary liberties. It may well be that, consciously or unconsciously, they
were a sort of compensation—something thrown into the
balance as a makeweight against the concessions that this and
the preceding government had made to the Africans. No doubt
the unrelenting pressure by the security authorities for an
extension of their powers was maintained and, in the prevailing
atmosphere, was hard to resist, especially as the ministers concerned were relatively inexperienced and less imbued with
deep convictions of the importance of liberty and justice than
their predecessors. Perhaps an indication of some of the thinking behind them is to be found in a statement by the Prime
Minister at the time. He said, in effect, that his government was
not content to follow the traditional British policy of waiting
till trouble arises and then dealing with it. He would see to it
that trouble did not arise. This is dangerous doctrine and strikes

at the heart of the rule of law. If the decision as to who is a potential trouble-maker is left to ministers or their subordinates, the outlook is grim for those who oppose them. Obviously there will be a predisposition to assume that their political opponents belong to this category. Moreover, each decision becomes a matter of personal judgment and thus depends upon the temperament and outlook of the person making it. If a nervous or suspicious official allows his imagination rein there is no limit to where it can carry him.

The culmination came in 1960, when the government published its Law and Order Maintenance Bill. An eminent lawyer described the proposals as vicious and a leading newspaper as hysterical and neither epithet was unjustified. It almost appeared as though someone had sat down with the Declaration of Human Rights and deliberately scrubbed out each in turn.

Here were some of the provisions:

The right of public assembly was circumscribed.

Officials or ministers were given complete control of public meetings and processions, and these could, in discretion, be altogether prohibited for a period. An individual could by order be prohibited from attending public gatherings.

A lawful meeting could, by order of a police officer, be made unlawful and dispersed, and he could forbid any person, however eminent, from addressing such a meeting.

A minister could ban any publication or series of publications and his order could not be varied or set aside by a court of law.

It was made an offence to wear uniforms or display flags with political objects, to 'jeer, or jibe' in certain circumstances, to say 'Hear, hear', to a subversive statement. So it went on.

Coupled with this Bill was another entitled the Emergency Powers Bill. Under this the government was empowered to declare a state of emergency and thereafter make regulations of a most sweeping nature. Amongst the provisions specifically envisaged was power to a minister to move people about the Colony or to arrest and detain them in his discretion.

It was claimed by the supporters of this legislation that every provision could be paralleled somewhere in the Commonwealth. This may have been true in a very general way, but in no Commonwealth country had all these repressive measures been collected together in one legal system. At the time I described it as an anthology of horrors—and it was not an inept description. Provisions had even been taken from Ghana, at the time constantly held up in Rhodesia as an example of oppressive government. Again, the Law and Order Maintenance Bill was not intended as emergency legislation to be invoked in times of national peril. It was to become part of the ordinary law of the land.

There were, moreover, two features of this Bill that were novel and which I felt were especially objectionable. For a large number of the numerous offences created minimum sentences were prescribed, which the courts were compelled to impose regardless of the circumstances of the case, and the Magistrates' courts were given a greatly increased jurisdiction, enabling them to deal with cases under the new law which otherwise would have gone to the High Court.

It is scarcely necessary to stress the difficulty that judges experience in assessing sentence; it is accepted that this is one of the most perplexing of the judicial functions. The circumstances in criminal cases vary infinitely. To lay down in advance the sentences to be imposed, many of them extremely severe, was an interference with the ordinary powers of the judiciary and was bound to lead to serious injustice.

To give special jurisdiction in cases under the new law to the Magistrates was completely illogical. These cases would have political undertones and in many of them strong emotions and prejudices would be aroused. The magistrates, generally speaking, had not the professional training and background of the judges. They were younger and less experienced and more subject to pressure by the government and the public. Nor was it an answer to suggest that their decisions would be the subject of appeal to or review by the High Court. There are many cases in which a higher court cannot interfere with the decision of a court of first instance, although it may be acutely unhappy about the decision. If more judges could not be appointed to deal with the anticipated expansion in the number of cases, the logical course would have been to give the magistrates a wider jurisdiction in more humdrum and less controversial cases and reserve to the High Court the power to deal with at least the more serious cases under the new law.

The cumulative effects of the security laws was to turn Rhodesia into a police state. The word has an emotional content and many white Rhodesians become very angry if it is used of their country. Yet, as I understand it, a 'police state' is a state in which the police and the executive are given or assume complete control over all political activity. In this sense it is manifestly true of the Rhodesia of today [1968]. Certainly the grosser physical abuses which have characterised some recent political states have not been widespread. It is sad to have to admit, however, that even these have not been entirely absent. Things have happened that would have been unthinkable a few years back. The arrest in the dark hours of the early morning. The repeated police visit at his place of employment or home of the suspect. Intimidatory measures such as these are not even a necessary part of the administration of the Acts. Hundreds of Africans have been detained without trial, many more restricted. Scores of people have been deported from or denied entry to the country. All political parties that had widespread African support have been banned. The only newspaper that could claim directly to represent African opinion has been banned, as have a number of publications in the nature of political commentaries. (These are of special interest because those who read them are in a position to judge how far the ban was justified. I can say categorically that of those I read, which included the newspaper, not one could properly be described as subversive.) Political meetings or other open political activities amongst the Africans have virtually ceased.

Public reaction to the legislation displayed a remarkable example of conditioning of the electorate. Earlier security legislation, that had involved relatively mild interference with the liberty of the subject, had provoked a strong and vocal reaction and vigorous protests were general and outspokenly worded. As more and more extreme measures were successively introduced the protests became more and more feeble, till only a few small groups continued the battle. Now they are so widely accepted, at least as a necessary evil, that it is difficult to arouse support even for a glaring individual case of their harsh application.

And for much of this a government had been responsible that professed itself liberal. That is what shook the confidence of the Africans to its foundations.

RHODESIAN FRONT SECURITY LEGISLATION

DOCUMENT 18. THE SECURITY SPHERE, FROM 'LAW AND THE
UNEQUAL SOCIETY: DISCRIMINATORY LEGISLATION UNDER THE
RHODESIAN FRONT FROM 1963–1969' BY PROFESSOR CLAIRE
PALLEY* (IN *Race*, VOL. XII, NO. 1, JULY 1970)

The Rhodesian Front inherited from Sir Edgar Whitehead an
apparatus of security laws. It is arguable that existing legislation gave the Front so much power that they could maintain
order without fresh legislation. Nonetheless from their accession
to power, a catalogue of ever more repressive legislation
evolved. Much of this legislation, largely modelled on South
African precedents, restricted legitimate political activity.
Later it became necessary to add to the armoury of restrictive
laws, powers to facilitate the suppression of opposition, which
would be encountered after U.D.I., and to preclude violent
overthrow of the régime. In fact, the security laws clearly fall
into several groups, each chronological stage involving a more
totalitarian approach: the earlier legislation is replaced as
loop-holes or as changed African opposition tactics provoke
new techniques to suppress them. Thus the first security laws
introduced by the Rhodesian Front are those designed to make
active political opposition by nationalists virtually impossible;
these laws are largely toughening-up amendments to the Law
and Order (Maintenance) Act. Then come laws designed to
control population movement, especially the influx of Africans
into towns, and to ensure that unemployed Africans are returned to the rural areas. Next in the catalogue come emergency
powers used to give the executive unfettered powers of government and power to suppress opposition—laws which become
even more Draconian with the advent of U.D.I. Lastly come
laws designed to counteract African insurgency and to deter
African guerrilla activity.

The stage of 'toughening-up' security laws occurred in 1963
and 1964, and was repeated early in 1970. Powers were given
to force the resignation from any organization of any person
who had been an officer or office-bearer of any unlawful
organization, e.g. the African National Congress, and police
powers of entry and search were extended. Public gatherings

* Professor Palley is an eminent Rhodesian authority on constitutional law.

on Sundays and public holidays were prohibited; a mandatory death penalty was imposed for offences against residential property through the media of petrol, paraffin, or explosives; the police were given powers of search of all persons leaving or entering Rhodesia; and whipping for political offences was introduced. Advocacy of or assistance to any body inside or outside Rhodesia in order to overthrow the Government by unconstitutional means, or to take-over or usurp the functions of government, or to attempt to coerce Government either by force, boycott, or civil disobedience, was made an offence carrying twenty years' imprisonment. Preventive detention was reintroduced (and invalidated by the Appellate Division of the High Court as being in conflict with the 1961 Constitution). Control of processions was tightened; penalties were imposed for civil disobedience, resistance to law, or use of force to further any political object; and the length of any period of restriction was extended from three to twelve months. Increased penalties were introduced for encumbering free passage in streets, for trespassing on property and refusing to leave, for resisting the police, and for committing any act likely to lead to a breach of the peace; and police powers of search of anyone carrying a bundle by night were reiterated. It became a criminal offence to depart from Rhodesia without a valid travel document and from other than a prescribed port. The granting of bail in political trials was further restricted. So was the use of trade union funds, services, or facilities for political purposes or for any political organization. The death penalty was introduced for unauthorized possession of explosives. Restriction orders were extended from twelve months to five years.

At the end of 1964 the Rhodesian Front introduced laws enabling influx control of Africans. Thus new controls were imposed on Africans residing in local government areas. A deterrent to Africans residing in towns was the imposition of fees and charges on lodgers in African townships. Any occupier of a house, who let a room to a lodger, became responsible for registering the lodger with the local authority, and for paying a fee of 15 shillings per month to the authority. Occupiers were to pay fees for their own children aged over 16 years who were living at home with them. In the event of default, the occupier became criminally liable. In conjunction with this measure, police powers of searching African townships were ruthlessly employed. African householders were (and are) summoned from their beds in the early hours of the morning for searches without warrant of their premises. If illegal lodgers were found the occupiers were prosecuted and the lodgers ejected, while the latter were frequently prosecuted under the Africans (Registration and Identification) Act—the pass law of Rhodesia. (Between 1965 and 1969 there were 69,356 criminal convictions under the Act.) The purpose was to push unemployed Africans out of the towns where they might be fuel for a possible explosion against the régime, and to force them to return to the rural areas. At the end of 1964 it was estimated that the African Township of Highfield had by this means had its population reduced from 100,000 to 70,000.

The Rhodesian Front Government decided early in 1964 that they could control events more effectively if they governed under emergency powers. From March 1964 to the date of writing only one week has passed in which there has been no proclamation of a state of emergency in some part of Rhodesia. Since 5 November 1965 at three-month intervals there have been fresh proclamations of states of emergency covering the entire country. Powers to make regulations during such times of emergency were further strengthened by the Emergency Powers Amendment Act Number 22 of 1967. Emergency Powers (Maintenance of Law and Order) Regulations have been issued with each proclamation. These Regulations have empowered the Commissioner of Police, and commissioned officers appointed by him as protecting authorities, to make orders controlling the movement of persons, their entry into and exit from areas, and their removal from, prohibition from, or restriction to particular areas; to declare places and areas as protected; to control traffic and to seize vehicles; to control the taking of photographs and the posting of notices; to control the distribution of newspapers, and printing or publishing; to control arms, to seize weapons, and to control gatherings. In addition the Minister of Law and Order was authorized to detain any person in a prison or other place if it appeared to him 'expedient in the public interest', while a police officer might without warrant detain any person for a period not in excess of 30 days if the officer had reason to believe there were grounds to justify such person's detention, or if the person failed to satisfy him as to his identity, had committed or was about to commit any offence under any law, or had acted or was about to act in a manner prejudicial to the maintenance of public order or the preservation of the peace. Any police officer might without warrant search or enter any premises, vehicle, vessel, or aircraft, and search any person. For the accommodation of any arrested or detained persons camps might be and were established by the Minister, who might alternatively direct that persons detained on his order should be lodged in prison. Communications with such persons were prohibited, as was the publication of any information concerning restricted or detained persons or places of restriction or detention.

Indeed the prohibitions contained in section 34 of the Emergency Powers (Maintenance of Law and Order) Regulations 1967 were so extensive that by denying a detained person all communication with or access to a legal adviser, they denied to him the means of challenging in a court of law any contravention of the Declaration of Rights, which were expressly provided for in section 80 of the 1965 'Constitution'. They were adversely reported upon by the Constitutional Council as being 'in excess of anything which could reasonably have been thought to be required' for dealing with the emergency and thus not justified under section 78 of the 1965 'Constitution' which permitted action otherwise in contravention of the Declaration in time of emergency. In order to create a good impression during negotiations for recognition by the British Government, Regulations in March 1967 provided for a Tribunal appointed by the Minister of Law and Order to review the detention orders in force and to report to him thereon. However, he was not obliged to give effect to any recommendations by the Tribunal. Again, although the Constitution Amendment Act Number 49 of 1966 had empowered the enactment of preventive detention legislation, the régime continued to rely on its emergency powers because it did not wish to prejudice the negotiations with the United Kingdom.

The reaction by the régime to incursions by African guerrillas was to secure the passage of the Law and Order (Maintenance)

Amendment Act Number 50 of 1967. The Act provided that any person who, with intent to endanger the maintenance of law and order in Rhodesia or in a neighbouring territory, possessed any arms of war, should be guilty of an offence carrying a mandatory death penalty, unless there were special circumstances peculiar to the offence, and not the offender, endorsed on the record by the High Court. Once found in possession of any ammunition, firearms, detonators, explosives, etc., a person was to be presumed to have intended to endanger law and order and, unless he proved beyond reasonable doubt that he had no such intention, a mandatory death sentence was to follow. Furthermore, any person who committed an act of sabotage or terrorism with like intent (again such intention was presumed once the act was committed and could only be rebutted by proof by the accused beyond reasonable doubt that he did not intend such results) was liable to be sentenced to death or imprisoned for a period not exceeding 30 years. Acts of terrorism or sabotage were so broadly defined as to include not only the furtherance of any political aim or the effecting of social or economic change by forcible means, but also the causing of serious bodily injury or the endangering of the safety of any person within Rhodesia, or the causing of substantial financial loss to any person or the Government of Rhodesia. Persons who aid, abet, incite, conspire in, or attempt any such offence are likewise liable to the penalties of section 48A. The régime ignored a Constitutional Council report that the Law and Order (Maintenance) Amendment Bill 1967 contravened section 72 (2) (a) of the 1965 'Constitution', which provided that every person charged with a criminal offence should be presumed to be innocent until he was proved, or had pleaded, guilty. A motion for assent by a two-thirds majority secured its passage. Subsequently by the Law and Order (Maintenance) Amendment Act 1968 the régime substituted a discretionary death sentence for the mandatory one for possession of arms of war. However, Mr Lardner-Burke, Minister of Law and Order, made it clear that his attitude had not changed:

I am perfectly satisfied that death is the only thing for these individuals when they come in, but it is for the courts to

decide. . . . Our main concern is the saving of the lives of
the security forces and therefore if the mandatory death
sentence is going to cause an individual to fight to the death
to kill our people I think it only right that we should reconsider the point.

Later withdrawal of censorship regulations became possible
because a private arrangement was reached with the Press.
An editorial in the *Rhodesia Herald* disclosed that there had
been agreement with the régime not to publish anything embarrassing about the sanctions war. The reality of self-imposed
censorship remained. In any event 'the Rhodesia Broadcasting
Corporation is subject to censorship and control of what is
published'.

Confidence in the determination of the courts to uphold
order led in February 1970 to the enactment of the Law
and Order (Maintenance) Amendment Act. This removed the
fetter on judicial discretion which had formerly necessitated
the imposition of mandatory minimum sentences for security
offences. At the same time the Act was designed 'to block
possible loopholes in the existing Act'. Thus the amending Act
made it an offence carrying a maximum of 20 years' imprisonment for any person to encourage or incite another person to
attend a course or undergo training for unlawful political
objectives. Again, since proof of intent to cause hostility 'on
account of race, religion or colour' had caused difficulty in the
courts, the Act made it an offence to make statements likely to
engender hostility against any group, section, or class of the
community of a particular race, religion, or colour. Similar
difficulties of proof in respect of publication of statements
likely to cause alarm and despondency among the public
were also remedied. It also became an offence for anyone to
permit to be heard in public a broadcast of a subversive
statement emanating from a radio station inside or outside
Rhodesia. Finally, in a reference to guerrilla activities, the Act
made it an offence knowingly to harbour or assist terrorists, or,
having harboured or assisted them, to refuse to disclose to the
police this fact within a reasonable time. The régime wished
to counter 'pressure and threats' by terrorists for shelter by
making it clear to the public that heavy penalties (5 years'

imprisonment and/or a £300 fine) will be imposed on anybody who is proved to have concealed or helped a person whom he knows to be a terrorist.

CENSORSHIP AND SEDITION

The following is the official record of the trial in which the editor of *Moto* (the Roman Catholic paper) was convicted. It contains the whole of the article written by the Bishop of Umtali, Dr Donal Lamont (alleged to contain subversive statements as defined by the Law and Order (Maintenance) Act).

DOCUMENT 19. COURT RECORD OF THE TRIAL OF *Moto*: ALBERT BRUNO PLANGGER V. THE STATE (FROM *Newsbrief Rhodesia*, MAY 1973)

HIGH COURT OF RHODESIA, APPELLATE DIVISION
MACDONALD, A. C. J. and LEWIS, A. J. P.
SALISBURY, 27 FEBRUARY and 23 MARCH, 1973.

N. J. McNally for the appellant.
R. R. Horn, for the respondent.

MACDONALD, A. C. J.: The appellant was convicted in the Regional magistrate's court of contravening s.44 (2) (a) of the Law and Order (Maintenance) Act (Cap. 39) which provides, *inter alia*, that 'any person who . . . causes to be printed any subversive statement shall be guilty of an offence . . .'.

The trial court found that the appellant, in his capacity as editor of a newspaper, had caused subversive statements to be printed in it. The findings that the statements were subversive and that the appellant had caused them to be printed were not challenged on appeal. The sole point raised was that the appellant escaped criminal liability under the proviso to s.44 (2).

The statements in question were published in an article in a Roman Catholic newspaper called 'Moto' (a Shona word meaning fire), printed partly in the vernacular and intended for African readers. It was published at the request of its author, the Roman Catholic Bishop of Umtali, Bishop Lamont.

The article reads as follows—the subversive statements complained of are in italics:

'The Report of the Pearce Commission revealed to all the

world what most of us knew already, namely that the present government does not enjoy the confidence of—to use the consecrated phrase—'the people of Rhodesia as a whole', and that it rules without their consent. It is as simple as that.

The African people detest now, and always have detested the government of the Rhodesia Front Party. They all do, no matter how much through fear they may dissimulate. Be they ordinary workers, minor civil servants, teachers, police, soldiers, even chiefs, in their heart of hearts, they regard the government as the oppressor and themselves as the oppressed.

This is the simple truth which Mr Ian Smith and his followers have long been trying to hide. That this hatred should be so real and so widespread is understandable, but that the governing minority should ignore it or deny that it exists, is utterly irresponsible and could prove disastrous.

The ill-mannered reaction of many of his European audience to Bishop Muzorewa's recent address in the Margolis Hall in Salisbury is symptomatic of the incredible ignorance and naïveté of the ruling minority. They simply will not recognise the plain fact that the African National Council truly represents the African people who outnumber them by over 20 to 1.

Won't See

They won't even see in Bishop Muzorewa's willingness to meet them, a sign of that good man's reasonableness and moderating influence. They close their eyes to the elementary truth that the future of Rhodesia is completely in the hands of the black African people.

Dogs and guns and internment and restriction are all that the Rhodesia Front Government has to keep it in power. The supporters of the régime who talk of keeping the country in civilised hands are so isolated and immature that they cannot read the signs of the times.

Bishop Muzorewa was stating clearly his people's mind when he said that having rejected the proposals there would be no change of heart. Incredibly, some silly people had actually suggested that the Africans should tell Britain that they had made a mistake in refusing the settlement terms! There will be no change of heart. That day has passed.

Reflects Feelings

The African People of Rhodesia cannot be expected to live uncomplainingly under a Constitution that is itself a mockery of law, being deliberately framed to keep the majority of the country's citizens in subjection for ages to come. Bishop Muzorewa very properly reflects his followers' feelings in this matter.

No-one who has any sense of justice can fail to sympathise with him. His efforts peacefully to wish to dismantle the unjust and institutionalised social structures which oppress his people, particularly deserve the support of all who call themselves christians.

To talk of preserving christianity while tolerating racial discrimination with its innumerable attendant injustices, is to make a mockery of the mission of Christ who founded His Church so that God's will be done on earth as it is in heaven.

God's will can hardly be said to be done when a whole people is kept in subjection through a system which differs not in essence but only in degree from the Nazi doctrine of racial superiority.

Masses of African People

Rhodesians must face the fact that those in government and those whose support keeps them in power, suffer from serious moral under-development, if they cannot see how unjust the system is. There simply can be no hope of permanent peace in their country under the present way of life, which is canonized in the 1969 Constitution. It must go.

The masses of the African people, that is to say, the people of Rhodesia as a whole, will not tolerate it much longer. Racial segregation must go. Job reservation must go. European privilege must go. Pious talk about talk must go, unless there be a civilised confrontation about the concrete issues which constitute the injustices inflicted daily on the African people.

Bishop Muzorewa and his followers have wisely and generously expressed their willingness to take part in such a meeting. To react to him and his offer as churlishly as many have done already, is ill-mannered in the extreme; to continue to act in this way would be the height of criminal folly.'

Section 44 (1) defines a subversive statement as meaning, *inter alia,* 'a statement which is likely . . . to excite disaffection against . . . the Government or Constitution of Rhodesia as by law established. . . .'

To say—

(i) that the African people of Rhodesia cannot be expected to live uncomplainingly under the present Constitution;

(ii) that the Constitution is 'a mockery of law';

(iii) that it is a Constitution 'deliberately framed to keep the majority of the country's citizens in subjection for ages to come';

(iv) that no-one with 'any sense of justice can fail to sympathise' with the 'wish to dismantle the unjust and institutionalised social structures which oppress' the African people;

(v) that 'a whole people is kept in subjection through a system which differs not in essence but only in degree from the Nazi doctrine of racial superiority';

(vi) that not to 'see how unjust the system is' is to 'suffer from serious moral under-development';

(vii) that there can be 'no hope of permanent peace in this country under the present way of life, which is canonized in the 1969 Constitution',

is to make a series of statements each one of which is likely to excite disaffection against the Constitution and/or the system of government established under it, and it is understandable in the circumstances that Mr McNally did not attempt to argue that the words complained of were not subversive.

Mr McNally did, however, submit that the magistrate should have found that the appellant had brought himself within the proviso, including the requirement that a subversive statement to avoid criminal liability must be 'made fairly, temperately, with decency and respect and without imputing any corrupt or improper motive'.

It was on this aspect of his argument that Mr McNally experienced the greatest difficulty. His difficulty arose from the fact that the appellant found himself unable to support the language used, and a perusal of his evidence shows that he was patently embarrassed by being placed in the position of having to do so. Throughout the appellant's cross-examination the struggle between his desire, on the one hand, loyally to support a bishop of his church and the substance of the Bishop's criticisms of the Constitution, and his desire, on the other hand, to fulfil the higher duty of giving a truthful answer to the simple question; 'Would you if you had written the article have used the language employed by the Bishop? clearly emerges. After unsuccessful efforts to parry the question put to him, the appellant admitted that he would not, had he written the article, have used the language employed by Bishop Lamont. The relevant passages from his evidence read as follows:

'*Q*. Because he is a bishop and a man of authority in the church and you are a priest and a man of less authority in the church, you would not have expressed yourself as strongly as he? Is that what you are saying? *A*. Yes, probably not as strongly. I could refer to things I have written myself as editor of this paper. I have expressed myself on similar matters in editorials and I did not write statements as strong.'

'*Q*. Can we then proceed on the basis that the article correctly reflects your attitude, in other words you agree with what is written and how it is written in that article? *A*. These are different statements. If I were asked "Will you give your signatures to those articles?'

'*Q*. What would your answer be? *A*. I would not give it.

'*Q*. Why not? *A*. Because I could not subscribe to the statement according to my knowledge and my experience.

'*Q*. Why would you not subscribe to it? *A*. I would not put my name there instead of his'.

THE COURT (MR HAMILTON): *Q*. You would not put your name there because you would not subscribe to the article as it is written? *A*. Because I would not express myself as forcibly as he does.' . . .

'*Q*. While on the "guns and dogs" and so on, is there any part of the passage charged that you would not subscribe to in the forcible terms in which it is expressed? *A*. There I would leave out the statement about the Nazi doctrine. If I were to refer to it, I would not put it like this. Although he refers to the doctrine as such and not to the system—there is a difference —If I referred to this I would . . .

'*Q*. You personally would not have referred to Nazism? Is that right? *A*. I would not say that.

'*Q*. What are you saying? *A*. You can refer to Nazi and you can refer to it in another way.

'*Q*. I am not quite sure whether you feel that that reference to Nazi doctrine?— *A*. This was singled out as a very strong statement. I agree that if I referred to the Nazis I would not have put it like this. If I wished to make a comparison with Nazi doctrine, very often people use the word "Third Reich" which is a common expression used by journalists if they want to avoid saying Nazi. It is probably less familiar to some people. Still you can refer to their doctrine of racial superiority as being in conflict with the pronouncements of ministers in this country.' . . .

'*Q*. There is no suggestion that anything about the Constitution is good or desirable, is there? *A*. There is no suggestion of this here.

'*Q*. Broadly is this your own genuine view? *A*. I would qualify that in my answer saying the article as such does not pick out any particular pieces of legislation. It says that with the objectionable features it cannot stand. If I were to change the Constitution, I would single out certain aspects.

'*Q*. Are you saying then that you would in a criticism of the Constitution make allowance for the fact that it was not all evil? *A*. Yes, I would.

'*Q*. Now did you consider that the publication of this article might possibly involve a contravention of the law? *A*. No, I was not aware of that. As I said before, I took it as a very provocative article, a very critical article, a very forceful article but remaining within the law.'

There was, however, no admission by the appellant that the language of the subversive statements fell outside the protection afforded by the proviso; on the contrary, he maintained that it did. Whether it does is a matter for judicial decision. In the case of S. *v*. Mutasa, 1970 (4) S.A. 610, I had occasion at p. 614 to emphasise the need in a multi-racial community for 'politicians of all races' to 'express themselves fairly, temperately, with decency and respect and without imputing any corrupt or improper motive if racial friction and public disorder are to be avoided'. I referred specifically to politicians because that was a case involving a politician, but what I said applies to anyone who ventures into the political field. The prevailing political climate calls for great circumspection in the choice of language if law and order is not to degenerate into civil strife. And the greater the position of influence occupied by a person expressing political views, the greater the need for circumspection.

The author of these statements, because of his high ecclesiastical position in a church who enjoys the respect not only of its members but also of non-members, is pre-eminently a person who must, of necessity, weigh his words when he ventures into the political field. Indeed, it is the assumption that a person occupying such an exalted position will always do so, which gives his every utterance so much weight and importance. Added to this is the fact that he is a European. While Africans might well be expected to treat with some degree of scepticism criticism levelled by Africans against European control of the system of government, it is not to be expected that the same degree of scepticism will be accorded to the statements of an apparently unbiased and impartial European occupying an ecclesiastical office the very nature of which could be expected to ensure that its incumbent is a person who will make statements 'fairly, temperately, with decency and with respect and without imputing any corrupt or improper motive'.

It is not difficult, indeed it is all too easy, to pinpoint the problems which exist in Rhodesia at the present time. Nor does it require more than minimal intellectual ability to criticise the evils which flow from these problems. What men of good-will in this country eagerly seek are concrete and practical solutions to the problems which exist. It is an acknowledgement of their complexity that what we are short of in this country is not destructive criticism based on the problems which admittedly exist, but concrete and practical proposals for their solution. It cannot be emphasised too strongly that to harp upon the known problems without offering concrete and practical solutions to them can only exacerbate the situation, and such conduct, if subversive, might well lead to the break-down of law and order.

I have studied the statements complained of in the charge with care. I regret that in my judgment they are unfair, intemperate and impute both a corrupt and improper motive to the framers of the Constitution.

The statements are unfair because they involve an all-embracing condemnation of the whole of the Constitution, without any attempt being made to discriminate between good and bad features in it. As the appellant himself said in his evidence: 'If I were to change the Constitution, I would single out certain aspects.'

'*Q*. Are you saying then that you would in a criticism of the Constitution make allowance for the fact that it was not all evil? *A*. Yes I would.'

The language used is intemperate because emotive words are used in a context which can only render the statements as a whole inflammatory in the extreme, and the choice of words is such as to leave no doubt that they were intended to inflame the minds of the African readers of the newspaper. Particularly intemperate is the attempt to equate the 'system' with 'Nazi doctrine of racial superiority'. The appellant, to his credit, did not attempt to defend the use of these intemperate words, on the contrary he admitted that had he written the article he would have left out 'the statement about Nazi doctrine'.

By suggesting that the Constitution was 'deliberately framed to keep the majority of the country's citizens in subjection for ages to come' the author imputed an improper motive to the Constitution and its framers.

The passages relied on in the charge must of course be read in the context of the article as a whole. Unhappily the effect of the remainder of the article is only to increase the subversive nature of the offending passages. It is not unfair to say that the article is a message of hate. Indeed, the offending passages read in the context of the whole article are such as to give the greatest comfort and encouragement to the enemies of 'the Government and Constitution of Rhodesia as by law established'.

Mr McNally made no attempt to argue that the article was designed to bring about the reformation of alleged defects and errors in the Constitution. It was not in the circumstances possible for him to do so. The article was published in a newspaper clearly intended for Africans who were said by the author to be the victims of injustice, and not for Europeans whom the writer held responsible for the injustice and the appellant frankly admitted that the primary purpose of the article was not to bring about reformation of any defects. His evidence on this aspect reads:

'*Q*. But as far as the reformation of the defects were concerned, it has to take a back seat, would you agree? *A*. Yes, I would agree.

'*Q*. It is not the predominant intention? *A*. That I would agree with.'

In my judgment there is no substance at all in the appeal against conviction.

An appeal has also been noted against sentence. The sentence imposed by the magistrate was five months' imprisonment with hard labour, the whole of which was suspended for three years on condition that during that period the appellant was not again convicted of contravening s.44 of the Act, or convicted of any offence under Part III of the Act and sentenced to imprisonment without the option of a fine or to a fine exceeding $50.

The appellant was placed in an invidious position by Bishop Lamont's written request for publication of the article in 'Moto'. The request included the following passage:

'. . . I feel that the Church of Umtali must be on record as having spoken in our own Catholic paper'.

Doubtful about the propriety of publishing the article, the appellant sought advice from his own bishop, the Catholic Bishop of Gwelo. Unhappily he received advice to comply with the request. In the circumstances this advice was unquestionably wrong.

The request, the nature of the request, the fact that the appellant sought the advice of his own bishop, and the fact that he received bad advice are all factors which mitigate the appellant's moral blame-worthiness, and the magistrate acted wisely when he decided in the circumstances to suspend prison sentence, the length of which not only appropriately reflected the very serious nature of the subversive statements printed by the appellant, but also provided an adequate deterrent against repetition of the offence. In my judgment, there are no grounds which would justify this court in altering the magistrate's sentence. I should mention that the Act provides for 'imprisonment for a period not exceeding five years' and does not permit the option of a fine.

I would dismiss both the appeal against conviction and the appeal against sentence.

LEWIS, A. J. P.: I agree.

Evans and Surgery, Pittman and Kerswell, attorneys for the appellant.

PART VI

Apartheid: The Ideological Basis

Unlike the South Africans, the Rhodesians have not yet provided themselves with an ideological framework for their policies of apartheid. Nor have they a comparable religious foundation on which to base their racialist practices. Relations between the two races have been variously described, ranging from a paternalistic sort of 'partnership' on the one side to a complete system of segregation on the other. The concept of 'parallel development', like the 'two pyramid' design, was favoured by most of the white 'Establishment': Sir Godfrey Huggins, Prime Minister for over twenty years, represented this point of view, particularly in his statement that the 'native' must be ruled by 'a benevolent white aristocracy'. In order to obtain British consent to Federation with the north, the emphasis shifted to 'partnership' between the African and the European, once defined by Huggins as a partnership of 'the rider and the horse'.

'Separate development', the slogan of the Rhodesian Front, makes no pretence of 'partnership'. The races are to be strictly segregated and the 'separate but equal' provision is to be applied to a society in which inequality prevails. Mr Smith's statement on 'separate development' only just stops short of the partition solution supported by many of his party followers.

As the Africans see it, the Rhodesian Front Government is moving towards the South African system of Bantustans, or separate African homelands, while concealing this objective under the less emotive term of 'provincialisation'.

'PARALLEL DEVELOPMENT'

DOCUMENT 20. *Native Policy in Southern Rhodesia*: STATEMENT BY THE HON. SIR GODFREY HUGGINS, PRIME MINISTER AND MINISTER OF NATIVE AFFAIRS, SALISBURY, 6 NOVEMBER 1941

After the recent attacks on Southern Rhodesia's Native policy a review of the position is necessary for general information. Before doing so it is necessary to look for the background of the problem, so that we may realise the *raison d'être* of the policy we have at present. . . .

Now let us examine the Native problem from the point of view of the alleged hardships imposed on him. The African is a British subject, entitled to equal treatment in the eyes of the law. There are special safeguards provided to ensure that the African does get just treatment at the hands of the law; thus an African charged with a serious crime is not tried before a judge and a common jury, but before a judge and two special assessors (generally two retired Native Commissioners) who are selected because of their special understanding of the African and who can be relied upon to appreciate the African point of view. Again, when a European is charged with a serious crime of violence against an African he is not tried before a judge and a common jury, but before a judge and a jury specially selected from among the more responsible citizens. The African complainant is thus ensured that the case is tried before men who will not allow any possible colour prejudice to interfere with the administration of justice. The African has his rights, and these are properly and adequately protected, and in his own areas he is a free man except that there are certain reservations in regard to the possession of European liquor and firearms, and the able-bodied has to pay a poll tax of £1 a year in exchange for which he has a free building site, arable and pasture land, rent free. The European does not pay a poll tax and is not allowed this privilege. The tax is paid into general revenue, but it is to this source that we look for funds for the Native Councils as they improve and increase their work and require more finance. This is the only special Native tax; the African contributes to revenue through ordinary taxation such as Customs, dog tax, motor vehicle tax, etc., and for this he receives the benefits of good administration and may be said to participate in all national expenditure (except European education and associated matters, for which he has a separate sum voted).

It must not be deduced from this that the poll tax is to be regarded as a permanent feature of our administration. The main difficulty in changing to another system of taxation is to find a means by which the Africans can contribute to the cost of administration, without placing a premium on loafing in the Reserves and contributing nothing to the common weal either by work or payment. As yet the African, after he has acquired enough wealth to purchase a wife or wives, has not the same incentive to earn money to support himself and his family as the European has—the family in many cases supports the man.

The requirements of the African in the Reserves are still small. Our critics must realise that administration and social services have to be paid for and if the majority sit back, because their requirements as yet are small, and do nothing to promote industry and create wealth there is no means of paying for essential services. Until the African has to work to live as the European must, either by producing crops, etc., for sale or by working for wages, I see no immediate possibility of replacing the poll tax by some other form of taxation.

This tax is a passing phase if we assume, as we do, that the African can be raised above his old environment. We can very well say that without European stimulus the African for the most part would do little or nothing and contribute little or nothing in his present stage of development.

The African has a vote the same as any European, the qualifications for a vote being the same as for a European. In the present state of development of the African this is not of much practical use as far as African representation in the House is concerned. It will probably be advisable in the future to introduce some alternative method of representation, which would be more direct and of more real value to the African, in place of his existing right to vote. If and when such an alternative method is introduced, no African should be eligible to be placed on the common voting roll, at all events until the general average knowledge of the Africans has been considerably raised, because in the African's present state of development the right to vote is likely to prove an embarrassment rather than a benefit to him.

It is interesting to note that in the neighbouring Protectorates the African has no right to vote for the election of members to the Legislative Council.

At present the rights of the African are chiefly protected by the good sense and sympathetic understanding of the European members of Parliament. In this regard a very marked improvement is noticeable in the atmosphere of the House since the first days of Responsible Government. Today there are many members who are always prepared to enter a debate as champions of the rights of the African, and I am satisfied that today the African is not suffering from any lack of proper representation in the House. There is, moreover, the additional safeguard, overlooked by professional critics, in the reservations contained in our Constitution.

In the white towns—what might be described as the white reserves as opposed to Native reserves—the African has to conform to white requirements. It should be noted that he is not obliged to go to a white town; he can earn outside the town what for him is a good living, if he does not like the restrictions in the towns. The major restriction is the pass law; this is a passing phase still necessary in the state of development the native has reached, but already we have provision for the more enlightened African to be exempt.

A great many of the native prosecutions are under the pass laws, due to the rather juvenile mentality of the African who will take a chance, like a school boy, and when found out put up with the consequences.

Other offences against the law are chiefly offences under municipal by-laws which apply to all races, and there is a very large number of convictions under the Roads and Road Traffic Act, a measure for the protection of life and limb of all races, regardless of colour.

The chief measures which protect the European standard against the less developed race are the Industrial Conciliation Act, and the Maize Control Act and the pass laws. The protection given by the first two Acts is incidental and not the main purpose of these Acts. The Industrial Conciliation Act only enshrines the principles of the Trade Unions in England, i.e., that there must be no scabs to break wage agreements. The Maize Control Act as it affects the African is an attempt to deal with an internal marketing problem, in the same way as the United Kingdom and other parts of the Empire attempted to deal with competition from goods produced by people whose wage-earners were content with a lower standard of living. The pass laws protect the dwellers in the white towns from the unrestricted lawlessness of a people many of whom are as yet unable to distinguish right from wrong, when removed from their tribal authority and customs, and assist in the administration of the African. It must be admitted, however, that some of the offenders can distinguish between right and wrong, but, in the manner of a child, take a chance that they may not be found out. This latter explanation accounts for most of the numerous minor offences. The necessity for the pass laws rests between these two reasons; I have already explained that exemption from this law has been provided.

We are endeavouring to restore authority to the Chiefs and to educate the Africans in administration by means of the Native Law and Courts Act and the Native Councils Act. If we are successful with Native Councils, I anticipate that the Chief's authority guided by his elders will pass into the hands of the Chief subject to the advice of his elected council. The Councils, apart from gradually introducing local self-government into the Reserves and Native Area, will form a basis from which a central native council will be elected and also, as soon as possible, provide the machinery for electing Europeans to represent them in Parliament, and, much later, for electing Africans to represent them. . . .

Conclusion

At the commencement I said that some statement of our policy was necessary owing to recent criticism, and I have dealt with most of this criticism in a general way. It will be noted that some of our critics omitted the twenty-one million odd acres in the Native Reserves. . . . I have tried to be fair, and the only way the policy in this outline varies from my previous statements is that I have visualised the possibility of the two parallel lines in our parallel development policy coming together in some very distant future. The reason for this change is that I appreciate you cannot plan for the unknown, and, as the possibilities of the African in the future are unknown, to state that the lines will never meet is stating what is not and cannot be known. All we can do is to plan on what is known, and change the plan as knowledge increases; we cannot foretell the future, especially when it is appreciated that there is no known reason why man should not inherit the earth for several millions of years, although his ultimate extinction appears to be inevitable.

To those who believe that the European has no right to survive in Africa this policy will make no appeal.

'SEPARATE DEVELOPMENT'

DOCUMENT 21. STATEMENT BY THE PRIME MINISTER, MR IAN SMITH (FROM RHODESIA, *Parliamentary Debates*, VOL. 68, 2 AUGUST 1967, COLS 457–64)

THE PRIME MINISTER: The motion before the House is that the House expresses its deep concern over Government's policy of separate development. . . . In fact, I find it very difficult to understand what all the concern is all about.

Let us face up to a few of the facts of life. Traditional ways of life and governmental organization all over the world, and particularly in Africa, are being overthrown, and are being replaced by concepts which profess to spring from liberalism, but which are in reality inspired and fostered by communism. —[HON. MEMBERS: Hear, hear.]—We know that this is the common enemy and hon. members opposite do not have very far to look to find evidence of this point I am making. They only have to look to a number of well-known countries which lie in the African continent to the north of us, countries where there is perpetual revolution, where people are perpetually being slaughtered, massacred and intimidated. All this evidence is there, ready, at hand for them to observe. I am surprised at how long it takes for them to learn the lesson and yet in contrast here in Rhodesia there is a different system. We are now being asked to express concern over this system, over retaining for ourselves our well-tried and our well-established ways to which we are all accustomed and which stamp us as one of the truly civilized countries on the continent of Africa.

I am disturbed at the facile approach adopted by a number of hon. members opposite in this debate, including the mover and the Leader of the Opposition. These hon. members have been trying to prove that a deep laid plot has been going on through the years whereby the European has deliberately adopted policies, particularly in relation to land, designed to keep the African in a perpetually inferior position. They have suggested that where laws have been passed providing for different treatment between the races, this has been done solely for the protection of the European at the expense of the African. I suggest to these hon. members that they are getting their history a little bit out of focus; in fact, even more I would suggest that they have got it completely upside down. The true position is the very reverse.

I suggest that they are conveniently ignoring the problems which have always been inherent in building up Rhodesia as a nation while keeping in balance all the economic, political and social forces which operate at any one time. I would suggest that they do not have the maturity to understand that a country cannot progress on a programme of fine slogans; it must progress on practical and realistic policies related to law and order, to public safety, to full employment, sound financial practices and the right of the individual to live as full and free a life as the circumstances of his environment permit him to do.—[MR HLABANGANA: Separate development does not offer that.]

From our earliest days, long before there was any of the present day fuss about so-called fundamental human freedoms, it was recognized instinctively that for the relatively sophisticated European community, one set of policies was right while for the relatively unsophisticated Africans a different case was necessary.—[AN HON. MEMBER: We accept that.]—What is important is to see that in the application of these policies successive Rhodesian Governments have acted with integrity and justice in providing for each individual community the maximum which the country's resources were able to provide. This is what is important. Witness to this is borne by a whole body of so-called racially discriminatory legislation which, in fact, protects the customary social life of the African against unwanted and unwelcome intrusions of European influence such as the African Marriages Act, the African Wills Act, and so on. Equally, there is other legislation which protects the Africans from economic exploitation such as, for example, the African Juveniles Employment Act and African Labour Regulations Act.

No one bothers, though, to mention legislation of this sort since this would weaken the case of those who try to see in the Land Apportionment Act the root of all the difference between the races. Certainly the Land Apportionment Act provides protection but this protection works both ways; it protects the African from the consequences of the superior economic skills of the European—and the Asian of course—and it ensures that at no time will the alarming position of the 1920's return when the price of land was too high for Africans and there was a danger that private African land ownership would never occur.

It is not denied that if this Act were not there unscrupulous Europeans, and the unscrupulous Asian, would perhaps be enabled to exploit the African; it is also not denied that perhaps there are some unscrupulous Europeans and perhaps some unscrupulous Asians who would wish to do this. But, fortunately, we have a responsible Government who are determined to ensure that this unscrupulous behaviour will not take place.

Certainly the Act also protects the European—do not let us deny this—in ensuring that the standards and values that he has set in matters of land ownership, occupation, etc., are not eroded. This is a comparatively new development because in the earlier days there was never any suggestion that it was possible for the African in any way to exploit the position as protected for the European. But because of everything that the European has done for the African, because of the advancement that has taken place, because of the fact that today there are many Africans with the ability, the education, the wealth —many of them with more wealth, I would submit, than you and I have today because of what the European has brought into this country and given to them—because of this it is now apparent, for the first time, that the European also needs some protection. Are we to assume that after everything has been given and after all the help that has been put at the door of the African that he is not prepared now as a *quid pro quo* to give the European some protection?—[HON. MEMBERS: *Inaudible interjections*.]—I would be very surprised if this was the view of responsible African opinion. I do not believe that this is so.

This is one of the things, of course, on which hon. members opposite remain silent, that there is a two-way trade here. They wish to have the protection of the European removed but they never offer to come forward and put their particular *quid pro quo* forward. Until they are prepared to come along and say that they wish to have no more protection then I do not believe they should come forward. This is a brazen attempt on their part, surely? I want to make it clear that if they did come forward and say they did not believe they wanted any more protection, that they wished to forego this, I do not think Government would accept this because I do not believe they would be speaking on behalf of the masses of the Africans. At any rate, surely, they should have the decency, the moral courage, that if they wished to ask us to give up what protection we have, they should be prepared to offer their own *quid pro quo*. This does not seem to be forthcoming.

I am surprised at how many hon. members referred to this new policy of ours. This is no new policy. I have said it many times before. I remember when I first came into Parliament, and this goes back quite a few years, long before any hon. members opposite came into Parliament, I remember listening to the then Prime Minister saying very clearly in this Chamber that the sheet anchor of the European and of civilization in Rhodesia was the Land Apportionment Act. This is not anything new that I have introduced or manufactured. This has always been the policy of this country. There is nothing new about this. If hon. members do not like the terminology they can choose any terminology they wish—a rose by any other name.

It is a fact that there was a suggestion made at the time of Federation that Rhodesia should deviate from their well-known and well-trodden path, and, in fact, the Federal Government tried to get the Rhodesian Government to do so. They were never really successful. Hon. members who were politically conscious in those days will recall that we used to have special provisions of extra-territorial areas in Southern Rhodesia so that we could cope with the new-fangled policy of the Federal Government. The Rhodesian Government moved about one-hundredth of an inch towards them and gave them these special areas, but no further. Then there was another serious attempt with the 1961 Constitution. There is no doubt that that had all the makings of a dramatic change, perhaps along the lines that hon. members opposite would wish, but this depended on interpretation and implementation. There is no doubt that if, at the ensuing election, the Government that used to sit on that side and to which some hon. members opposite belonged, if they had been returned I think there would have been a dramatic change, but fortunately the people of Rhodesia came to their senses in time and prevented such an occurrence. So we have never deviated, never, from this particular path. . . .

From what I have said, I think it is clear that this Government is merely following the path trodden by its predecessors. I have been asked by the mover of this motion to state Government policy. That is very simple. Government policy is to continue along the traditional Rhodesian path—you can call it what you wish, you can call it separate development, you can call it the traditional road. There used to be arguments about whether we should call the Federal policy partnership or co-operation, and so on, but it was obviously bad whatever you called it. Fortunately our inherent policy is obviously good, whatever you call it. This is our policy, with no sudden changes in direction, to ensure that the separate communities have the opportunity of preserving their own identities, traditions and customs while promoting the full economic development of all people in Rhodesia, including those in the Tribal Trust Lands. Through the application of community development principles and practices, which are being slowly and carefully evolved, each geographical entity of the people will have the opportunity to organize so as to assess and meet its own needs within the overall framework of our national development.—[MR GONDO: How is it going to affect the University.]—It is as simple as that Mr Speaker. That, in a nutshell, is what I have to say.

In conclusion, I believe that I have taken a positive and a

constructive approach to our well-tried and proven policy, showing how, by sticking to the traditional line, we can not only preserve our values but we can also raise our standards.

'PROVINCIALISATION'

DOCUMENT 22. 'PROVINCIALIZATION: RHODESIAN FRONT DESIGN OF DEEPENING APARTHEID', BY THE REV. CANAAN BANANA, DEPUTY PRESIDENT OF THE AFRICAN NATIONAL COUNCIL (FROM *Moto*, 26 AUGUST 1972)

The policy of provincialization is a brain child of the Rhodesia Front as a result of political intercourse with the Nationalist Party of South Africa. It has clearly the influence and stresses from the Bantustan policy adopted and implemented by their counterpart, the Nationalist Party—a policy that is proving more unnatural and unworkable even in South Africa where it was born.

Provincialization can therefore be defined precisely as the Rhodesian Front's design of deepening apartheid.

It is the logical application of the Land Tenure Act—a most vicious piece of legislation which is being used to deprive Africans of land in urban areas now so designated European areas.

The basic philosophy behind the policy of provincialization is to stem the tide and ambition of African nationalists by attempting to establish African leadership to lead in their own areas, away from competition with Europeans in the urban centres. It is intended to direct African energies away from their desire and demands for political power in the national government and to turn them away from demanding a fair treatment in return for their exploited labour in the major industrial and commercial centres.

Futile Attempt

It is a futile attempt by the RF to neutralise and then divert the wishes of the African people to achieve quasi-political independence in their own areas under European rule, hoping that this will ensure permanent white domination.

The thinking behind this policy clearly shows an acceptance

of the fact that the present suppression of the black people by the white minority throughout this land has frustrated the African people. History throughout the North of Africa bears print of the results of the policies of imperialism and colonialism in Africa.

Chiefs Rule

Previous colonial régimes in this country tended to discourage traditional rule by the chiefs so that tribal laws or custom could be absorbed by the so-called rule of law in the western concept. But political events since the days of the now defunct Central African Federation have brought about direct conflict between black nationalism and white nationalism.

And since it is pretty obvious that a formula of co-existence between European domination and African independence cannot be found, the RF and its followers is now being forced by prevailing circumstances to isolate and divide the African people through a system that is bound to engender even more hostility.

The chieftainship, being the weakest system in modern politics is being manipulated and used as a link between the exploited poor African and the régime in power today. There is open talk of increasing the power of chiefs over their people.

Strictly speaking, if such powers are to assist the chiefs, they cannot assist them in their traditional role as traditional custom never emanates from Parliament, but from the African people themselves through their tribal culture and beliefs.

The truth of the matter is that in Rhodesia, and unfortunately, the role of the chiefs has long been seriously negated to the extent that they no longer act as true traditional leaders but have, by and large, become a mere extension of the Ministry of Internal Affairs.

Need to Examine

There is need to examine whether this separatist policy can succeed. The rural areas have been allowed to deteriorate to the present state where 75 per cent of the arable land is now virtually desert land.

This failure has been brought about by successive white régimes and their special advisors who must have either suffered from ignorance of the needs of the tribal people, and their right approach to the development of their land, which is the inferior part of the total land in the country anywhere, or a deliberate economic device to keep the African masses at subsistence level.

The crucial question to be raised is: If successive so-called European technical experts through the Natural Resources Board failed to develop correct economic and land management in rural areas what chances do the chiefs have in this respect?

So long as the RF continues to gamble with the true needs of our people, and country at this alarming rate, for its sinister political motives, there will be no hope for progressive society in this land. In fact the inherent danger in this system is that there is enshrined within it seeds of a revolution.

African Agriculture

In order to prepare for the implementation of the provincialization policy, in its recent moves the RF régime has placed African Agriculture under the department of Internal Affairs —Tribal Trust Lands, the chiefs, the tribal courts are all under this ministry.

This clearly means that the Internal Affairs Department will be in a position to formulate and dictate terms in the formation of the proposed provincial assemblies. We are aware that it is the régime's intention to stir tribal and ethnic differences between the two major African tribes.

The provincial assemblies will be used to press discriminatory rules between relatives and prevent the so-called undesirable Africans to visit TTLs. It is quite plain that the Department of Internal Affairs will hatch all sorts of evil practices to persecute the African people and pass them over to provincial assemblies for a rubber stamp.

Through this system the RF will have achieved, at last to the final conclusion, its dream to use an organized body of Africans to directly persecute its own fellow-men under the false assumption that this would avert a direct white-black confrontation.

If provincialization was required by Africans why did it not come from the Africans themselves? It is, therefore, clear that this is an imposition from the RF Congress now to be implemented against the wishes of the African people, and ultimately at the peril of the minority whites.

Economic Blackmail

The creation of so-called Industrial Complexes at Seke, Ntabazinduna and Zinunya by Tilcor, in order to stop the influx of Africans into the so-called European area, is economic blackmail. Africans will be directed by the provincial assemblies to look for work in their own designated tribal areas, or to wait until Industry can be brought into their areas in the unforeseeable future.

Provincial assemblies can order the expulsion of the masses of unemployed from urban areas. The apartheid ideological approach in this matter ignores all economic considerations.

Professor Houghton has argued that: 'The optimum location of a factory in Southern Africa depends upon a combination of the proportion of its output destined for the inland markets and the difference between the railway tariff on its raw materials and its finished products.'

Because of the alarming lack of adequate infrastructure in the TTLs transport costs will be high enough to stop any meaningful economic development in these areas. The railway tariff system is designed to serve European interests only. The low agricultural production in the TTLs is due to deterioration in soil fertility and the general congestion of people and stock in relation to available land have contributed to the poverty that prevails in the TTLs.

It, therefore, goes without saying that a dying economy in the TTLs cannot support industrial expansion extended to its borders to serve the RF ideological concept and the interests of the European population in general.

There can be no remedy that can come from the RF régime's inept economic policies of creating poverty areas in the TTLs. The RF's attempts are merely ideological and not real. To pretend that provincialization can instil economic development is the biggest joke ever mooted in living memory.

The Morality

The ethics of provincialization is based on the false concept that
the white man holds the mantle of the God fatherhood of the
black man, and that he alone knows what is right for the black
man, and that the black man must remain in permanent servi-
tude.

It is a highly aggressive policy that is intended to assassinate
the humanity of black people and make them feel less human.
This system does severe damage to the soul and personality of
black people. It neutralises their potential resources that could
be allowed free development and utilization for the general
good of the whole country.

It is now up to all thinking people of this country, black and
white, to marshal all the courage of their convictions and resist
the band wagon of the RF with dangerous policies that threaten
the very foundation of our nation.

PART VII

Apartheid: The Practical Application

In practice, the doctrine of separate development is applied to every aspect of Rhodesian society. This situation has developed over a period of nearly half a century, during which an increasing number of European settlers, uninhibited by restraints from the colonial power, has succeeded in imposing a system which guarantees the continuation of white supremacy.

Perhaps of most significance, in a country with an economy based on agriculture, is the inequality in the apportionment of land between the races. This division, first legalised by the Land Apportionment Act of 1930, continues to this day.

A similar inequality—in wages, in job opportunities, in apprenticeships, in effective collective bargaining—prevents all but a few of the Africans from ever obtaining either a fair share of the country's economic potentialities or the earnings and property necessary to qualify for the right to vote and thereby to exercise any real influence on the prevailing political system.

Separate education facilities, which are nowhere near 'equal', especially in terms of access to secondary education, also prevent the Africans from qualifying for the skilled jobs and professions and, again, for the educational requirements to vote.

Social segregation is everywhere in evidence, whether explicit, as prescribed by law, or implicit, as practiced within the social context. Its intensification by the Rhodesian Front Government's legislative and administrative measures has led to a complete polarisation of Rhodesian society.

THE LAND QUESTION: THE EFFECTS OF APPORTIONMENT

A former agricultural officer in Southern Rhodesia in the 1950s criticises the effects of the two main land laws in operation in the country—the Land Apportionment Act and the Land Husbandry Act. These laws prevailed until the consolidation of land law within the Land Tenure Act of 1969, enacted by the Rhodesian Front Government.

DOCUMENT 23. *Land in Southern Rhodesia* BY K. E. E. BROWN, SINOIA, SOUTHERN RHODESIA, MARCH 1959 (AFRICA BUREAU, 1959)

In many parts of the country it is quite embarrassing (if you are a European) to drive through a European Area into a Native Area. The change in soil-type coincides almost exactly with the boundary-line and is startlingly obvious; an example of this is on the Salisbury to Shamva road, passing into Chinamhora Reserve.

Moreover, most of the Native Areas are sited well away from existing main-roads and railways, making transport to markets a difficult problem, while most of the European Areas are adjacent to a main road, a railway or both. For example, one can travel the main north road from Salisbury to Chirundu, or from Salisbury to Odzi, or from Salisbury nearly to Bulawayo, all by road or rail, without passing through any Native Area.

It is thus easy to appreciate the unfairness and injustice of the Act. Exactly half of the land of the Colony has been allocated to the non-Africans—who comprise only about one-eighth of the total population—and this contains nearly all the fertile soil, is close to markets, and is well-served by roads and railways (all the Urban Areas are also in the European Area, of course). Forty-one per cent is allocated to an African population of more than $2\frac{1}{4}$ million, and most of it is poor, infertile soil, remote from main roads, railways and markets. The remaining 9 per cent is forest or unallocated areas.

It may be argued that the Land Apportionment Act merely allocated to the Africans those areas which, due to an abundance of natural water supplies and other features, they had always inhabited and cultivated; and retained for European occupation those which, due to lack of water, the Africans had never inhabited anyway.

To a certain extent this is true (though it is by no means true of the Matabeleland section of the Colony); many—though by no means all—of the more fertile areas of the country are without adequate natural water supplies, and in many cases the Africans did not inhabit them before the Europeans came. . . .

The Native Reserves

These reserves and special areas were originally set aside to ensure adequate areas of suitable land where the indigenous inhabitants of the Colony could live and develop without undue interference, and especially with protection against the more unscrupulous type of European who might take advantage of the Africans' ignorance to exploit them. This aim—to protect the less-advanced African—was (and is) a praiseworthy one, and there is still a case for protected areas for Africans: if there were no land apportionment, many rural Africans would still fall prey to unscrupulous speculators and lose their land.

Since the original Land Apportionment Act in 1930, however, the situation in the Reserves and in the country as a whole has radically altered. There has been a huge increase in the African population: in 1901 the African population was estimated to be only 550,000; in 1926 it was 936,000; and in 1957 it was 2,282,823. The result of this increase in population is that today most of the Reserves in the country are over-populated and overstocked: this in turn has led to exhaustion of both arable and grazing land, and to severe soil erosion. For example, Zwimba Reserve in Sinoia District is 201,600 acres in extent, has an estimated population of 28,500 (i.e. seven acres of arable and grazing per person) and a cattle-population of over 20,000 (ten acres to one beast). Over most of the Reserve the fertility of the arable lands is exhausted and they are badly eroded, and in all but a few areas the Reserve is overstocked with bush-encroachment and erosion in the grazing lands. Zwimba is a typical Reserve with typical problems.

When the Reserves were first allocated, the African population was small enough to enable the traditional system of

'shifting cultivation' to continue. While this system was waste-
ful economically, due to lack of proper stumping, manure, etc.,
it is recognized today that, from a conservation point of view,
and particularly on sandveld soils, the system was almost
perfect.

The Native Reserves and Special Native Areas of Southern
Rhodesia together occupy an area of just over 30 million acres.
Of this about 60 to 70 per cent—some 20 million acres—is
suitable for cultivation, the rest being waste land, steep land,
wet land, vleis, roads, villages, etc. Under the old system of
shifting cultivation this area could support at subsistence level
a population of only 660,000 (about a quarter of the present
African population). Even under a properly managed long
ley system with fertilizers and correct tillage methods, the
present area could not support more than half the African
population at a reasonable standard of living. Not more than
5 million acres would be down to crops in any one year. To
attain a reasonable standard of living from the land on typical
Reserve soil it may be reckoned that four acres of crops per
head of population is needed. Thus about $1\frac{1}{4}$ million people
could be supported—approximately half of a population which
is rapidly increasing.

The Land Husbandry Act

The main objects of the Act are as follows (in the words of the
official pamphlet [*What the Native Land Husbandry Act Means to
the Rural African and to Southern Rhodesia*]):

(i) To provide for a reasonable standard of good husbandry and for the protection of natural resources by all
Africans using the land: the Act contains power to enforce
these provisions.

(ii) To limit the number of stock in any area to its carrying capacity and, as far as is practicable, to relate stock
holding to arable land holding as a means of improving
farming practice.

(iii) To allocate individual rights in the arable land and
in the communal grazings as far as possible in terms of
conomic units; and where this is not possible, due to

population, to prevent further fragmentation and to provide for the aggregation of fragmentary holdings into economic units.

(iv) To provide individual security of tenure of arable land and individual security of grazing rights in the communal grazings.

(v) To provide for the setting aside of land for towns and business centres in the Reserves.

These five points are in themselves quite laudable and comparatively innocent, but are they in fact the main purposes of the Act; and how do they work in practice?

Land Conservation

From an agricultural and conservation point of view the Land Husbandry Act is a bad measure. It entrenches and 'legalises' the practices of centralization and continuous cultivation on soils which are quite unsuitable for them. Thus it perpetuates all the serious erosion problems in the Native Reserves. In most cases the arable holding to be allocated per family under the Act is eight acres, two of which are supposed to be used for a grass or legume ley and the remainder for crops. Thus the proportion of ley to crops is 1:4, the reverse of what it should be. . . .

Even if, in theory, erosion and soil exhaustion could be halted under the Land Husbandry Act system, that is without long leys but with special methods of good tillage, manuring, conservation works, etc., in practice it would still be a hopeless proposition for two reasons:

(i) the majority of arable areas in the Reserves are already so eroded and so exhausted of fertility that nothing short of a 12 or 15 year rest to grass will restore them to a state of structure and fertility which would enable economic crop-production to commence.

(ii) the majority of the inhabitants of the Reserves, due to lack of equipment, knowledge and correct outlook, are just not ready for, or capable of adopting, such practices and special measures. . . .

We conclude then that the arable provided under the Land

Husbandry Act is inadequate for the needs of anyone who wishes to make a *living* from the land (as opposed to an existence). . . .

Psychological Factors

Just as important as the technical considerations is the psychological or 'human' factor involved, and, even if the Land Husbandry Act could be justified on other counts, it would still be psychologically a bad piece of legislation. In most Reserves men with six or eight acres of sand soil can see with their own eyes across their own Reserve boundary-line thousands of acres of European farmland, mostly undeveloped and often virtually unused. Very often the soil is better than that of the Reserve, and sometimes the change in soil-type coincides almost exactly with the boundary. Most European farms consist of thousands of acres. The minimum economic holding for a European farmer is considered to be 750 acres; under the Land Husbandry Act that for an African farmer is about 50 acres (eight acres of arable and 40 to 50 acres of communal grazing): this gives a ratio between European and African of about 1:15. While it is acknowledged that there is at present *some* difference in the basic living needs of Europeans and Africans, this figure of 1:15 is quite out of proportion to all relevant facts, and it frankly smacks of exploitation and oppression. There is no shortage of land in Southern Rhodesia—in fact the Government has great difficulty in getting the land settled with Europeans. Yet the African population is 'crying out' for land and Africans in Southern Rhodesia are suffering untold hardships from the Government's policy of confining them to the miserable allocations of granite sands that exist in most Native Reserves.

It is often argued that, if the Africans were given more land, they would only ruin it as they have already ruined that which they already have. This is a fallacy. The fact is indisputable, that when, before the advent of the Europeans, Africans had abundant land, the *erosion they caused was negligible* and the *soil maintained its fertility and structure*. It is the coming of the Europeans which has changed this and caused most of the soil erosion and soil exhaustion in the Reserves; there have been three stages, (i) by the Land Apportionment Act which limits the land of the African population, (ii) by the huge increase in the African population, an increase which would not have occurred had there been no European occupation, and (iii) by the continuous cultivation policy which for nearly a generation has been encouraged by the Native Agriculture Department and applied to soils which are quite incapable of sustaining it. The fact that the majority of rural Africans are not yet expert agriculturalists increases the amount of damage done on such soils when land is restricted. If the majority *were* expert farmers, there would from an agricultural point of view be more excuse for limiting their land; the fact that they are not is all the more reason for *increasing* the Native Areas.

Human Rights

The Land Husbandry Act strengthens the hand of the Land Apportionment Act in interfering with and denying to the African population certain basic human rights. The Act has been described by African leaders in this country as 'cruel' and 'vicious', and to a large extent these descriptions of it are true. Many of those involved in the initiation and implementation of the Act are men of high integrity and sincerity of purpose who sincerely believe that the Act is intended solely to arrest the erosion process in the Reserves and to promote good farming methods. But are these, in fact, the main aims of the Act?

In view of the Southern Rhodesia Government's established Native Policy and its past record of legislation in this sphere (e.g. the Pass Laws and the Masters and Servants Act), it seems highly probable that two other main objects of the Act are: (i) to ensure an abundant supply of cheap labour for European industry and agriculture, and (ii) to tighten control over the African population. If these are *not* the purposes of the Act, they are certainly—or will be in the near future—the effects of it.

The original purpose of the Reserves was to provide protected areas where Africans could live and farm in a tribal or semi-tribal manner, unmolested by Europeans. Up to the time of the Land Husbandry Act, it was a recognized precept throughout the Colony that every indigenous African had the right to reside in the Reserve, and, with the permission of the Chief, to cultivate lands there. Now, under the Act, this basic right of Africans to reside and plough their own areas has been destroyed: once the land has been allocated, no man without a farming right is allowed to have lands in the Reserve. He may be allowed to reside there (with the acquiescence of the Chief and the Native Commissioner), but he will be allowed no means of subsistence off the land. . . .

Spokesmen for the Southern Rhodesia Government will readily admit that one aim of the Land Husbandry Act is to force 'loafers', either to farm properly in the Reserve, or to go and work in European industry or agriculture, and also to stop the present practice of Africans alternating for different periods between town and country, between work and 'loafing in the Reserves'. . . . If the Southern Rhodesia Government wishes to stabilise labour in industry and agriculture, it could be done by improving African wages, housing and conditions of work. (Indeed, investigation inevitably shows that it is deficiencies in the above spheres that force the African worker to live his double life of alternating between town and country.) If the Government wishes to discourage indolence in the Reserves, it should explore more humane methods, such as the improvement of health facilities, education and incentives to work. . . .

The Government itself anticipates fewer right-holders with larger holdings, and this, together with the natural population increase, will gradually force more and more Africans out of the Reserves and into the urban areas or European farms to seek a livelihood. Will European industry and agriculture be able to absorb all these people? One estimate is that there will be an annual surplus of at least 50,000 from the Reserves, of whom industry will only be able to absorb 20,000 or 25,000. It is impossible to predict whether industry and agriculture will be able to expand at the required rate. Should depression or a major recession come, the surplus African population would have no safeguards against poverty and unemployment. The prospect of a large workless and rightless population in the urban areas is not one to inspire complacency. . . .

THE LAND QUESTION: THE REMOVAL OF THE AFRICANS

The case of the eviction of the Tangwena people from their homelands by the Rhodesian Front Government is described by Mr Guy Clutton-Brock, who was himself evicted following the closure of the multi-racial 'Cold Comfort Farm', which he founded and helped to manage.

DOCUMENT 24. *Rekayi Tangwena: Let Tangwena Be* BY GUY CLUTTON-BROCK, SALISBURY, JULY 1969

The Court Cases

In spite of the protection given to them under section 93 of the Land Apportionment Act, Rekayi and many of his people have come under increasing pressure to sign Labour Agreements or leave the land and their homes. On 17-9-66 Rekayi received a month's notice to quit.

On 5th May 1967 Rekayi was summoned to appear before the Magistrate at Inyanga Court, charged 'that upon or about the period extending from the 1st November 1966 to 30th April 1967 and at or near Inyanga in the Province of Manicaland, the said Rekayi, being an African did wrongfully and unlawfully occupy land in a European area. . . .'

In court, Rekayi conducted his own defence through the court interpreter. With his elders as witnesses, he disputed the boundaries now drawn, although far from clearly marked except on a map not easily obtained. He affirmed that the boundaries now fixed by the surveyor differed from those which the Chief had agreed with the European settlers in the past and which had reserved the Chief's area. Rekayi, however, was found guilty and fined £30 or 3 months imprisonment with hard labour, of which the payment of £20 or 2 months imprisonment was suspended on condition that he ceased to occupy the land in question by 31st July 1967. Rekayi paid the fine and did not move.

On 3rd November 1967 he was again summoned to Inyanga Magistrates court on the charge that he 'being an African did wrongfully and unlawfully occupy land in a European area'.

On this occasion he was defended by Advocate R. H. B. Pringle. After the case had continued over nearly 3 months with 5 remands, Rekayi was again found guilty and fined £30 or 3 months imprisonment with hard labour.

In the course of these proceedings Rekayi and anything from a handful to a hundred of his people (varying somewhat according to the weather) walked the 40 miles there and back across the hills and valleys on each of the 8 occasions (a total distance of perhaps 320 miles), in order to defend himself and so also to defend his people. No more than a handful of supporters could enter the tiny court room; the rest sat around in the yard outside the court, the men listening at the windows, the women suckling their babies. At the end of the proceedings Rekayi walked out into the yard and offered himself for prison with supporters close behind ready to join him. On second thoughts he lodged an appeal to the High Court, so continued on bail.

Rekayi's appeal against his conviction was heard in the Appellate Division of the High Court of Rhodesia at Salisbury on 13th and 14th June 1968. Advocate R. H. B. Pringle again represented Rekayi. In their judgement, Sir Vincent Quenet, the Acting Chief Justice, Mr Justice Macdonald and Mr Justice Lewis, allowed the appeal, quashed the conviction and set aside the sentence. (The previous conviction and sentence were also subsequently set aside.) In their judgement the judges accepted that, as a matter of probability, African occupation of the land in question occurred even before the Crown acquired the land. They pointed out that 'the so-called ambiguity in section 93 (3) relied upon by the Crown would lead not only to absurdity but to manifest injustice. We were asked to disregard clear language, improperly admit an ambiguity and adopt a construction which would put those who had occupied land for more than half a century in a worse position than persons who on the 10th January, 1952, had been in occupation for only a few weeks. Section 45 (1) of the 1923 Constitution made provision for persons such as the appellant and there is nothing in the present Act which indicates that during the intervening years the lawmaker's concern for such persons had become less keen. Indeed, the language of section 93 (3) clearly expresses an intention to give protection until such time as a proclamation is made. The protection, in my view, confers a right which can be vindicated in answer to a prosecution in terms of Section 42 (1) (a) of the Act or in any action for ejectment for trespass or in similar proceedings.'

The court was full to hear the Appeal proceedings. Some 40 members of the Tangwena tribe working in Salisbury clearly took the day off to hear the appeal of their Chief. Rekayi was vindicated in the judgement of the High Court. He was occupying his home land lawfully, being protected by the Land Apportionment Act. No one had the right to evict him nor any of his people who were living there prior to 1905, unless a Proclamation was first made by the Governor in terms of Section 86 of the Act.

The Proclamation

On 21st February 1969 a 'Proclamation by His Excellency Clifford Walter Dupont, Esquire, Officer Administering the Government and Commander-in-Chief in and over Rhodesia' was published in the Gazette as 'Rhodesia Government Notice No. 134 of 1969'. This directed that 36 named men, who included Rekayi, 'together with every person who is a member of the families of, or lives with, the said squatters ... shall permanently depart with all their property from the land described ... by 31st August, 1969, and those of such squatters so named or described as aforsaid who are indigenous Africans shall move to the land described ...'.

A Government Statement

On 19th May 1969 a statement by the Ministry of Internal Affairs was published in the Rhodesia Herald giving 'the story of these tribesmen as it was known to the Ministry'. A subsequent letter to the Rhodesia Herald (14-6-69) commented and pointed out that the 'story' was 'substantially misleading'; it appeared to contain 'serious mistakes of fact and law as well as significant omissions'. This record of Rekayi explains this assertion but two points need emphasis.

The statement refers a number of times to the land which Tangwena and those living at Tsatse's kraal are 'illegally occupying', referring to them as 'illegal tenants'. The legality of the occupation of the land by the Tangwena, however, has only once been tested. This was in the case of Rekayi. In the judgement of the High Court, he was shown to be neither a tenant nor to be occupying the land illegally. He held statutory rights of occupation and was not liable to be evicted. The letter to the Rhodesia Herald (14-6-69) commented:

> It raises serious issues for the ordinary citizen when such a judgement, given in the High Court, is apparently not accepted or is disregarded in a statement subsequently issued by a Government department—when something declared lawful by the High Court is declared to be illegal by a Ministry.

A substantial part of the Ministry's statement is devoted to an explanation of the 'labour agreement' system. It states: 'To understand the Tangwena issue it is necessary to understand "labour agreements" in Rhodesia.' As is shown by the High Court judgement, the question of labour agreements is quite irrelevant to the Tangwena case. It has nothing to do with Tangwena's right of occupation which is derived from Section 93 of the Land Apportionment Act. The statement ends its section on labour agreements by saying:

> Because of these facts and also because others failed to comply with the requirements of their labour agreement on Gaeresi Ranch due notice was given to them . . . and they were told to leave. . . . This was ignored . . . a small group led by Rekayi is now putting forward the story related in the letters to the Press soliciting sympathy and seeking to blame the Land Apportionment Act for their difficulty.

So far as Rekayi is concerned and those also protected by Section 93 of the Act, the notice was not 'due' but was unlawful. As lawful occupiers, they were not liable to be evicted. The notice was rightly ignored. Rekayi had not been blaming the Land Apportionment Act for the difficulties raised in connection with his occupation; he has in fact been relying upon a section of it for protection from those seeking to evict him.

The statement ends with a curious sort of 'sermon':

> It must be appreciated that land tenure problems are not solved as Rekayi apparently thinks, by ignoring the laws

of the land or by changing them to suit individual circumstances without regard to the legal rights of other individuals. Rekayi and his people know the law and like other citizens are expected to comply with it.

Rekayi, in these exact words, might well have addressed those government officials and others who have been trying over recent years to evict him apparently without lawful reason. He has in fact taken the necessary steps to acquaint himself with the law, has complied with it and has expected others to do the same.

The Quinton Report

The Report of the Select Committee on the Resettlement of Natives is the most recent authoritative report on land settlement. It was presented to the Legislative Assembly on 16th August, 1960. Mr H. J. Quinton was the Chairman and it is generally known as 'The Quinton Report'. The Committee consisted of Members of Parliament, including members of the Opposition Dominion Party, a predecessor of the Rhodesian Front. This Report, which was unanimous, outlines the main features of the Land Apportionment Act. It underlines its grave disadvantages to the social and economic development of the country. It emphasises that removals, such as those proposed for the Tangwena, go against the trends which are necessary to promote the development of the country.

In paragraph 143 it points out that the cost of moving a family approximately 50 miles is not less than £200, and that the country cannot afford this cost. It is economic folly to move populations from one place to another unless by so doing productivity is markedly increased. It is foolish to spend large sums moving Africans from a subsistence economy in one area to again a subsistence economy in new surroundings.

In paragraph 144 the report states that the Committee cannot see the advantage in shuttling Africans from one category of land to another merely because the circumstances under which they occupy a particular piece of land do not coincide with the particular conditions laid down for the occupation of that land. It points out that Government might well incur the displeasure of the Africans for uprooting them from known surroundings for no apparent reason and moving them to new areas where they would be no better off.

In paragraphs 172 and 173 it states that between 1936 and 1959, 113,000 Africans were compulsorily moved from the European area and that to preserve the barriers created by the Land Apportionment Act, millions of £'s of badly needed capital were spent for ideological, rather than productive, purposes. The economic arguments against such movements of people were valid.

In paragraph 174 the Committee recommended that all energies and funds should be devoted to increasing the prosperity of existing areas rather than opening up any further areas to which people would be moved.

In paragraph 234 it says: 'NO GOOD PURPOSE WOULD BE SERVED BY MOVING ANY AFRICANS FROM THE LAND THEY ARE NOW OCCUPYING.'

In paragraph 235 it says that the solution appears to be to leave them where they are and to supply to each particular area the pattern of development which circumstances dictate.

In paragraph 250 the Committee recommends that where Africans have occupied what are regarded as European farms for 20 years, they should be permitted to purchase the land provided that the owners are prepared to sell.

In paragraph 312 the Committee makes the observation that people are more important than land and that the immediate welfare of people living at a low level of poverty must not be by-passed.

The actions of Rekayi and his suggestions would appear to be in line with the policy recommended by the last authoritative government report concerning the Land Apportionment Act and land settlement.

The Views of Rekayi

Rekayi pours out his views strongly and with feeling, speaking on behalf of his people:

'I would like to make it clear that I do not want to move from my area even if I am forced. I inherited it from my forefathers who were found there by Rhodes and the early Europeans. Before my father died he said to me: "This is your area where you will live after my death." He showed me the boundaries. I want government to recognise our traditional boundaries, to be friends to my people and to protect us. I know this won't impress Europeans because they can easily leave their inheritance and settle down in a new area. But there are some Europeans who still live at their homes as they have done in the past. But if I leave this area, I cut off all ties with my past and my ancestors and there is no one who can carry them on. The early Europeans came and found me and my ancestors on this land and Mr Hanmer came and saw me on this land. He did not fight or conquer me. We only gave him permission to settle down with us in a friendly way. But now he wants to evict us and says that the land belongs to the Company which we did not know before.

'We intended to live well with the Europeans. We agreed with them from Rhodes onwards. They recognised our right of occupation in the early days. We agreed the boundaries with them which were stated clearly. They were marked by features which we knew. The early Europeans offered us a new way of life. This is not a new way of life for us to be turned out. It is not according to our custom to move. Our whole life is based on land. Any good government should mediate fairly in this dispute and not side with one man unfairly. We would have looked for assistance to government in the past. Now it seems impossible as it looks as though the government is urging the Company to get us off the land. We have all been children of the government in the past. Now it seems the government is eliminating us as its children.

'I was cleared by the court from breaking the Land Apportionment Act. Now the Government has made an order so that if I do not obey it they can say that I disobeyed the order. But the Government itself has broken the law in UDI. If I disobey their order, I am just following the example of government. . . .'

THE LAND QUESTION: THE RHODESIAN FRONT SOLUTION

The Rhodesian Front Government's case for preserving the division of land into racial areas is made by the Minister of

Lands, Mr Philip van Heerden, during the Second Reading of the Land Tenure Bill. In the referendum to which he refers, the predominantly white electorate endorsed the proposals for a new constitution, embodying provisions for land tenure, by a vote of 54,724 (73 per cent) to 20,776 (27 per cent) the previous June. In the same referendum, the vote in favour of a republic was carried by an even larger majority.

DOCUMENT 25. STATEMENT BY THE MINISTER OF LANDS (FROM RHODESIA *Parliamentary Debates*, VOL. 75, 15 OCTOBER 1969, COLS 1472–1500)

THE MINISTER OF LANDS: The Land Apportionment Act has been the cornerstone of the land policies of successive Governments since 1931. The Act has been amended many times, but the basic principles which it enshrined have remained unchanged and have served Rhodesia well. However, the time has arrived for these principles to be re-stated, and where necessary rationalized, and for the rights of all Rhodesians to be established beyond dispute along the lines accepted by an overwhelming majority of the electorate in the referendum last June.

One important reason why the position requires review has been the lack of constitutional guarantees concerning the total extent of the European area and the total extent of the African area. Although the extent of the native reserves or Tribal Trust Lands as they are now called, has been specially protected against encroachment, the Native Purchase Area and the European Area have not enjoyed similar protection. The result of this has been that the total acreage of land reserved for the exclusive use of Africans has risen from 29,000,000 acres in 1930 to 44,400,000 acres today, while the European area has been reduced over the same period from 49,100,000 acres to 35,600,000 acres.

And here I should perhaps take the opportunity of commenting upon the frequently voiced criticism that even the existing apportionment of land as between Africans and Europeans is unfair having regard to their respective numbers. Criticism of this kind completely ignores the economic facts. For example, it ignores the fact that some 650,000 African workers live in the

European area, mostly with their families, and enjoy a far higher standard of living than most Africans living in the African area. It ignores the fact that in 1968 the 44,400,000 acres of African area produced crops and livestock of an estimated gross value of £27,400,000 of which only £3,500,000 went into the money economy, while the 35,600,000 acres of the European area produced crops and livestock to the value of £64,100,000 of which £59,200,000 went into the money economy. It ignores the fact that other fields of economic activity such as mining, secondary industry and the distributive trades, almost all of which are confined to the European area, contributed 85 per cent of the gross domestic product. In short, it ignores the fact that it is European enterprise, initiative and expertise on which the economic advancement of both Europeans and Africans depends, and will continue to depend for many years to come.

Furthermore, it is not enough to prevent any further encroachment of the European area which produces almost the whole of Rhodesia's wealth. We must reverse the trend and help the African people to improve its contribution to the national economy. We must try to ease off the braking effect of the Tribal Trust Lands on the growth of the economy as a whole.

Although a small number of Africans have shown a commendable determination to improve their lot through hard work and good farming practices, it is nevertheless a fact that the great majority have done little to lift themselves above the subsistence level.—[MR RUBATIKA: *Inaudible interjection.*]

This Government, like others before it, has given every encouragement to Africans to raise their living standards and move towards a cash economy, but with a disappointing response. Nevertheless, we are not daunted by past failures, for there are signs of an awakening, and the good example set by a few Purchase Area farmers and tribesmen, in many cases helped by their European neighbours, is bound to have an influence on others in the long run.

The creation of the Tribal Trust Land Development Corporation, is yet another move towards the orderly development of the Tribal Trust Land for the benefit of tribesmen. We can look forward to the time when there will be a steady and increasing demand by tribesmen for the establishment of industry on Trust Land. Indeed, I say without hesitation that the establishment of industries in the Tribal Trust Lands, is regarded by the Government as a vital development if this country is to progress, and if it is to feed, clothe and provide shelter for the rapidly increasing population.

To establish industry in the Tribal Trust Lands will require a great amount of capital and skill which, as matters stand at present, only Europeans can provide; but no European businessman will invest in the Tribal Trust Land without security of tenure, and a flexible approach must be adopted to allow him to have this, subject to suitable safeguards. The Bill provides the flexibility required, and with goodwill on the part of all sections of the community, I believe that we can look forward to the future of the Tribal Trust Lands with confidence, in the knowledge that great achievements in agriculture, mining and industry lie within our grasp. . . .

The main objectives of the Bill are to divide the major portion of the land in Rhodesia into two equal areas, in one of which the interests of Europeans, and in the other of which the interests of Africans, will be paramount; to create a national area where the interests of neither Europeans nor Africans will prevail over those of the other race; to set out the rights of Europeans and Africans in their respective areas, and to ensure that there will be no erosion of these rights in the future; and last but not least, to eliminate racial friction arising out of the ownership, occupation, and use of land. In furtherance of these aims, the ownership of land will generally be confined to persons of the race in whose area the land is situated. . . .

Part I of the Bill provides for the classification of all the land in Rhodesia into European, African, and National Areas, the land assigned to each category being listed in the First, Second, and Third Schedules. The European and African Areas each comprise 45,000,000 acres, while a little over 6,500,000 acres are to be included in the National Area. . . .

While one of the objectives of the Bill is to ensure equality as between the extent of the European Area and that of the African Area, some alterations of boundaries will obviously be required from time to time. These will become necessary because of changing circumstances, and in pursuance of the long-term objective of removing small islands of land owned by persons of one race within the area of the other race. The Bill accordingly makes provision for transfers and exchanges of land between one Area and another. Furthermore, in order to allow some flexibility it permits a two per cent variation either side of equality in the case of the European and African areas, and also a two per cent variation in the extent of the National Area, from that fixed on the day on which the Act comes into operation. Provided the two per cent variation is not exceeded, land may be transferred by the President from one Area to another, on the recommendation of the boards of trustees whose composition and functions I will now describe.

While, in the past, there has been a board of trustees charged with safeguarding Tribal Trust Land and the interests of tribesmen, there has been no equivalent board for the Purchase Area or for Unreserved Land; nor has there been any similar board looking after European land and the interests of Europeans.

It is now proposed to rectify these omissions, and the Bill provides for the establishment of two boards of trustees, namely, a board of trustees for the European Area and a board of trustees for the African Area. So, for the first time, there will be boards of trustees holding powers of trusteeship for the benefit of both communities, and, moreover, the board of trustees for the African Area will assume the additional responsibility of safeguarding Purchase Land and the interests of Africans on that land.

The transfer of land by the President from one Area to another, will be subject to the specific recommendation of the boards. The boards will have a common chairman and will be the Chief Justice, or, failing him, any other judge of the High Court or a retired judge of the High Court appointed with the approval of the Chief Justice.

One of the main duties of the boards, will be to see that the two per cent. variation either side of equality in the extent of the European and African Areas is not exceeded. They will also be required to ensure that persons who are displaced by any land transfers are resettled or reasonably compensated. . . .

I come now to the fundamental principle of this Bill, which is that the interests of Europeans are paramount in the

European Area and the interests of Africans are paramount in the African Area. This principle is enshrined in Parts II, III and IV, thereby ensuring full security of tenure for each race in its own area.

It is recognized, however, that each race cannot be self-sufficient in its own area, and that it is necessary for persons of one race to own, lease, and occupy land in the area of the other race, subject to strict control on a fully reciprocal basis, and the provisions which deal with this aspect are also contained in Parts II, III and IV.

Before proceeding any further, I want to make it clear that in terms of this Bill the European, Asian and Coloured communities are all regarded as Europeans, as they have always been for land apportionment purposes. However, as hon. members know, proposals designed to avoid friction and discord between these communities, particularly in relation to residential areas, are under consideration by the Government at present. These will be dealt with otherwise than through this Bill and there is nothing in the Bill to prevent the introduction of any such arrangements.

I will deal first with the ownership of land in the European Area by Africans, and in the African Area by Europeans.

The circumstances in which a European may own land in the African Area, and an African may own land in the European Area, are strictly circumscribed and are limited, in the main, to the acquisition of residential accommodation in a non-racial residential area, or in a township specially set aside for Europeans in the African Area, or for Africans in the European Area. The procedures for establishing areas of this kind are set out in great detail in the Bill, to ensure that these exceptions to the principles on which the Bill is founded will not be lightly invoked.

Bearing in mind that the points of contact between the races occur mostly at local level, the power to authorize persons of one race to occupy land in the other's area, or to prohibit them from doing so, is being vested in local authorities, with provision for call-in powers by the appropriate Minister in cases where national policy may become involved.

In dealing with the occupation of land in one area by persons of the other race, the Bill requires the adoption of more stringent procedures for urban land than it does for rural land. This is because the points of contact between the races in the rural areas are more natural and thus less likely to cause friction than in the urban areas. . . .

One of the difficulties experienced in administering the Land Apportionment Act was to give rapid practical effect to the power vested in the Officer Administering the Government to remove illegal occupants from land. It will be obvious that powers are needed to enable persons who are unlawfully occupying land to be speedily removed or evicted, and the Bill lays down the procedure to be followed in these cases. . . .

Special provision has been made to deal with attempts to evade or avoid the intent or purposes of the Bill. I trust that this provision will seldom have to be used. If, however, the Minister is of the opinion that a scheme or arrangement has been entered into for the purpose of evading or avoiding the intent or purposes of the Act or of the Land Apportionment Act, and he is satisfied that the ownership, lease or occupation of the land by virtue of the scheme or the arrangement is contrary to the general principles embodied in this Bill, he may declare that the persons concerned are unlawfully occupying land or that the ownership or lease of the land is unlawful. Once the Minister has made such a declaration, the persons who are then unlawfully occupying the land may be evicted or removed from it, while those owning or leasing the land must dispose of it or terminate their lease within whatever period the Minister may specify. . . .

I commend it to hon. members and the country as a measure which not only fulfils Rhodesia's needs today, but which is also, I believe, sufficiently flexible to satisfy the country's requirements for many years to come. It attempts to lay down and entrench the basic principles of land tenure and to provide a firm foundation on which Rhodesians of all races can plan ahead, invest their savings and press on with development in the knowledge that their land rights are secure. It will, too, provide the stability which will encourage immigrants and foreign investors to come and join us in developing the great potential of this wonderful country. In conclusion, it will help to ensure that Rhodesians of all races will live in harmony, free from the friction which, elsewhere in the world, is increasingly impairing friendly relationships between people with different backgrounds and traditions.

LABOUR AND TRADE UNIONS: 'INDUSTRIAL CONCILIATION'

A European trade union leader gives a favourable, although qualified, account of the Industrial Conciliation Act of 1959, which, for the first time, allowed for African membership of trade unions. The main qualification is the provision for 'vertical' unions—the restriction by law of the activities of a particular trade union to one industry only. The alternative—'horizontal' unions—would permit a trade union to function in more than one industry, thereby increasing its potential membership and bargaining power.

DOCUMENT 26. 'THE NEW INDUSTRIAL CONCILIATION BILL: POSITIVE STEP TOWARDS PARTNERSHIP' BY PETER GIBBS, GENERAL SECRETARY, NATIONAL INDUSTRIAL COUNCIL FOR THE ENGINEER- ING INDUSTRY (IN *Central African Examiner*, 28 FEBRUARY 1959)

It is now nearly five years since the Southern Rhodesian Government of Mr Garfield Todd, by introducing the Native Industrial Workers' Unions Bill in 1954, set in motion a process of national cerebration that has finally produced the third Industrial Conciliation Bill. Like many processes of sustained thought it has been a painful exercise, involving two select committees of Parliament and an incalculable volume of debate, official and unofficial—occasionally informed, more often quite irrelevant—but the climax of the argument seems to be in sight at last in the debate on the second reading of the latest Bill.

To judge the merits of the new Industrial Conciliation Bill its origins must be understood. The process of thought that has given birth to the Bill started virtually in the opposite direction from that in which it has finally settled down, for the original Native Industrial Workers' Union Bill proposed blatantly to create workers' unions on a specifically racial basis.

At the time the proposal seemed reasonable enough as a short-term remedy for the difficulties that were facing the

Native Labour Boards. The boards had been set up to deter-
mine conditions of employment for Africans and it seemed
logical that, if they were to take evidence from people claiming
to represent unions of African workers, these unions should be
properly recognized. So the Bill provided for African workers'
unions to be registered so that they could speak to the labour
boards for those they represented, but the unions would be
given no powers to negotiate direct with the employers; they
could, in time, win the right to submit to the Government
names of Africans who might be nominated—but not necessarily appointed—to the boards, but that was as far as the
proposals took them.

To those who looked more than a few years ahead the
proposals of the Native Industrial Workers' Unions Bill were
clearly inadequate, even dangerous. As the African developed
he would not only demand, he would earn, the right to negotiate with his employers. So the life of the system of labour
boards, imposing arbitrary conditions—as distinct from industrial councils negotiating freely between employers and employees—must inevitably have had its limits. The boards might
have gone on fulfilling their purpose for years, but in time a
situation would have emerged when the African, graduated at
last to take his part in a negotiating system, would have been
firmly entrenched in exclusively racial unions, set up by law,
with all the seeds of discord that such a state of affairs must
necessarily have implied.

So, when the inevitable was realized—that the African
would one day be participating in negotiation—the process of
thought swung abruptly round in the other direction, and even
the first new Industrial Conciliation Bill, presented to Parliament in 1956 following the report of the select committee on the
Native Industrial Workers' Unions Bill, purported to integrate
the African workers into the industrial conciliation system.

But even this Bill was a little hesitant in committing itself
too radically to the principle of integration, for although it no
longer excluded the African from the system it left to the option
of each trade union the admission of members of more than one
race, and thereby left the door open for the establishment of
unions on racial divisions, which was just what the select
committee had so expressly rejected.

The second Bill, which followed in 1957 after the first had been sent to yet another select committee, tried bravely to remove this apparent hesitancy by inserting a clause which purported to prohibit trade unions from excluding anybody from membership on grounds of race, but somehow the admirable intention of the select committee got mauled in the process of drafting, for when the Bill appeared there still remained a convenient loophole which would allow the registration of two or more trade unions, each with members of different races, but each representing the same occupational interests.

Now in the latest Bill, the third, at present before the Southern Rhodesian House, this funk-hole has been carefully blocked up by the draughtsmen, and there can only be one trade union representing a particular occupational interest and that union must be open to workers of any race—provided, of course, that the workers qualify for membership by themselves being concerned in the interests for which the particular union is registered. And any trade union is free to circumscribe those interests as widely or narrowly as it likes.

If the Bill is passed African workers will in future be subject to the same labour legislation as non-Africans, and in any collective instruments involved in determining conditions of employment—such as trade unions, employers' associations, industrial councils—the races will be integrated and distinctions will be drawn only along those lines where distinctions are justified—that is to say, between workers carrying out different occupations or performing them on different levels of skill.

Those who seek to establish trade unions can be as exclusive as they like, limiting membership to those with whatever skill or qualification they choose to nominate, but if the prospective member has the necessary skill or qualification for membership then the colour of his skin will be irrelevant. Acceptance of this principle must surely constitute the most sincere and positive step towards racial partnership that has yet been attempted in this part of the world.

Of course, there will be those ready to point out, rightly enough, that the passage of the Bill by itself will not drive Africans against their inclination to join trade unions already dominated by Europeans. Nor, by the same token, will it immediately remove those widespread European prejudices that exist today against African advancement in industry. In fact, there is bound to be a period of hesitancy—in many instances of mutual suspicion—before any positive signs arise of the races becoming integrated in negotiating machinery; which integration, let it be remembered, the Bill merely provides for and does not itself effect.

But the value of legislation lies not in what happens immediately but in the long run; and if the Bill is passed it is safe to predict that, because the legacy of arbitrary distinction between races in labour legislation will have been removed, before many years have elapsed negotiations between employers and employees will be taking place quite spontaneously without any racial considerations.

As for the mechanics of the Bill itself, the measure is unavoidably complex. But over the five years that have passed during its incubation each of its detailed aspects has been argued out exhaustively enough and it is fair to say that those who will be concerned with its application and administration are satisfied with its provisions—with one glaring exception.

That one exception arises from an eccentric inspiration which beguiled the sponsors of the first Bill in 1956. This inspiration was happily discarded by the select committee in the second Bill in 1957, but now in the third Bill it has come to life again. The idea is to restrict by law the activities of a particular trade union to one industry only; during the lively discussions that have followed since the idea first took shape in someone's inventive imagination, the principle has come to be known as the system of 'vertical' unions; the alternative system, whereby a trade union can function in more than one industry, has been christened 'horizontal'.

As far as can be gathered, the only purpose behind this 'vertical' idea is to prevent the formation of trade unions which would represent too great a number of workers, who would thereby wield too great a power and might attempt to hold the country to ransom by calling widespread strikes. But provision is made in the Bill anyway for the federation of trade unions, and, if the workers in two or more industries have the sinister desire to act collectively, the mere fact that they have been forced to belong to different trade unions is unlikely to deter them.

151

And there are potent arguments against 'vertical' unions. Certain occupations must inevitably overlap in two or more industries, and workers in these occupations will move periodically from one industry to another. So if the trade unions are 'vertical', every time such a worker moves he must transfer from one union to another if he wishes representation on the industrial council in the industry in which he is now working. The impracticability of the situation is obvious.

To say, as the Minister of Labour said in his address introducing the second reading of the Bill, '[the principle] will in no way affect the right of a trade union to have members in industries other than that for which it is registered', is merely to avoid the issue. The issue is not whether a trade union is prepared to have members in other industries, but whether it is fair on a worker to compel him to pay subscriptions to two unions so that he may maintain his continuity of membership in one, in order to participate in its benefits, and at the same time be represented by the other on the industrial council of the industry in which he is working.

To insist on separate trade unions in each industry will in many instances compel the formation of two or more unions where one could well fulfil the need. The establishment and maintenance of local trade unions—divorced from outside influences as they will be required, quite rightly, to be—will be difficult enough from the economic aspect in any event; if the new Industrial Conciliation Act insists on a multiplicity of small, completely unassociated unions—as many provisions of the Bill are at pains to see that they shall be—trade unionism in this country may be frustrated almost to the point of proscription.

It seems such a pity that a good measure like this third Bill, after all the painful thought that has been given to it, should have its prospects of working successfully jeopardized by what is really nothing more than a whim. So far as can be ascertained from wide enquiries, nobody but the Government itself supports the principle of compulsory 'vertical' unions. But in actual effect very much of what the Government is aiming at—which is the classification of trade unions by industries—would result by what might be called a process of natural selection.

On the other hand, compulsion would in many instances

cause anomalies and hardships without any compensating advantages. And the Government itself has already accepted that 'horizontal' unions are not necessarily as dangerous as they would make them out to be, for otherwise why have they agreed, by including a special saving in the Bill, that any union already registered in more than one industry shall remain so?

But whether trade unions should be 'horizontal' or 'vertical' is largely a matter of detail and will presumably be decided at the committee stage of the Bill. What is important is that a generally acceptable measure has been proposed at last so that the mental exertions of the past five years have not been altogether in vain.

LABOUR AND TRADE UNIONS: AN AFRICAN TRADE UNION VIEW

The President of the African Trades Union Congress criticises the wage structure, the employment opportunities, the inadequate system of social security and the restrictions on trade union membership for Africans engaged in rural and domestic occupations. He proposes a number of reforms which would improve the conditions of Africans in employment and extend to those who have been excluded the opportunity of qualifying for trade union membership.

The statement is remarkably free of any criticism of the political framework within which the economic conditions prevail.

DOCUMENT 27. 'LABOUR PROBLEMS IN RHODESIA: A TRADE UNION VIEWPOINT', BY P. F. SITHOLE, PRESIDENT OF THE AFRICAN TRADES UNION CONGRESS (FROM *Rhodesian Journal of Economics*, VOL. VI, NO. 4, DECEMBER 1972)

I. *The Basic Problem: Structural Malformation*

The wage sector of the economy is of paramount importance as an employer of African workers. In March of this year, an estimated 824,000 workers, or approximately 60 per cent of the adult male African population were employed in this sector, although 331,900 of these were working on the farms in the

White areas. In 1971, African labourers earned an estimated $244 million, an amount of great importance to the dependent households, and to the economy as a whole. The contribution of African workers to the country's economic welfare is fundamental, and the problems associated with employment conditions are therefore very important to all sectors of our community.

However, despite the fact that large numbers are employed and that their aggregate earnings are substantial, it is fairly safe to say that this employment is, from the point of view of the individual worker, highly unstable, and the conditions under which the vast majority of the workers are employed are most unsatisfactory.

In June of 1971, a survey conducted by the Central Statistical Office revealed that 35 per cent of those workers employed received a cash wage of less than $10 per month, and a further 39 per cent received between $10 and $30. Over 90 per cent earned less than $50, an amount which almost certainly is inadequate to maintain a family in decent living conditions. Apart from wages, other conditions of employment need to be considered. The housing situation is highly unsatisfactory. The townships are overcrowded, and the fact that many workers are forced either to lodge, or if they are fortunate enough to have been allocated a house, to take in lodgers to supplement the meagre earnings that they are able to glean from employers, means that family life deteriorates, and workers regard the townships as unsuitable as areas in which to raise families. The pension schemes that operate cover a very small proportion of the work-force, and are such that an even smaller number can look forward to retirement on the proceeds of pensions accumulated during a lifetime of toil in industry. There is no adequate system of social security, and the threat of unemployment, resulting even by chance out of accident, is a very real one that haunts workers constantly.

The conditions in the Tribal Trust Lands, however, are even worse, and there is a constant drift to the towns as the rural people seek wages as a supplement to their low incomes which have been declining on a *per capita* basis for more than a decade.
. . .

Workers in industry are viewed essentially as migrants, their employment is seen as temporary, and the rural areas are expected not only to ultimately absorb returning workers at the end of their industrial working lives, but also to act as an 'accommodation mechanism' for labour not required in the modern sector. The extra dependents whom the rural areas are forced to cater for reinforce the problems associated with basic subsistence, improving standards of living and comprehensive and successful agricultural reform. The entire process of economic development is frustrated and a large sector of the society becomes increasingly impoverished. The resulting situation is unsatisfactory for the workers and it must ultimately endanger the stability of the economy itself. It can only be solved by comprehensive reform, involving an increase in the employment generating capacity of the industrial sector, a removal of restrictions on the upward mobility of African employees in the modern sector and positive measures designed to increase the productive capacity of the rural areas.

II. Remedies: A General Statement

The employment capacity of the industrial sector can only be expanded by the dual expedient of increasing the technical training facilities available to all levels of skill and adopting revised methods of production enabling a larger number of semi-skilled workers to be employed in the productive process. Technical training is and must continue to be a responsibility of government. It is incomprehensible to me how a government, supposedly acting in the interests of all the people in the country, can justify a policy under which manpower requirements are continuously met through immigration in a situation in which there is both widespread unemployment and a shaky economic foundation to the immigration policy. If industry is expanding in such a way that employment opportunities are being developed for our people, the failure to take steps to equip these people to fill the available vacancies is, in my opinion, very short-sighted and a serious error of judgement. The system by which European artisan groups, assisted by Government policy, have resisted what is emotionally called 'job fragmentation', has further inhibited the development of a broadly-based technical training programme. 'Job fragmentation' is often used as a phrase designed to discredit what in reality is nothing more than the adoption of techniques more suited to our situation in which we have a relative abundance of labour. The plea for the 'maintenance of standards' is little more than a shallow attempt of a self-interested worker group to bolster up outdated privileges when these cannot be maintained in the face of honest productive competition. I would like to assure the European artisan group that their place in industry is not being challenged. I do not suggest that these skilled workers should be replaced, but rather that they should find their place in the redefined technical hierarchy of modern industry. The skilled technician-artisan is indispensable, but not within the outdated craft concept of industrial arrangement. What is needed is the adoption of training techniques capable of producing skills suited to the changing pattern of industrial technology, and in this system the higher technical skills will grow in importance. But in the final analysis, if the European artisan is to retain his present privileged position he must rely on his productive capacity, and should not expect protection behind artificial barriers erected by industrial councils as a means of effecting a permanent guarantee of highly paid employment.

I do not think that I am being either radical or unrealistic in calling for the adoption of rational and modern productive methods, and for training facilities geared to serve those methods, but I would at this stage come back to my earlier point; namely, that industrial reform must be viewed as a supplement to, and must be accompanied by, agricultural reform.

In very broad terms, official efforts with regard to agricultural development have been incomplete and ineffective. There is no formal comprehensive development programme around which efforts may be focused. There is little attention being given at present to a broadly based incomes or employment policy. On the European farms, workers are denied fundamental rights of collective bargaining, and this is justified by reference to the fact that their conditions of employment are regulated by the Master and Servants Act. It is interesting and sad to note that the basic features of this legislation were originally introduced in the Cape Province of South Africa in 1856, were adopted for Rhodesian use in 1891 and were probably somewhat antiquated even then. The Master and Servants Act is totally unsatisfactory as the basis on which to cater for a large work-force in a country claiming to be both modern and progressive. It is an insult to African workers that they should be denied basic human rights of association on the spurious grounds that they are better served by a paternalistic system under which wages are set unilaterally. Both the working conditions and real earnings on these farms have deteriorated to such an extent that many work-seekers would rather face the prospect of unemployment in the towns with the hope, however faint, of eventually gaining some employment, than the certainty of sustained poverty on the farms. It is not surprising, therefore, that the Rhodesian African Labour Supply Commission continues to act as a labour recruitment bureaux for this sector. I have already described how dangerous the situation is for the stable development of the economy, but I am amazed and dismayed that much of the comment offered on the problem is more often directed against the reluctance of African workers to enter such employment than towards concrete measures designed to improve worker productivity and thereby bolster wages.

In the rural areas, the efforts of TILCOR, amongst others, are perhaps best described as 'patchy'. I do not mean to criticize specifically the actual methods employed by the officials of that organisation, since they are operating with limited financial resources in something of a developmental vacuum. My basic objection is to the entire concept of TILCOR as a suitably financed, technically equipped and sufficiently substantial vehicle for effecting development in the TTLs. The total investment in that organization, standing in stark contrast to tobacco subsidies, is symptomatic of the actual level of development effort and suitably reflects the inadequacy of that effort.

III. Remedies: Positive Policy Suggestions

I am fully aware, in suggesting possible policy measures that might be taken to overcome these serious labour problems of one important governing principle. That is that no single group or institution should in itself be expected to undertake desired reforms. The effort required must inevitably involve a concerted joint approach by the state, by employer organisations and by worker groups.

With this principle in mind, I would suggest that the following measures might go at least some of the way towards solving our current labour problems.

(i) It is necessary, by establishing a pension and social security system, to encourage the formation of a permanent, stable, urban industrial working class, relating to an industrial life-style and active in the promotion of new working and recreational habits.

(ii) The employment generating capacity of the industrial sector must be increased, particularly in regard to the local population, by the provision of training facilities for local persons in preference to the policy of importing required skills, by extending the coverage of such training facilities, and by adopting modern productive methods capable of being performed by workers with an intermediate level of skill under the overall supervision of more skilled technicians. The methods where possible should be labour-intensive and training facilities should be sufficiently flexible to cater for new or changed production methods.

(iii) A comprehensive and detailed programme for reforming the productivity of labour in both European and African areas should be implemented, but it must be realised that such a programme would have to be integrated with other developmental initiatives in the economy, that it would involve considerable expense and that effective reform may only be achieved with some sacrifice in the rate of growth of the centralised industrial complexes. None of these factors should prejudice the adoption of such a programme, which would have to be viewed from the point of view of benefits secured in the long run.

(iv) The stabilisation of the working population can only be achieved if wage rates allow for a decent standard of living for all workers in the country. We, in the trade union movement, have long felt the need for the establishment of some minimum level of wages that would be regarded as necessary according to some objective measure, and are at present pursuing initiatives into the establishment of a poverty datum line. I do not intend to speculate over the level at which such a line would eventually be drawn, but in the absence of a fuller study, I would suggest that no worker is able to maintain a family on less than $15 per week at today's prices. We should be aiming at this wage rate as a minimum for all workers within a short time period, and it is a wage that could be paid by employers in commerce and industry provided that they took proper initiatives to introduce new and improved methods of production. For too long in Rhodesia, labour has been forced to take up the slack of managerial inefficiencies, and when employers have been faced with inadequate or declining profit margins, they have not turned to improvements in internal efficiency or to methods for boosting productivity, but have rather taken the easy way out by restraining the rate of advance of wages. This situation must end if Rhodesia is to aspire eventually to the full development of internal markets for her industrial output.

(v) In the final analysis, a number of diverse policy measures have to be co-ordinated in a single comprehensive development programme, and although such a step appears distant from current government thinking on the matter, I offer it as perhaps the only way by which Rhodesia's labour problems can be effectively solved in the shortest possible period of time.

LABOUR AND TRADE UNIONS: RACIAL OR NON-RACIAL?

A South African financial journal analyses the provision for non-racial trade unions in Rhodesia, as compared with the South African system of legalised segregation. The labour 'calm' is attributed to the provision for African contact with employers through the Industrial Councils and Boards and, more significantly, to the large reservoir of unemployed Africans available to replace any recalcitrant worker. Equally significant are the repressive laws preventing political activities by trade union members and financial assistance from organisations based outside Rhodesia.

DOCUMENT 28. 'RHODESIA'S LABOUR CALM' (FROM THE *Financial Mail*, JOHANNESBURG, 5 APRIL 1973)

South African employers and their government, tinkering around to fit the country's so-called traditional way of life to the labour negotiating machinery of a modern economy, might well look North for an example.

By no means can Rhodesians claim all the answers. Living cost data, for instance, are way behind SA's. So are wages.

But at least the Rhodesians have Africans in *registered* unions, have had them for years, and don't, for the moment at least, regard labour unrest as a fact of life.

Still the situation has its paradoxes.

On the one hand, the Industrial Conciliation Act of 1960 expressly prohibits 'the exclusion of any person from membership of a trade union on the grounds of race or colour'.

Yet, more often than not trade unions divide along racial lines.

Then there's no doubt that African wage levels in commerce and industry are well below minimum income needs for urban subsistence. Yet strikes and stoppages are still relatively rare.

As the existence of about 14 registered multi-racial trade unions suggests, the Act has fostered a degree of co-operation across the colour line. But the 19 or so purely African unions and 17 White unions also give the impression that co-operation is the exception rather than the rule.

All the same, it would be wrong to interpret this Black-White division as deliberate defiance of the Act.

On the contrary, racially divided trade unions are the unintentional consequence of a traditional employment pattern (no different from SA's) in which skilled jobs are held mainly by Whites, and unskilled entirely by Africans.

Indeed, this well-intentioned Act can unintentionally help entrench the Whites' position, given their inevitable desire to retain skills in their own hands.

For it defines trade union representation by occupation, by industry and by area, so not only drawing the line between skilled (White) unions and unskilled (Black) unions, but reinforcing race barriers in a particular industry in a specific area.

One unfortunate result is that an unskilled Black and a skilled White, working at the same bench but belonging to different trade unions, are often more conscious of their differences than their similarities.

The White artisan, through his union, resists any 'fragmentation' (breaking down of job classifications) of his job for fear that the Black man working alongside him might eventually replace him at a lower wage. Or, if the White does agree to fragmentation, the African's advancement into the resulting semi-skilled job tends to be localised.

So, while job fragmentation may be the rule in the Umtali building industry, it tends to be the exception elsewhere.

Fragmentation indeed is the major unresolved issue on the Rhodesian labour scene. If White employers argue for it, they are concerned with the skilled labour shortage (an 8·6% vacancy rate for journeymen and an average 4·1% for all sectors). If White unions argue against it, they maintain that fragmentation would undermine the 'rate for the job'.

Predictably, government sits squarely atop the nearest fence.

Minister of Labour, Ian McLean is opposed to any 'massive' fragmentation because it 'will inevitably lead to a lowering of standards'. But he concedes that 'with technological advances taking place almost daily, it would be quite unrealistic to apply inflexible rules.'

White unions cannot be saddled with all the blame for blocking African advancement. Job fragmentation has become a fiery issue precisely because employers themselves have failed to train Africans up to better skills.

Here they're more to blame than their South African fellows.

Spreading the culpability fairly, the combined effect of White union resistance, government indifference, and employers' neglect has been to limit African advancement into skilled jobs.

Of the 2,181 apprentices in employment at the end of 1971, only 59 were African and 148 Coloured and Asian. Moreover, the situation is being aggravated by the Rhodesian Front's 'non-selective' immigration policy, which generally seems to result in a mediocre White immigrant displacing a local African from his job.

Africans also suffer from a weak negotiating platform. Their unions draw their support mainly from poorly paid and only partially urbanised unskilled workers who have yet to realise the full value of collective bargaining.

Furthermore, registered African unions often lack sound financial backing, and consequently the necessary expertise, to negotiate with employer organisations at Industrial Council level. Notable exceptions, however, are the clothing and textile unions, with a solid history of expert bargaining.

The unvarnished truth is that the African trade union movement has yet to get off the ground. In 1971, registered trade unions participating in Industrial Councils represented a mere 5·2% of the total urban African work force of about 790,000.

The 15 or so African trade unions yet to become 'representative' enough to achieve registration have no power to negotiate direct with employers, but are allowed to submit evidence to Industrial Boards (equivalent to SA Wage Boards), made up of three ministerial appointees representing employers and employee interests and an independent member with a casting vote.

In 1971 these boards (35 in all) represented only about 17·2% of the total African labour force.

The difference between an Industrial Council and an Industrial Board is this: a Council 'freely' negotiates a wage agreement in which the Minister may only interfere under rare circumstances when the 'public interest' is affected: a Board submits recommendations to the Minister who may decide to go against them when framing wage regulations.

Few represented

Either way, Boards and Councils together represent at most only a quarter of the total African work force, a factor that could account for the low level of African wages.

The fact that Rhodesia has no official poverty datum line, and that private organisations and individuals have only half-heartedly done the sums to establish one, also complicates matters. Employer and employee negotiate in a vacuum, with no real idea of an acceptable minimum objective.

The nearest Rhodesia ever got to a PDL was in 1958, when the Plewman Commission calculated the minimum income needed for subsistence in Salisbury at R$12·70 monthly for a single person, R$21 for a married man and R$31 monthly for a married man with two children.

These sums assumed that housing, hospitalisation, and education were free.

Since 1958, however, the African consumer price index has risen by 37%, housing rentals for single-storey married accommodation (two to four rooms) are now anything from 50c to R$15 monthly more than the compulsory R$3 monthly rental subsidy paid by employers, while education (costing from R$6·10 to R$10 p.a. a child) and hospitalisation are anything but free.

As a final straw, the African pays sales tax just like anyone else.

With the CoL increases, and if additional rental, education and other charges are put in at a highly conservative R$1 (single) and R$5 (married) monthly, then the PDL now reads: R$19 monthly (single), R$35 (married) and R$50 (married with two children).

That's not the end of it. The size of an urban African family in Rhodesia is not a maximum of four persons, but an average of six. Feed that into a computation and the minimum African wage for a family head works out close on the R$60 monthly calculated by the African trade unions.

There is some reason why this should be so much lower than the R$82·19 calculated by the Johannesburg Chamber of Commerce for the head of a family of five in Soweto. Rhodesian workers enjoy cheaper meat, live closer to work, and can buy cheaper and better clothing, wood and other items.

All the same, it tots up to a minimum average income of R$720 p.a., a pay target that only two sectors get anywhere near: transport (R$717) and finance and insurance (R$744). The rest, like industry (R$484), electricity (R$486), construction (R$478) and commerce (R$480) fall distressingly short.

Rhodesia's much publicised unemployment burden, together with the lack of influx control and a profitable farming industry (both factors focusing the whole problem on the cities) really offer little incentive to employers to pay African employees much above levels already negotiated through Industrial Councils or recommended to the Minister through the Boards.

So the statutory minimum wage levels for a general labourer may be taken as close to actual wages, excluding the R$3 monthly housing subsidy. On this premise, African wages are generally pitched above the minimum of R$19 that a single person should be getting, but even in the more progressive firms still slightly below the subsistence level for a married person.

Lack of advancement and low wages, taken together, would account in turn for the big gap between Black and White wages. This has been growing wider each year in actual terms over the six years to 1971, though the ratio of White to Black wages (10·5:1 in 1965, and 10·8:1 in 1971) has not changed strikingly.

Two trends are showing up.

First, the skilled labour shortage has forced employers to bid up White wages in an effort to win skills, widening the gap discernibly in sectors like industry, mining, electricity, commerce and transport.

In industry, White wages have risen from 6·9 times African wages in 1965 to 7·8 times in 1971. In other sectors like construction, and finance and insurance, where African advancement into higher positions has been more noticeable, the gap has decreased slightly (in insurance from 4·9 to 4·4 times).

Even so, the overall gap is wide enough to give cause for concern. The wonder is that industrial unrest has been so restricted.

Work stoppages because of employer-employee disputes in 1971 involved only 947 employees (or slightly over 0·1%) of a total White and African working force of about 894,000. Of these, only 115 were Africans (about 0·01%) from a total force of 790,000.

There are two basic explanations. African contact with employers through the Industrial Councils and Boards, though limited, nevertheless gives Africans a chance to voice their frustrations and grievances in a manner that is seldom practicable here.

Second, the mere presence of a large number of African jobless in the cities tends to discourage Africans who have jobs from being too vociferous in their demands. There's always the fear that a replacement is waiting outside the factory gate.

When serious trouble does break out (as during the Pearce Commission visit), it is generally aligned with politics.

But, as last year's bus drivers strike bears out, the pressure for better pay is increasing. The best that Rhodesian employers can do is not to resist it, but to recognise that Africans have a case.

For a start, there is scope for an immediate 20% increase in wages. This would only entail a 1·8% rise in manufacturing industry's gross operating costs and would in any case probably be absorbed by better productivity.

Minimum needs

Over the longer term, a 50% increase in African wages over present levels would enable most African workers to at least meet minimum subsistence needs, while the resultant 4·8% rise in gross operating costs could conceivably be balanced by better training techniques.

Even if they can't manage a phased programme for hiking wages, employers should at least stimulate co-operation through the existing negotiating machinery.

But they must also help improve the machinery itself. They could agree to provide pay deduction facilities for union dues for the African unions. . . .

Finally, government could assist by ensuring that leaders of embryo trade unions receive a modicum of training.

LABOUR AND TRADE UNIONS: INFRINGEMENT OF TRADE UNION RIGHTS

The United Nations Commission on Human Rights appointed a Working Group of Experts to investigate the rights accorded to African workers in Rhodesia. The Reports of the Group reveal the manner in which these rights have been infringed by the legislation prevailing in that country and, in particular, by the new Industrial Conciliation Act of 1971. The International Labour Office (ILO) also participated in the enquiry and its findings were incorporated in the reports.

DOCUMENT 29. *Trade Union Rights, and Allegations Regarding Infringements, in Southern Africa,* REPORTS OF THE *Ad Hoc* WORKING GROUP OF EXPERTS OF THE COMMISSION ON HUMAN RIGHTS (UNITED NATIONS ECONOMIC AND SOCIAL COUNCIL, E/4953, E/5245, 19 FEBRUARY 1971, 23 FEBRUARY 1973)

Summary of Relevant Laws

100. It will be recalled that, in 1969, the illegal régime adopted a new 'Constitution' which became effective in March 1970.

101. This illegal 'Constitution' includes a 'Declaration of Rights'. This is of significance to trade unions. It purports to protect the right to life (paragraph 1 (i)); the right to personal liberty (paragraph 2 (i)); the right to protection from slavery and forced labour (paragraph 3 (i)); the right to protection from inhuman treatment (paragraph 4 (i)); the right to protection from search and entry (paragraph 6 (ii)) and the right of every person to the protection of the law.

102. Of particular interest to the inquiry on trade union rights is the declaration on freedom of assembly and association which is contained in paragraph 9 (i) (b). It provides that 'no person shall be hindered in the enjoyment of his freedom of peaceful assembly and association, that is to say, his right to assemble freely and associate with other persons and, in particular, to form or belong to trade unions or other associations for the protection of his interests'.

103. This declaration, however, contains a saving clause the application of which may render the provision as a whole largely ineffective, stating that 'no law shall be construed to be inconsistent with sub-paragraph (1) of this paragraph to the extent that the law in question makes provision which is necessary in the interests of defence, public safety, public order, public morality or public health, or the economic interests of the State or to protect the rights and freedoms of other persons or which impose restrictions upon public officers which are necessary in the public interest'.

104. Similarly, the right to 'protection from discrimination on the ground of race, tribe, political opinion, colour or creed' (paragraph 10 (i) of the 'Constitution') is made ineffective by sub-paragraph (2), which states that 'a law shall not be construed to discriminate unjustly to the extent that it permits different treatment of persons or communities if such treatment is fair and will promote harmonious relations between such persons or communities by making due allowance for economic, social or cultural differences between them'.

105. It will also be recalled that the main law governing trade unions in Southern Rhodesia is the Industrial Conciliation Act 1959, as amended. Its main provisions may be briefly summarized as follows: although the Industrial Conciliation Act purports to give trade union rights to workers, it does not apply

to farm workers, domestic servants, and to a large number of government employees. It permits the establishment of trade union branches on a racial basis; it restricts the growth of strong unions by the prohibition of horizontal membership; it imposes conditions under which strike action may lawfully be taken. It compels union officials to answer any questions, however incriminating, which may be put to them by the registrar of trade unions or any authorized officer. 'Any person who refuses or fails to answer any question put to him by the registrar or authorized officer shall be guilty of an offence.' Section 11 of the law prohibits trade unions in Rhodesia from accepting assistance from the international trade union movement. Assistance is given so wide a definition that it includes 'any services, donations, loans, travel vouchers or tickets'.

106. Brief reference should further be made to the emergency and security legislation which is designed primarily to curb the political and social aspirations of Africans. Among other things, the Law and Order (Maintenance) Act prohibits workers from taking strike action by widening the definition of 'public order' and 'essential service' to include basically all the main industries and services where the majority of workers are employed. 'Essential service' is defined to include 'any transport service; coal mining; communication and any service relating to the production, supply, delivery or distribution of food, fuel and coal'. It empowers the police to prohibit the holding of meetings; to record speeches made at trade union meetings; and to detain any person for periods up to five years without trial.

107. The Emergency Power (Maintenance of Law and Order) Regulations of 1968 provide, *inter alia*, for the control of printing, publishing and distributing newspapers and other publications; for the removal of persons from one area to another; for the restriction of individuals to specified areas; and for the arrest and search of persons without warrant.

108. The Emergency Power (Industrial Relations) Regulations of 1968 empower the Minister to release any employer from certain of his obligations under the Industrial Conciliation Act. Section 3 (1) of the Regulations reads:

Notwithstanding anything to the contrary contained in the principal Act (the principal Act being the Industrial

Conciliation Act) the Minister may, on application by an employer, grant to such employer exemption from the provisions of any employment regulations in respect of any one or more of the following matters: (a) hours of work; ... (c) remuneration of an employee who is weekly or monthly paid where such remuneration is not determined by the time worked; (d) taking of leave.

109. Reference should also be made to the Land Tenure Act, which was enacted in 1969. The Act contains provisions which seriously affect trade unions. Section 11 (2) of the Act provides that 'no member of one race may occupy land in the area of another race'. A trade union is deemed to be African 'if the majority of members in such a union are Africans'. The Minister may, under Section 72, authorize a voluntary association ('voluntary association' as defined in the Act includes trade unions) to occupy land in European or African areas as the case may be, irrespective of the race of the member of the association. This concession may be granted at the discretion of the Minister (clause 5) who has power to cancel it. Pursuant to this provision, in March 1970 eight unions were evicted from their offices in Salisbury because this is a European area. They had to move to African townships seven–ten miles away.
110. The Act further creates loop-holes which may permit what appears to be some form of forced labour or slavery. Special attention is drawn to section 2 (1), in which the term 'employee' is defined as 'a person who is *bona fide* employed by another person to undertake work or perform duties for that other person, but does not include a person who is employed in terms of an agricultural labour agreement'.

Recent Legislative Developments

77. The most recent amendment to the Act was enacted in January 1971 ('Industrial Conciliation Amendment Act No. 79 of 1971') and its provisions relevant to this inquiry are examined in detail below. The Act makes provision for the registration and regulation of trade unions and employers' organizations; and for the regulation by agreement and by arbitration of conditions of employment and other matters of

mutual interest to employers and employees. Were it not for the constraints discussed below, the main objects of the Act as set out in the preamble would appear to be the creation of rather standard machinery for the appointment of industrial boards, and the prescription of the powers and duties of these boards; and provision for the making of employment regulations in industry. The industrial boards and their role in industrial relations are examined in the section below on the right to collective bargaining. There are, however, several legal and political obstacles by the force of several general and security laws as well as by the imposed statutory requirements imposed by the Industrial Conciliation Act, which hinder the full and free exercise of trade union rights. Among these legal constraints are the prohibition of meetings in certain circumstances; restrictions on trade union leadership as to who can and who cannot be a leader or officer of a trade union; and restrictions on the scope of permitted trade union functions.

'Industrial Conciliation Amendment Act No. 79 of 1971'

78. Section 11 of the new 'Act' adds a further dimension to the restrictions on those eligible to leadership of trade unions by extending the prohibition to persons who have been convicted of political offences or offences arising from trade union action, which in Rhodesia may be secured with considerable ease under the 'Law and Order (Maintenance) Act' or under the 'Unlawful Organisations Act'. The relevant clause reads:

44(3) No person upon whom, on or after the date of commencement of Part I of the Industrial Conciliation Amendment Act, 1971, a sentence of imprisonment for a term of three months or more has been imposed, whether or not the sentence has been suspended, on conviction of any offence under the Law and Order (Maintenance) Act (chapter 39) or the Unlawful Organisations Act (chapter 81), shall be an official or an office-bearer of, or be employed in an administrative or clerical capacity or any other capacity prescribed by regulation, by a registered trade union or employers' organisation, within the period of ten years from the time of conviction.

79. Section 14 of the new 'Act' adds further encroachment upon the unions' independence and freedom of action. It requires that 'the secretary of every registered trade union shall, within three months after the end of each financial year, forward to an auditor the books of account of the union concerned and shall within thirty days after receipt by him of the auditor's report forward to the registrar a true copy of such report and of the statement of income and expenditure and of the balance sheet to which such report relates'. The intention of this provision, it would appear, is to strengthen the 1967 amendment which prohibits trade unions from accepting assistance of any kind from any organisation specified by the Minister who shall refuse such approval if in his opinion the purpose or intended use of such assistance is not in the public interest. Another encroachment upon the affairs of the unions by the Government which the new Act introduces is the requirement that '(e) where the union organisation concerned has conducted a ballot on any proposal to declare or take part in or in the continuation of a strike or lock out, shall forthwith after the completion of the ballot, forward by registered post to the registrar a copy of the proposal and a statement of the number of ballot papers issued, ballot papers returned, votes cast for the proposal, votes cast against the proposal and spoiled ballot papers'. This appears to be an unwarranted interference in the unions' internal affairs. Here again the intention of this provision becomes clear when account is taken of section 122 (2) (9) (ii), which requires that any proposal to take strike action must be supported by not less than 51 per cent of the membership who are in good standing and have indicated by ballot that they support the proposal to declare a strike.

80. Section 45 of the 1971 Act places the right of the workers to strike in doubt. It not only lays down an elaborate procedure to be followed as a condition to engage in a lawful strike in support of a dispute but above all it gives the 'President' power to declare that the award of the arbitrator is binding on the parties to the dispute even when they have declared their intention not to be bound by the said award as provided by the procedure laid down in the Industrial Conciliation Act. Once the President has so declared, it becomes unlawful for any party to the dispute to engage in a strike. . . .

EDUCATION: THE TWO SYSTEMS

The Judges Commission, Rhodesia's first multi-racial Royal Commission, was appointed during the last year of the Whitehead United Federal Party Government to report on the state of the Colony's educational system. While rejecting racial integration in the schools as 'untimely', it advocated equality of opportunity and access to the country's educational facilities. Education was to become 'equal' but to remain 'separate'.

DOCUMENT 30. *Report of the Southern Rhodesia Education Commission, 1962* (C.S.R. 37–1963), *The Judges' Report*

Opinion on the Two Systems

96. In every part of this rapidly evolving social system we have proof in evidence of the belief, among the African public, among the leaders and teachers of most religious bodies, and among part of the European public, that all young citizens can claim a common heritage and a future of equal citizenship. Without being obsessed by the importance of our mission, we do feel that on the educational system now rests almost the whole weight of responsibility for allowing the newer patterns of a common life to come into being.

97. Our sense of destiny in this connexion is strengthened by the degree of anxiety now at large concerning the obstinate failure of the African and non-African systems of schooling to grow together. This is clearly an anxiety of recent growth, since we note a marked lack of stress on race distinctions and their implications in the Kerr Report of 1951. . . .

Equality of Opportunity and Access

118. If there is one matter on which nearly all people seem to be agreed it is that to offer to compel children of different racial backgrounds to attend the same schools is as untimely and as ignorant of realities as it is outmoded to compel all of them to undergo their school courses in watertight containers. It may indeed be many years before any form of education for Africans becomes compulsory.

119. Thus it may be thought pusillanimous for the Commission to leave the arena of educational politics to those who are better acclimatized to it, and to look at some of the non-political aspects. For the subject of the common uses of educational resources is, however it is looked at, one which would make the strongest appeal to a society that is deeply committed to both African advancement and to the survival of the economic and cultural structure attributable to generations of European effort. . . .

121. A policy which favours the use of the country's taxable resources, to say nothing of its reserves of professional manpower in the schools, to hand out different measures of educational value according to the racial origins of the recipients invites, in this year of grace, the adoption of a philosophy of distributive justice which each and every member of this Commission warmly repudiates.

Education and the Whole Economy

958. . . . According to the Central Statistical Office calculations of the percentage contribution of education (as enjoyed by all races) to the gross domestic product of Southern Rhodesia, education's share was 3·7 per cent in 1961 and 3·9 per cent in 1962.

959. . . . Although the impact of education on the budget resources of Central African governments is large, its share in the division of the national product is low compared with highly industrialised countries, where the figure may be as high as 8 per cent, representing an expenditure incurred on behalf of a much smaller fraction of the whole population than that which, as we note above, demands attention in Southern Rhodesia. There can be no present fear that the territory is over-straining its real resources in providing for the culture and opportunity of the younger generation: in fact, very much the reverse. . . .

Fee Income

962. . . . Rather than recommend that rural Africans be freed from fee payments, we have to ask that urban Africans and

non-Africans should pay too. And our requirement, for some years to come, would be the payment of fees by all. . . .

Local Taxation

963. . . . Education may well make itself the largest burden on the local rating system in most cases. Could it be uniformly charged? We believe not. Capacity to pay must be brought into account. . . . A remote and poorly provisioned area with a population engaged solely in subsistence farming would in common justice require a large measure of support from central funds. It could not be left to stew in its own juice. The idea of local self-sufficiency in social services was discredited and abandoned long ago.

Fees and the State

964. . . . European families have for long escaped the financial responsibilities which have fallen upon African families on behalf of their young. If offered the choice between continued segregation at a high price and the chances of some racial admixture at a relatively trifling price, some Europeans would certainly opt for the former. We mention this, having learnt to be realists in racialist matters, and would offer them what they wish, as we would grant similar rights to Africans. . . .

The International Measuring Rod

985. . . . Southern Rhodesia, with the help of the Central Statistical Office, has been able to organise a powerful presentation of its progress and intentions within the economic setting—impressive, in as much as operations in the primary school field compare well with the record elsewhere; although it is mortifying to note that, by UNESCO methods of calculation, access to secondary type education is substantially easier for Africans in Basutoland, Ghana, Kenya, Western Nigeria, Swaziland and Uganda, than for those in Rhodesia.

A Projection of the Annual Cost to the National Treasury

994. . . . Unless substantial help were forthcoming from abroad, the allowance made by the UNESCO tables for the

expansion of the educational budget—a virtual doubling of available revenue in a period of 10 years—would be insufficient in Southern Rhodesia. At a constant value of the £1, more than two and a half times the size of the current education budget for African education would be needed by 1972 in order to achieve the anticipated expansion in the Addis Ababa [UNESCO] formula.

995. We must recommend, accordingly, that any forward planning for the education of Africans on the scale desiderated by the UNESCO formula should seek financial backing from the national treasury at a rate of expansion representing an annual increment of not less than 11 per cent. . . .

EDUCATION: 'NEW PLAN' FOR AFRICANS

The Rhodesian Front Government announced a 'new plan' for African education in April 1966. While expenditure was to remain at about 2 per cent of the gross national product and be equally divided between the unequal black and white school population, a different type of education was envisaged for Africans. The Minister of Education puts the case for reducing African primary education from 8 to 7 years, for a vocational-type secondary education for Africans and for increased financial contributions from parents and local communities.

DOCUMENT 31. AFRICAN EDUCATION: MINISTERIAL STATEMENT (FROM RHODESIA *Parliamentary Debates*, VOL. 63, 20 APRIL 1966, COLS 1847–60)

MINISTER OF EDUCATION [Mr A. P. Smith]: The proposal is that a sum equal to approximately 2 per cent of the gross national product be allocated each year to African education. It is considered that such an amount is the maximum that central Government can allow, and the rate of educational development mentioned hereafter is based on this amount.

However, it is pointed out that if any local community wishes to develop at a greater rate than is envisaged, they could do so provided trained teachers are available, and any sum in excess of central Government's contribution was raised from local government sources, school fees, or by any other appropriate means. It must be appreciated that the local community must also give an undertaking that their support will be continual.

At the present time approximately 2 per cent of the gross national product is spent on African education, that is £6,600,000, and slightly less is spent on European education. The total Education Vote of over £12,500,000 represents about 22 per cent of the national budget and is considered a very generous allowance. . . .

The present type of education is what might be called the traditional British colonial education for backward people with literacy as a main consideration. The vast majority of the pupils leave school without having reached a stage at which they have any clear idea of the relationship between their schooling and any future possible employment.

Approximately 45 per cent proceed no further than the end of the lower primary course, and of those who complete the full eight-year primary course slightly less than 25 per cent find places in secondary schools. From the point of view of the great majority, therefore, there is no 'purpose' other than literacy.

It is now proposed to introduce a new system which will firstly, provide a full course of primary education commencing from 1969; secondly, provide a two-year course leading to Junior Certificate designed to prepare pupils for the type of employment likely to be available at the end of the two years, in other words a two-year course of vocational preparation. Approximately a third of the time in this course would be devoted to handwork and to activities suited to the area in which the school is situated. Pupils would leave school at the age of approximately 16 years. This two-year course will be provided in a new type of junior secondary school. Approximately 37½ per cent of those leaving primary schools will be accommodated in these new schools by 1974. The first entry will be in 1970; thirdly, provide a four-year course of formal secondary education for approximately 12½ per cent of those completing their primary education, followed by a further course for those suitable to proceed to form VI work and university entrance. Fourthly, provide correspondence courses supervised by a mentor in classrooms for the 50 per cent which cannot be accommodated in secondary schools. The cost of the course to be met by the pupil. . . .

Purpose in education, in terms of the parents' demand, can only be achieved if the last two years of schooling are directed towards the probable type of employment which will be available. The parents must be brought to realize that their children must enter work at this stage. It is in commerce, industry and agriculture that work must be sought whereby the economy can be strengthened and developed.

To achieve the 'purpose' in education the establishment of a relationship between the school and the area in which it is situated is a first and essential requirement. The two last years of schooling in the junior secondary schools can be described as 'an ecological secondary education course'.

In urban areas, trade and industry must accept that its labour force will largely be drawn from the school-leavers in the area, and to this end there should be established a youth placement organization, under the aegis of the Ministry of Labour, whereby trade and industry indicate the types of training they would wish and the types of jobs offering.

The schools should be able, by the requisite activities and by aptitude testing, to provide the labour to meet the demands of industry.

In rural areas where agricultural operations in their widest sense are likely to provide a livelihood it will be essential to link the two final years of schooling to agricultural activities. Equally, a relationship should be established between the parents and farmers and the school and the agricultural extension services. . . .

In order to allow the introduction of a full primary course in 1969 and yet maintain the present development, it may be necessary for Government to raise fees from pupils in both the Government and the aided system. The proposal is that these be called registration fees, as distinct from school fees, which will continue to be determined and raised by the school authorities. . . .

The missions have contributed the advice and management for the primary system and have established a large part of the secondary system; the parents have built the buildings and teachers' houses for the primary system and bought the books and equipment, the Government has paid the teachers' salary grants, controlled the syllabuses, provided the inspectorate, and been directly responsible for urban education and a part of the secondary system.

Thus it has happened that Government has been mainly responsible for providing the schools in the urban areas and the missions in the rural areas, with only very limited scope for local government bodies to step in in areas where missionary enterprise has not done so, mainly in African Purchase Areas.

In the future we are planning for the admission into the partnership of a fourth partner—the local government councils. This has been strongly urged by the Judges Commission and there is no doubt about the intensity of the desire to participate in the educational field.

Local government councils must be permitted, indeed encouraged, to assume responsibility in all areas for the provision of primary schools and, having learned what such responsibilities entail, to go further and establish junior secondary schools and all boarding accommodation. . . .

Central Government will be responsible for the provision of all additional senior secondary schools. It is hoped that the missions will continue to co-operate with Government and also with local government councils. Only by co-operation between the parents, the voluntary organizations and the Government has the present system of African education become possible. Each has contributed to the best of its ability.

For this system to continue and to meet the challenges of the future it is essential that African local government contribute its initiative, enthusiasm and resources.

Last year the African education vote stood at £6,600,000, but in addition it is estimated that the parents and the voluntary organisations raised an additional £2,500,000. . . .

Whilst conceding that we have done much in the field of primary education, our critics have had much to say about the lack of opportunity in secondary education. In fact this Government has been accused of deliberately withholding secondary education from our African people in order to deprive them of the franchise. This is, of course, complete nonsense—our record in the provision of secondary education speaks for itself.

Forty-five new secondary schools have been established during the three years since we won the December 1962 election. In the three years prior to that only 18 new secondary schools were established. During the period of our administration the number of Africans in secondary schools has almost doubled and the number in sixth forms has more than trebled.

As a first priority we have endeavoured to give a basic education to all our people. Of necessity this has cost a great deal in primary education, with the result that we have had little available for secondary education.

Nevertheless, we have managed to give secondary education to nearly 25 per cent of those leaving the primary schools, and I think it must be conceded that among this 25 per cent are the ones who are most likely to benefit from further education. . . .

Our immediate problem is to curtail the amount spent by Government on ever increasing costs of primary education in order to devote more money to secondary education. One obvious means of doing this is to open up the primary field to the energies and resources of local government bodies and other voluntary agencies.

There are two further means of curtailing the amount spent on primary education. Firstly as a result of improved teacher training we will be able to reduce the period of primary education from eight to seven years, and secondly, we propose to introduce a degree of double sessioning.

However, these measures of themselves may not be sufficient to enable us to afford the educational system we desire and so it has been decided to provide for the introduction of the small registration fees already mentioned.

As a result, we are able to offer full primary to all by 1969—this is about five years earlier than was previously envisaged—and at the same time give the African teachers an increase in their salaries.—[HON. MEMBERS: Hear, hear.]

EDUCATION: AFRICAN OBJECTIONS

An attack on the Government's education policy by the African nationalist party ZAPU.

DOCUMENT 32. 'AFRICAN EDUCATION', BY THE ZIMBABWE AFRICAN PEOPLE'S UNION (FROM *Zimbabwe Review*, LUSAKA, 30 AUGUST 1969)

There is, currently, consideration of what is called an African Education Report in the Rhodesian régime's Parliament. A select parliamentary committee prepared the report [Rhodesia Parliament, Select Committee on Education, *Third Report*, S.C. 5–1969]. The purported object of the committee was to make a thorough collection of information on the existing structure of African education and its content. It is not difficult to guess that the régime wants to enter into a more precise and miserly form of 'Bantu education'.

Our interest lies in the mentality revealed by the whole set of so-called parliamentarians. It is shocking and confirms the urgent necessity of removing these elements from further polluting the thinking of the Zimbabwe population. In broad terms the consensus of opinion is that the base of African elementary education should be narrowed and its progress upwards should taper as it produces professional men. We have never regarded African education as run by the settlers as anything near satisfactory to say the least. Its re-examination by the régime must not, however, be misinterpreted for a sign of progress. . . . The fact of the matter is that the settler régime wants to keep the Africans completely out of beneficial and self-reliant education.

Ninety per cent of African education hitherto was conducted by Christian missionaries. It was started by the missionaries for their own purpose mainly, of course—and not by the régime. Because of the strides made by the Africans largely on their own efforts, the settler régimes have all along sought to take absolute control of the education from the missionaries whilst at the same time harshly discouraging any independent African initiative to establish schools of their own. Each measure of control by the régime has meant reducing the pace of African education. It is little wonder that the more open fascists, the Rhodesian Front, are making it abundantly clear that in their view there are too many Africans entering school at elementary level and this base should be reduced drastically. They are calling for taking over completely the management of African schools presently managed by religious missionaries.

The other urgent point conceived by the régime is that whilst the régime's control will be maintained in the management, the financing of African schools at the primary level must not be catered for by state revenue but should be surrendered to Bantustan types of councils under the supervision of chiefs.

Not surprising is the emphasis that African education should concentrate on preaching the dignity of manual labour. Following on this is the requirement that the curriculum for African education should be geared towards producing labour for industry and farms. The settler mental disease revealed itself most in using the economy as the excuse for limiting expenditure on African education and blaming African birth-rate for straining the country's finances. Adding absurdity to this perverse logic one settler argued in Parliament that immigration of Europeans must be increased in order to help finance African education. All these stupid arguments of the settlers make precise comment of the fact that if there are any people who have failed to benefit from education over the years, it is the settlers themselves.

EDUCATION: AN INTERNATIONAL APPRAISAL

UNESCO examines the Rhodesian educational system and reports on its inequalities.

DOCUMENT 33. *The Elimination of Racial Discrimination* (UNITED NATIONS ECONOMIC AND SOCIAL COUNCIL, COMMISSION ON HUMAN RIGHTS, E/CN. 4/1110, 25 JANUARY 1973)

In Rhodesia, several factors operate to ensure that education, below university level, is separate for the various population groups. Of these, the most important are the legal provisions.

The Land Apportionment Act of 1941 with its amendments of 1944, 1945, 1950, 1951, 1960, 1961 and 1970 determined not only the proportion of land to be held by each racial group, but also where the various groups were entitled to live. Thus, even when Africans lived on land in an area designated for European holding, they were grouped in 'African township' areas. While, if Europeans lived in an area designated for African holding they lived in a 'European township area'.

An African may not own, lease or occupy land in the European area except in so far as part of that area has been created as a non-racial residential area, but even where this is so, the 'non-racial' qualification may be revoked by the appropriate Minister by notice in the *Gazette*. Education in urban areas follows the rules of occupation and is covered by the Land Tenure Act.

The Act itself therefore provides for racial segregation of educational facilities in urban areas.

Since there are limitations on the number of Africans allowed to move into urban areas, this in turn limits the number of Africans who can attend schools within these areas.

In addition, regulations governing the administration of Tribal Trust Land lay the foundation, not only for purely African schools but also for rural African schools established on a tribal basis.

Beside these laws, local government by-laws may impose additional restraints on the use of premises within their areas.

Separation is further emphasized by differing administrative responsibilities as between Africans and Europeans. The first is under the Central Government.

The Constitution of the Federation of Rhodesia and Nyasaland (1953) and the Federal Acts relating to school provision and school attendance solidified the customary division of administration as between African education and European education. The former remained a local matter. The latter came under federal control. This in fact meant that there continued to be—and in fact the Constitution provided for—a budgetary distinction between the two types of education.

Both Legislation and custom were based on the premises of a dual society. White Rhodesians are given an education which would prepare them to fill the middle and upper echelons of government, the public service and the private sector. This education is as good as any provided in Europe, for on it depends the maintenance of the present Rhodesian social structure. Top level posts are held by Europeans, either native-born white Rhodesians or by immigrants from Europe. Since the structure depends on increased immigration from Europe the Rhodesian Government has done much to ensure that they could be attracted by the provision of a social and economic status in Rhodesia which is better than in their former home countries.

African education on the other hand is geared to providing the semi-skilled labour necessary for industrial development but not educated to compete with white Rhodesians for top level posts.

Missions were responsible for the greater part of African

education but even then education was closely directed by Government.

The policy of the present Government is, while maintaining the present structure of non-African education, to transfer African education from the missions to 'responsible' community boards and councils, themselves politically controlled by the Central Government. This was done, not only to ensure the political direction of African education, but also through community taxation to force Africans to contribute a greater share of the financing of their education particularly at primary school level.

The trend in finance then is that this should increasingly be found from the poorest sector of the community rather than from all-over taxation.

On 14 December 1966 Government policy was announced:

(i) As from 1 January 1967, in under-developed areas, new primary schools would only be opened under the authority of community boards or local governments.

(ii) From 1 January 1968, no new primary schools or additional streams in existing primary schools would be authorized unless local government existed in the areas and had assumed responsibility for new schools in those areas.

(iii) From 1 January 1970, development of grades 6 and 7 in mission schools in Tribal Trust Lands and in Purchase areas would be at the cost of the missions concerned.

In fact in 1970 there was a 5 per cent cut in the Government contribution to teachers' salaries in the aided sector. Missions found it impossible to work with this cut in already seriously under-financed schools and there was a considerable transfer of administration either to councils or community boards or, in an intermediate stage, to a government-sponsored school.

Even before 1970, part of the finance for African primary education was raised by the communities themselves. This was done by voluntary building labour and by the registration fee which is payable in addition to school fees.

Registration fees had jumped from $143,400 in 1967–1968 to $248,600 in 1970–1971. In addition the African Education Amendment Act of 1970 provided for a levy to be paid in respect of each pupil attending a sponsored school. The money for this levy is required to cover the 5 per cent cut in the grant for teachers.

It was estimated that this would mean an additional fee of $1·25 to $1·50 per African pupil.

In January 1967, instead of there being one teacher for each primary class up to grade 5, four teachers were required to teach the five classes and the primary course was reduced from eight to seven years.

It should be noted that in 1964 boarding grants for Africans in central primary schools and equipment grants to primary schools were withdrawn. Unaided upper primary schools were being built and staffed by African communities themselves. Of 305 additional upper primary schools constructed in 1963, 215 were unaided.

A summary of Government expenditure on African education shows that it rose from $11,351,546 in 1963–1964 to $17,104,380 in 1969–1970. However, some key sectors should be examined.

Government teacher training *drops* from $306,674 in 1963–1964 to $245,282 in 1969–1970.

Government primary education rises from $1,623,036 in 1963–1964 to $1,865,732 in 1969–1970.

Aid to teacher training in non-government schools *drops* from $364,566 in 1963–1964 to $281,092 in 1969–1970.

Even where increases are present they are modified by increases in salaries, the purchasing power of the Rhodesian dollar and an increasing population.

The most telling argument for discrimination is the comparison in expenditure as between African education and non-African education.

	African	*Non-African*
Population	4,817,950	252,414
Total education—Vote 1971	$21,400,000	$20,299,000
Approx. expenditure per head of population	$5	$80

In 1970 the Government declared its target for African post-primary school places. This was to be 50 per cent of African primary school *leavers*. Even if all children who entered primary school completed, the target of the Government was to leave half of these without further education.

In fact, there is a high drop out throughout the primary course, with an average of 37·204 per cent of African pupils who started primary school completing. It is 50 per cent of this

37·204 per cent who will receive post-primary education. In other words 81 per cent of the intake of African [primary] schools will not get post-primary education. The 50 per cent however would not go to academic secondary schools. Only 12 1/2 per cent of primary school leavers would. Thirty-seven and one half per cent would go to a new type of secondary school geared to semi-skilled labour, untrained to become apprentices and unable to proceed to higher education.

This semi-skilled labour would not be mobile, but would be closely tied in rural areas to the implementation of the aims of the Tribal Trust Land Development Co-operation.

In line with this policy government academic secondary provision increases between 1961 and 1966 and remains steady after that.

In fact, total enrolments: primary, junior secondary and secondary show a declining percentage decrease from 1962 to 1968. In 1969 and 1970, not only is there a *percentage* decrease, there is a decrease in absolute numbers.

While most African pupils would have left school after four years of *primary* education, most Europeans would have left after at least four years of *secondary* education. While in 1969, 605 European students of a population of 252,414 would have left after the upper sixth, 180 African students of a population of 4,817,950 were *registered* in the upper sixth.

In addition European students may qualify for university through the MVI. This is not available for Africans. In addition to the 605 European students leaving after upper sixth, 929 left after MVI.

An examination of Rhodesian education shows discrimination against Africans at every level. Moreover, this discrimination is increasing and is reflected in administration, finance, school provisions, extra curricular activities, pupil-teacher ratio and syllabus.

It in turn affects which high level posts Africans are qualified to hold and the pace of their political advance since the last is tied to educational and economic criteria.

A SEGREGATED SOCIETY: 'POLARISATION'

The role of the Church in opposing many of the apartheid measures of the Rhodesian Front régime has been a significant one. This is analysed by the late Jack Halpern, a former editor of the *Central African Examiner*. Particular attention is given to the 1969 Constitution, the Land Tenure Act and their effects on the 'polarisation' of Rhodesian society.

DOCUMENT 34. 'POLARISATION IN RHODESIA: STATE, CHURCH AND PEOPLE' BY JACK HALPERN (FROM *The World Today*, VOL. 27, NO. I, JANUARY 1971)

> We have reached a point of no return. . . . Justice is more important than law and order, and can sometimes be incompatible with it. . . . The Christian faith is completely contrary to the prevailing philosophy of those who hold sway in this country.
> Fundamental freedom is now endangered. . . . We cannot in conscience and we will not in practice accept any limitation of our freedom to deal with all people, irrespective of race, as members of the one human family. . . . We are now compelled to declare 'We must obey God rather than men'.

These are not the words of the acknowledged political leaders of Rhodesia's Africans: of ZAPU's Joshua Nkomo, who is a Methodist lay preacher and is now in the sixth year of banning and restriction without charge or trial, or of ZANU's Rev. Ndabaninge Sithole, still serving a jail sentence for actively opposing Ian Smith's rebel régime. Nor are they statements by the remnants of the always tiny handful of truly committed liberals amongst Rhodesia's white population: of someone like Guy Clutton-Brock who, because he has been instrumental in maintaining a multiracial co-operative on Cold Comfort Farm, whose land is reserved for Europeans only, was two months ago arbitrarily deprived of his Rhodesian nationality as an obvious prelude to his expulsion.

Instead, the statements quoted are by bishops of what have long been regarded as Rhodesia's leading white Establishment churches: the first by the Anglican Bishop of Matabeleland, and the second collectively by the five Roman Catholic bishops of Rhodesia. And their particular significance lies in the fact that, as the Rhodesian Front's policies and actions continue deliberately to polarize Rhodesia's life and peoples, the churches have become the guardians of national public morality. It is not a role which they have sought. Indeed, they could justifiably be criticized—and have been so criticized by African Nationalist leaders who are practising Christians—for having remained far too long an integral part of the white Establishment. But, as polarization has been pushed further and further, with internal African political opposition gagged and bound whilst almost all whites in effect range themselves inside the Rhodesian Front's *laager* and the old liberal voices fall largely silent, church leaders—always excepting those of the Dutch Reformed Church—are filling their new role with courage.

The statements quoted were made by the bishops after Mr Smith's Government declared Rhodesia to be a Republic on 2 March 1970, thus bringing into effect a new Constitution. This Constitution is designed, in Mr Smith's own words, to 'entrench Rhodesia's government in civilized hands for all time'. It therefore explicitly rules out majority rule for ever, providing instead for infinitely retardable progress by Rhodesia's 5 million Africans towards parity of legislative representation with the 234,000 whites. The pattern officially adopted by the Rhodesian Front party is one designed to polarize the Africans internally as well as *vis-à-vis* the whites. Three provincial assemblies are planned—one for the Mashona, one for the Matabele, and one for whites who, for this purpose, would include Rhodesia's 25,000 Asians and Coloured or mixed-race people. A multiracial House of Assembly, elected by voters on racially separated African and white rolls, is to exercise central control.

Clearly, it is this House of Assembly which matters and its purpose is reflected in the way it has been constituted under the Republican Constitution. Whites have been given 50 seats, based on voting qualifications which none of the 90,000 white electorate should have any difficulty in meeting. Urban Africans, after meeting much more difficult requirements, are permitted to elect 8 representatives, and tribal chiefs and authorities nominate a further 8. Any increase in African representation is to be related to African contributions to personal income tax. At present only 947 Africans in the whole of Rhodesia earn sufficient to be subject to such tax and, not surprisingly, their contribution is only 0·7 per cent of the total. Even if one were very optimistically to assume that this African share will grow steadily by 0·1 per cent per annum (which is twice the growth over the past five years), it would, under the present constitutional formula, be 230 years before the *present* 24 per cent African representation is 'justified', and some 500 years before parity could be reached. And whites, of course, continue to control the economy, education, jobs, and taxation.

It remained for the churches to put the issues clearly. With the exception of the Roman Catholics on the one hand and the Dutch Reformed Church on the other, most important churches, including some African separatist ones, are members of the Christian Council of Rhodesia. This Council, incidentally, is the only 'established' church body—except for the Methodist Church (U.K.)—in which Africans occupy top positions. Here, too, white church leaders can join with others in pronouncements which most of their white congregations, and most of their missionaries, would object to and very likely reject.

Before the June 1969 referendum, the Christian Council publicly denied the basic principles of the constitutional proposals: 'No government that wished to rule as the servant of the people would be satisfied with these proposals as the basis for its power.' The Roman Catholic bishops were even more explicit about the Front's proposals:

> In many respects they are completely contrary to Christian teaching—they are calculated to destroy every possibility of achieving the common good . . . and can only breed hatred and violence. If they should be implemented, it will be extremely difficult for us effectively to counsel moderation to a people who have been patient for so long under discriminatory laws and are now presented with such provocation.

In the event, hardly any of the 6,634 'qualified' Africans took part in the referendum, and the new Constitution was approved by 54,724 votes to 20,776 and the Republic by 61,130 votes to 14,327.

The subsequent announcement that Rhodesia would become a Republic on 2 March 1970, with an election based on the 1969 Constitution to follow, brought unequivocal opposition from Protestant and Catholic leaders, including the statements quoted at the beginning of this article. But these had no discernible effect on the general election held in April. The Rhodesian Front overwhelmingly won all 50 white seats. . . .

Were it not for the previous and equally outspoken opposition of the churches to UDI, it could be said by sceptics that they have spoken so clearly now because their own lives and organizations are being attacked, especially by the replacement of the *Land Apportionment Act* by the *Land Tenure Act*, which became operative at the same time as the new Constitution. . . .

The Government has now gone further, carrying the 'separate development' ideology of its Constitution to a legal conclusion with the *Land Tenure Act*. A clean division is made between African and white land, with 44·9 million acres for whites (of whom only 54,000 live on farms) and 45·2 million acres for Africans. On paper a Bantustan-type Industrial Development body has also been created. The Act states that the interest—as approved by the Government—of each race shall be paramount in its own area and that neither race may own or occupy land in the area of the other race except by permit issued solely at his own discretion by a Government Minister. Crucially, this discretion may be delegated to local authorities, and the Act therefore makes all activities and all occasions of association between members of the two major races dependent upon official permission. It gives the Minister, local councils, and officials power to control attendance on a racial basis at schools, hospitals, churches, parks, or any place to which the public is admitted. As Sir Robert Tredgold, the former Chief Justice of the Federation of Rhodesia and Nyasaland, said in an interview last November: 'The Act is so dependent on the discretionary decisions of individuals or small groups that it is almost the negation of law. *No further legislation, only administrative action, would be needed for the full introduction of apartheid in Rhodesia*' (italics added). . . .

Once again, only the church leaders have taken a stand. Heavily engaged in educational and other work on lands either owned or leased by them in what are now 'Africans-only' areas, they refuse to register, as the Government has suggested, as Voluntary Associations which, under the Act, would allow them to continue operating, although only at the Minister's discretion, with mixed congregations, or schools, in both racial areas. Seventeen Roman Catholic and Protestant Church leaders, representing most of Rhodesia's churches, stated on 28 April 1970:

> We affirm that the new Constitution and the *Land Tenure Act* cannot be reconciled with the Christian faith, since they entrench separation and discrimination solely on the basis of race . . . we will not register as Voluntary Associations.

On the following day Rhodesia's five Roman Catholic bishops said that the new 'legislation now in force will effectively close all these [church and mission] institutions'. With church leaders prepared to translate belief into action, the Government avoided a physical confrontation by the device of 'deeming' the churches to have registered as voluntary associations, saving face by reminding them that church activities which could lead to racial friction could mean Ministerial withdrawal of this status. . . .

One other use to which the régime is putting the *Land Tenure Act*—the harrying of the still legal African trade unions —should be mentioned, as it is relevant to the mounting problem of African unemployment, the progressive removal of Africans from such skilled jobs as they have been able to secure, the exclusion in practice of Africans from industrial apprenticeships, and the crisis in African education. Over the past decade, Rhodesia's African population has increased by an estimated 1·3 million. But, as the President of the Associated Chambers of Commerce told his 1970 congress: 'Unemployment and underemployment are without doubt the most fundamental problems facing Rhodesia in the long term. . . . Since 1960 the number of Africans in employment has risen by only 50,000 and work-seekers by roughly 400,000.' The 1969 Report of the Secretary for African Education stated: 'In the modern sector of our economy it is plain that only a small proportion of school-leavers at any level are likely to find jobs for which they are fitted.' Perhaps Mr Ian Smith's otherwise surprising statement last year that 'For any African who is prepared to work we have jobs waiting for him' is related to the strong suggestion made in 1969 by the Select Committee on African Education that *'the Division of African Education change their policy and include in the curriculum for all primary schools the inculcation of the dignity of labour'* (italics in the Committee's report).

In any event, an acute crisis now faces African primary education. Economies have already been made in the number of teachers employed. Now, as of 1 January 1971, the Government, which allocates 2 per cent of the gross national income to white education and only the same amount to African education, will pay only 95 per cent instead of the whole of African primary-school teachers' salaries. The churches, who have been responsible for 90 per cent of African primary-school management, have not been able to find the extra 5 per cent of salaries and, being unwilling to increase fees, have for the most part withdrawn from school management. The Government has decreed that the schools should become local community schools, with none allowed to operate unless the parents, or some other body, pay the extra 5 per cent salary. A heavy falling-off of school enrolment and length of attendance is expected. Meanwhile, the Government plans to spend the money 'saved' on 'secondary education'. In fact, this is a bogus description; the schools being put up are Junior Schools offering only two years' education.

There is no reason, other than the rise of guerrilla resistance, to doubt the continuing validity of the Roman Catholic bishops' pastoral letter shortly after UDI: 'It is simply quite untrue to say that the masses are content . . . or that they have consented by their silence. Their silence is the silence of fear, of disappointment, of hopelessness. It is a dangerous silence. . .'

A SEGREGATED SOCIETY: 'SEPARATE BUT EQUAL'

As one of the earlier measures of social segregation enacted by the Rhodesian Front Government, the Municipal Amendment Act of 1967 provided municipal authorities with the power to make by-laws to establish and regulate separate facilities for the races and to prevent the use of the same facilities by different racial groups. The amenities involved included parks, sports and recreation grounds, swimming baths and public sanitary conveniences; and these were to be provided 'equitably' in accordance with the requirements of each race.

After the Constitutional Council, established by the 1961 (and retained by the 1965) Constitution to report on legislation contravening the Declaration of Rights, had reported that the Bill was in conflict with that Declaration, the Legislative Assembly, on the recommendation of the Minister of Local Government, re-enacted the Bill by a two-thirds majority vote. Under subsequent amendments to the Act (December 1972), the Minister of Local Government determined whether the facilities provided are 'equitable according to the needs of each race'.

DOCUMENT 35A. MUNICIPAL AMENDMENT ACT, NO. 51, 1967 (FROM *The Statute Law of Rhodesia, 1967* SALISBURY: GOVERNMENT PRINTER, 1968)

Amendment of section 277 of Cap. 125.	34. Section 277 of the principal Act is amended— (h) by the repeal of paragraph (60) and the substitution of—
(Recreation grounds)	'(60) for regulating and maintaining— (a) parks and public places of recreation; and (b) recreation, athletic and sports grounds; established by the council, and for making charges in connection therewith, and, where separate such parks, places or grounds are provided for the use of particular races, for prohibiting the use thereof by members of other races;
(Sanitary conveniences and swimming baths)	(60A) (a) for requiring the establishment of separate public sanitary conveniences for separate races, so, however, that such conveniences

shall be afforded equitably according to the needs of each such race;

(b) for controlling and regulating public sanitary conveniences and public swimming baths;

(c) where separate public sanitary conveniences or public swimming baths are provided for the use of particular races, for prohibiting the use thereof by members of other races;

Provided that no by-laws shall be made under this sub-paragraph unless the facilities to which they relate are afforded equitably according to the needs of each such race;

For the avoidance of doubt it is hereby declared that for the purposes of this paragraph 'public sanitary convenience' means any sanitary convenience to which the public have access, whether by right or otherwise, and whether or not such convenience is referred to elsewhere in this Act.'

DOCUMENT 35B. MINISTERIAL STATEMENT ON THE CONSTITUTIONAL COUNCIL'S REPORT THAT THE MUNICIPAL AMENDMENT BILL CONTRAVENED THE DECLARATION OF RIGHTS (FROM RHODESIA *Parliamentary Debates*, VOL. 69, 7 NOVEMBER 1967, COLS 1084–104)

Minister of Local Government and Housing [Mr Mark Partridge]: ... The Constitutional Council has reported that, in its opinion, to the extent that clauses 30 (b) and 34 (h) of the Municipal Amendment Act Bill (A.B. 43A, 1967) empowers municipalities to provide separate amenities on a racial basis and to make prohibitions in this regard, they are inconsistent with section 76 of the Declaration of Rights. . . . It is my intention, following my motion that the House 'takes note' of the Council's report on the Municipal Amendment Bill, to move that notwithstanding the adverse report the Bill be submitted for the assent of the Officer Administering the Government. . . . I would be failing in my duty if I did not make it clear that the Government does not accept the interpretation which the Council has given to the Declaration of Rights in this particular instance.

If one accepts the Council's view of this matter, there can, as I see it, under our Constitution be no differentiation on racial grounds at all, unless the measure is saved by subsection 3, 4 or 5 of section 76 of the Declaration of Rights. . . .

I would like to explain once again the connexion in the Bill between clauses 30 (b) and 34 (h). Clause 30 (b) relates to section 256(7) of the principal Act, which gives a municipal council the power to provide various facilities, including public lavatories and, by implication, swimming baths . . . Clause 34, paragraph (h) gives a municipal council power to make by-laws controlling the facilities provided by them, and also, in paragraph (60A) (a) for requiring persons other than the municipal council to establish separate public sanitary conveniences for separate races. Examination of these two clauses will show that wherever provision is made for anything to be done for separate races, the proviso, which I shall call the 'separate but equal' proviso, always operates so that the facilities must be afforded equitably according to the needs of each race. . . . The result is, therefore, that all these powers, both to provide facilities and to make by-laws, are qualified by the 'separate but equal' proviso. . . .

Although the Council were aware that it was my intention to ensure that separate facilities would be equitably provided, they still regard the Bill as discriminatory because (a) the separation would be based on race alone; and (b) the injury to the person's dignity would not be removed. . . .

Turning now to the Bill, if where separate facilities are

provided they are provided equitably according to the needs of each race and each race is prohibited from using the facilities provided for members of other races, then firstly, the same restriction applies to each of the races and, secondly, no one race is prejudiced.

It would be fanciful to argue that prejudice in the sense contemplated by the Constitution could be caused merely by feelings of inferiority on the part of one race, for if persons choose to feel inferior then no conditions could ever be applied to their particular race alone for they would always argue that the condition was only applied because they were regarded as inferior, yet the Constitution expressly contemplates that, in some cases, conditions can be applied to one race and not to others. . . .

Summing up, therefore, I repeat that before the Constitutional Council can say this Bill is discriminatory they must be able to say that by or as an inevitable consequence of the Bill —not the by-laws—persons of a particular race will be prejudiced by being subjected to a restriction which does not apply to persons of another race.

A SEGREGATED SOCIETY: MEASURES OF RACIAL DISCRIMINATION

The United Nations Secretariat reports on recent discriminatory legislation in Rhodesia.

DOCUMENT 36. INTENSIFICATION OF RACIAL SEGREGATION IN SOUTHERN RHODESIA: EXCERPTS FROM A WORKING PAPER ON SOUTHERN RHODESIA PREPARED BY THE UN SECRETARIAT (FROM *Objective: Justice*, VOL. 5, NO. 2, APRIL–JUNE 1973)

In the aftermath of the Pearce Commission's report, the illegal régime proceeded with full implementation of the 1969 illegal 'Constitution' and with the original platform of the Rhodesian Front (the 'Government party') calling for greater separation of the races along the lines of the *apartheid* system practised in South Africa, including, in particular, a programme of 'provincialization'. This concept involves the delegation of greater local governing powers to tribal authorities, similar to the Bantustan and homeland system of South Africa, and the investing of greater powers in the chiefs, while simultaneously limiting the influence of elected tribal representatives in the 'House of Assembly'. . . .

On 24 November, the illegal régime published in the 'Government Gazette' a 'Regional Authorities Bill' calling for the establishment of local authorities and enumerating their proposed functions. These included the right to levy taxes on people and property; the authority to acquire, sell, lease or exchange any of its property; the power to make by-laws; and the authority to raise loans within the country on conditions laid down by the 'Minister of Internal Affairs' in consultation with the 'Minister of Finance'. The 'Bill' envisages that these local authorities would gradually become involved in certain decisions within the framework of central government policy, for example: health, education, communications and water supply, and would also act in an advisory capacity to the 'Government' on all matters within the area of their jurisdiction. The 'Minister of Internal Affairs', however, would retain the power to make regulations over a number of essential matters, including the method of appointing or electing members, the qualifications and disqualifications of members, the appointment of advisory officials and other procedures. . . .

Segregation at bars

A regulation prohibiting Africans from being served in bars in white areas after 7 p.m. on weekdays and after 1 p.m. on Saturdays and all hours on Sundays and holidays came into effect on 1 November; it was introduced under the 'Land Tenure Act'.

As a result of an appeal by three hotels and an African journalist, the regulation was overruled on 16 November by the Rhodesian High Court which judged that the regulations were *ultra vires* the 'Land Tenure Act' and had no force or effect. The 'Government' therefore appealed the ruling. On 15 December, the appellate division of the Rhodesian High Court dismissed the 'Government's' appeal against the High Court ruling, although, on the previous day, the 'House of Assembly' had approved an amendment to the 'Land Tenure Act' broadening the terms of the 'Act' to allow the imposition of curbs on African patronage of establishments serving liquor in white areas. The judges, ruling in terms of the unamended 'Land Tenure Act', found that there was nothing in the 'Act' that would empower the 'Minister of Lands' to alter the Liquor Act of 1961 which gave Africans the right to buy alcoholic beverages in European areas. Mr Justice MacDonald, the Judge President, said in his judgment that the drinking regulations profoundly altered the rights conferred to Africans by statute in 1961 and curtailed the rights of some whites under the Liquor Act to serve all races.

On the same day, the Senate approved an amendment to the 'Land Tenure Act' to empower the 'Government' to make regulations affecting the rights of Africans under the Liquor Act of 1961. In January 1973, new regulations were published in the 'Government Gazette' reintroducing curbs on Africans drinking in European areas.

African registration

The illegal régime tabled in the 'House of Assembly' on 17 November 1972 the 'African (Registration and Identification) Amendment Bill' requiring all Africans over 16 to carry a registration or identity certificate at all times and to apply for special permission to leave the country. The 'Bill', introduced by Mr Lance Smith, 'Minister of Internal Affairs', provides for a maximum fine of \$R100 or one year in prison or both for failure to carry valid identity documents. It also provides that Africans leaving the country must surrender their identity papers and apply for their reissuance upon return. (Present legislation requires that all Africans over 16 must be registered, but does not require them to carry identity documents.) The 'Bill' further enables the illegal régime to deport foreign Africans who have no registration certificates and to refuse to grant such certificates.

The 'African (Registration and Identification) Amendment Bill' has come under severe attack from various groups, including the African National Council, African members of the 'House of Assembly', leading clergymen and the Centre Party. The Reverend Canaan Banana, of the African National Council, stated that the repercussions of such legislation were bound to be graver than the Rhodesian Front was prepared to anticipate. It was clear that the illegal régime was choosing a collision course out of desperation and therefore had to bear full responsibility for the consequences for their actions. The Reverend Banana also stated that the 'Bill' was designed to 'intimidate Africans into conniving with a corrupt system of government'.

The Anglican Bishops of Matabeleland and Mashonaland, the Roman Catholic Bishops and the Rabbi of Bulawayo, in separate communications on 21 November, appealed to the 'Minister of Internal Affairs' to withdraw the 'Bill', which they unanimously labelled *apartheid*. The clergymen agreed that to impose the burden of identification on one section of the population was discriminatory, oppressive and degrading. . . .

Restrictions on school attendance

The illegal régime tabled in the 'House of Assembly' on 17 November 1972, an 'Education Bill' consolidating existing legislation from which was omitted a clause proposed by the Roman Catholic churches safeguarding the Africans' right to attend interracial private schools. The clause, which was dropped without consultation with representatives of the Church, stated that nothing in the 'Bill' would preclude the admission, attendance and instruction of African children at private schools. The omission of the clause met with strong protest, among other groups, from the Catholic Bishops' Conference.

Restrictions on public meetings

On 23 November 1972, the illegal régime tabled in the 'House of Assembly' the 'African Affairs Amendment (No. 2) Bill' prohibiting the holding of unauthorised public meetings throughout the African area as defined in the 'Land Tenure Act', instead of only in the Tribal Trust Lands and other tribal areas as at present. The 'Bill' would also extend the powers of district commissioners to prohibit individuals from holding or addressing meetings. In addition, the 'Bill' would require that any white person employed at a religious mission in the Tribal

Trust Lands or other tribal areas obtain written permission from the 'Secretary for Internal Affairs' or the provincial or district commissioner to enter or be in any Tribal Trust Land. The 'Secretary for Internal Affairs' would retain the authority to ban anyone, whether white or African, from entering or remaining in any Tribal Trust Land or other tribal area if he believed that the presence of such an individual was against the public interest or the interest of Africans living there. The 'Bill' would remove an existing provision requiring that prohibition notices be tabled in the 'House of Assembly'.

Control over urban areas

A proposed amendment to the 'Vagrancy Act', known as the 'Vagrancy Amendment Bill', was published in the 'Government Gazette' on 24 November 1972. The amendment, which would empower the district commissioner to prohibit 'vagrants' from entering urban areas, defined as a vagrant: (a) any person found in an urban area who is not lawfully resident in that area or who is not employed by such a person; (b) any person who is idle or disorderly; and (c) any person who lives on the earnings of prostitution. The 'Bill' would further empower the district commissioner to endorse the identification certificate of the prohibited person with the particulars of the order banning him from urban areas. . . .

Segregated postal facilities

In December 1972, the illegal régime introduced in the 'House of Assembly' the 'Post and Telecommunications (Amendment) Bill', which, *inter alia*, would provide for separate facilities in post offices for different 'classes' of persons. Under the terms of the 'Bill', the classes of persons would be determined by occupation, language, or any other class the 'Minister of Posts' might consider desirable.

Occupation of Tribal Trust Land

On 5 December, the illegal régime introduced in the 'House of Assembly' the following amendments to the 'Land Tenure Act':

(a) a provision which would allow wives and children of mixed marriages to apply for permission to live in the 'racial' area of their husbands and fathers; (b) a provision which would enable the 'Government' to acquire Tribal Trust Land for 'public purposes', such as defence, mineral development, transport or communications; (c) a provision which would require 'non-tribesmen' wishing in the future to live in Tribal Trust Land to obtain a permit from the 'Minister of Internal Affairs' (the provision would not affect persons already resident in the Tribal Trust Lands, who would be deemed to have been issued with permits); (d) a provision which would permit *bona fide* religious, educational or charitable institutions to own and maintain interracial premises in either white or African areas. Apart from attendance at church, however, such occupation would be allowed only subject to the granting of a special permit.

PART VIII

The Independence Issue

THE ISSUES BETWEEN BRITAIN AND RHODESIA

After the Rhodesian Front Government's Unilateral Declaration of Independence, the British Government published all of the correspondence between the two Governments on the issue of granting independence to Rhodesia on the basis of the then prevailing 1961 Constitution. In releasing what would otherwise have been regarded as confidential exchanges between Commonwealth Governments, the Labour Government made the case that, first, every effort had been made to reach a settlement of the independence issue with the Rhodesian Front Government, and second, both the Conservative and the Labour Governments were committed to a policy of withholding independence until the Rhodesian Government agreed to broaden the basis of their franchise and representation and establish their claim that independence on the basis of the 1961 Constitution was acceptable to 'the people of Rhodesia as a whole'.

The correspondence continued for over two years, beginning with the exchanges between the first Rhodesian Front Prime Minister, Winston Field, and the Minister responsible for the Central Africa Office, Mr R. A. Butler. Mr Smith, after replacing Field as Prime Minister in April 1964, continued to plead the Rhodesian case for independence in correspondence with the Conservative Prime Minister (Sir Alec Douglas-Home) and Commonwealth Secretary (Mr Duncan Sandys) and, after the October 1964 British election, with the Labour Prime Minister (Mr Wilson) and Commonwealth Secretary (Mr Bottomley).

It is evident from the British side of the correspondence that the 1961 Constitution, with its highly restricted franchise, was never intended as an independence constitution, and that no promise to this effect had been made in order to get the Rhodesians first to accept that Constitution; second, to agree to the dissolution of the Federation, or third, to participate in the conference to dissolve the Federation in 1963. This point is made in the letters of both Sir Alec Douglas-Home (16 September 1964) and Mr Wilson (21 October 1965). Both British Governments also warned the Rhodesians of the dire consequences of a UDI (see the letter of Sandys to Field in February 1964 and the Labour Government's statement of 27 October 1964, in next document). Again, both British Governments rejected as 'not proved' the Rhodesian claim that they had a mandate for independence—based on the approval of an Indaba (conference) of Chiefs in October 1964 and a virtually all white referendum in November 1964. The conditions for independence established by both British Governments are embodied in a set of 'Five Principles', first set out in full in Mr Bottomley's letter of 21 September 1965, but containing points made in the correspondence of the previous Conservative Government.

The case made in most of the Rhodesian correspondence was that the Conservative Government had promised them independence under the 1961 Constitution; that they had a mandate from the Rhodesian people in the form of the consent of the Chiefs and the European electorate; and that negotiations for independence with a Labour Government were not possible unless that Government repudiated their pledge of NIBMAR (no independence before majority African rule) contained in the letter from Mr Wilson to an African leader, Dr Mutasa, during the 1964 general election.

DOCUMENT 37. *Southern Rhodesia: Documents Relating to the Negotiations between the United Kingdom and Southern Rhodesian Governments, November 1963–November 1965* (CMND 2807, 1965)

Message dated 22 February, 1964, from the Secretary of State for Commonwealth Relations, the Right Hon. Duncan Sandys, M.P., to the Prime Minister of Southern Rhodesia, the Hon. Winston Field, C.M.G., M.B.E., M.P.

5. You say that 'whilst Southern Rhodesia would wish to be independent within the Commonwealth, its Government is not

wedded irrevocably to this'. I am afraid, however, that your willingness to forgo Commonwealth membership would do nothing to solve the problem. The question of Southern Rhodesia's membership of the Commonwealth is not the issue. What we are concerned with is the likely reactions of other Commonwealth Governments to a decision by the British Government to grant independence to Southern Rhodesia, at a point of time when the franchise is incomparably more restricted than that of any territory which has acquired independence in the last 50 years.

6. The Press here have been reporting from different sources, that Southern Rhodesia may be contemplating a unilateral declaration of independence. I sincerely hope that these reports are without foundation. For I cannot believe that those who may be thinking like this, have fully weighed the likely consequences.

7. International reaction would be sharp and immediate. The issue would be raised at once in the United Nations; and we, of course, would not be able to offer any justification. The whole Commonwealth would be deeply disturbed and the attitude of the newer members would be extremely antagonistic. Commonwealth and foreign Governments, with one or two exceptions, would almost certainly refuse to recognise Southern Rhodesia's independence or to enter into relations with her. The African Nationalists in Southern Rhodesia would probably set up a Government in exile, which many countries would recognise. Thus isolated, Southern Rhodesia would increasingly become a target for subversion, trade boycotts, air transport bans and other hostile activities, organised in other African States.

8. In particular, the relations between Southern Rhodesia and Northern Rhodesia, which have made such a promising start with the agreements on Kariba, the Rhodesia Railways and the Central African Airways, would be in danger of serious disruption.

9. A unilateral declaration of independence by Southern Rhodesia would not, of course, make Southern Rhodesia legally independent. To take such action would be outside the Constitution which Southern Rhodesia Ministers are pledged to work. The British Government would, therefore, be bound to take the view that this had no legal or constitutional validity.

10. You emphasise that your Government sets great store 'on retaining, as an independent State, a special relationship with the Crown and with Britain'. Far from our being able to create a new and special relationship between our two countries, I fear that feeling in Britain and in the rest of the Commonwealth would be so unfavourable that we should be pressed to regard Southern Rhodesia as being in a state of revolt and to have no official dealings with her Government. . . .

Message dated 16 September, 1964, from the Prime Minister, the Right Hon. Sir Alec Douglas-Home, Kt, M.P., to the Prime Minister of Southern Rhodesia, the Hon. Ian Smith, M.P.

In the course of our talks you told me that you had been under the impression that the British Government had, in 1961, given to the Government of Southern Rhodesia an undertaking that if the Federation were dissolved, Southern Rhodesia would be granted immediate independence on the basis of her existing Constitution and franchise. I am writing to confirm what I said to you, namely that no undertaking, explicit or implicit, was given about the British Government's intentions regarding Southern Rhodesia's independence in the event of the dissolution of the Federation, which we were not at that time contemplating; nor was any such undertaking asked for.

Sir Edgar Whitehead confirmed this in a speech in your Legislative Assembly, on 25 August, in which he said that 'no agreement was made with Her Majesty's Government to the effect that after the Federal break-up, if such happened, we would necessarily be granted sovereign independence without any further change'. . . .

Message dated 25 November, 1964, from the Prime Minister of Rhodesia, the Hon. Ian Smith, M.P., to the Prime Minister, the Right Hon. Harold Wilson, O.B.E., M.P.

3. I am at one with you in your desire to find a way forward through frank talks in confidence between our Governments and I am still willing to go to London for this purpose as soon as I am convinced that we, both of us, accept the basic proposition

that there is common ground between us to enable us by negotiation to find a way in which, as you so rightly say, the people of Rhodesia can move together in harmony towards a stable future as an independent State within the Commonwealth. You have volunteered the assurance that your Government has no preconceived plan that you wish to impose on our country. I find it difficult to reconcile this assurance, welcome as it is, with a statement made by you in a letter which you sent as Leader of the Labour Party to Mr E. C. Mutasa, Salisbury, on 2 October, 1964, in which you say that the Labour Party is totally opposed to granting independence to Southern Rhodesia as long as the Government of that country remains under the control of a white minority. This letter has received wide publicity in this country and your High Commissioner has obtained for me an assurance that the letter itself is authentic. The statement implies that Rhodesia will not be granted independence by a British Labour Government until the Government of the country is under African control and, *a fortiori*, until the terms for independence have been accepted by an African Government. If we meet for discussions I shall reaffirm my acknowledgment that independence must be based on general consent and I shall stand by the results of the October indaba with the chiefs and headmen and the referendum of the electorate as incontestable proof that the majority of the population of this country support my Government's request for independence on the basis of the present Constitution and franchise. I can see common ground, to be explored by negotiation based on statesmanship and understanding, but not on the uncompromising assertion contained in your letter to Mr Mutasa. I regret that I cannot agree that the letter to Mr Mutasa has been superseded by the subsequent correspondence between us unless I am told that this letter, and what I believe it implies, is not British Government policy today. I do not think I am being unreasonable in asking for a specific answer on this point before deciding whether to accept your invitation to go to London for discussions with you. The fact that your Government has not specified any conditions as to how your hopes of a peaceful transition to African majority rule should be achieved or the period of time in which it should take place seems to be beside the point.

Message dated 27 November, 1964, from the Prime Minister, the Right Hon. Harold Wilson, O.B.E., M.P., to the Prime Minister of Rhodesia, the Hon. Ian Smith, M.P.

Thank you for your message of 25 November.

I have said that we lay down no prior conditions for the talks. It would appear that, for your part, you are seeking to lay down two. First, that I should make plain whether or not the British Government intends to insist on African majority rule in Rhodesia as a pre-condition of independence. Secondly, that I should recognise in advance that your position in the talks will be that independence on the basis of the present Constitution and franchise has been incontestably proved to be the wish of the majority of the population.

We have an open mind on the timing of independence in relation to progress towards majority rule, to which, as I have said, we wish to see a peaceful transition, but the granting of independence must be on a basis acceptable to the people of the country as a whole. As we have already informed you, we cannot accept that it has been demonstrated that independence on the present Constitution and franchise would do so. . . .

Message dated 21 September, 1965, from the Secretary of State for Commonwealth Relations, the Right Hon. Arthur Bottomley, O.B.E., M.P., to the Prime Minister of Rhodesia, the Hon. Ian Smith, M.P.

3. . . . In your talks with the Lord Chancellor and myself last February you agreed to explore the possibility of a negotiated settlement. We subsequently explained to you the principles on which we would need to be satisfied before we were able to contemplate the grant of independence. They were and are as follows:

(i) the principle and intention of unimpeded progress to majority rule, already enshrined in the 1961 Constitution, would have to be maintained and guaranteed.

(ii) There would also have to be guarantees against retrogressive amendment of the Constitution.

(iii) There would have to be immediate improvement in the political status of the African population.

(iv) There would have to be progress towards ending racial discrimination.

(v) The British Government would need to be satisfied that any basis proposed for independence was acceptable to the people of Rhodesia as a whole (on which you had acknowledged our right to be satisfied.)

4. You agreed at the time that discussions should proceed on the basis of these principles. There have since been extensive and lengthy explorations between us, but there has been no substantial move on your side towards meeting us on these criteria. Your talks with the Minister of State in July confirmed the wide gap which remained to be bridged, particularly on the question of effective constitutional safeguards. In so far as the possibility of a second Chamber was explored in this context the proposal put forward on your side was for a small nominated Senate with a minority of Africans. You have also suggested as an alternative to a Senate that Africans in the House of Representatives should have a 'blocking quarter' of the seats, though you would not agree that the additional two seats this would require should be elected on the B roll. On this basis, the vote of one African member could constitute the sole margin of constitutional safeguard. You will recall that the Minister of State made it plain that, from our point of view, there would have to be cast-iron safeguards providing a predominantly elected African voice in these affairs. . . .

6. I was therefore surprised to receive from our High Commissioner his report of your interview with him on 11 September. As you put it to him, your position on the five principles set out above appears now to be as follows:

(i) The Rhodesian Government are unable to accept the principle of unimpeded progress towards majority rule enshrined in the 1961 Constitution.

(ii) They cannot accept any form of constitutional safeguard which would prevent the Europeans in Rhodesia from altering the Constitution if they deem it necessary to prevent the emergence of an African Government.

(iii) The only measure of African advancement which the Rhodesian Government will contemplate (apart from any advance implicit in your safeguard proposals) is some form of adult suffrage on the existing B roll, provided cross-voting is abolished.

(iv) There are no specific steps which your Government will

take towards ending racial discrimination, and you will not amend or repeal the Land Apportionment Act.

(v) The Rhodesian Government are not prepared to contemplate any process of consultation with African opinion within Rhodesia which might result in rejection of proposals for a basis of independence reached in negotiations between the two Governments. . . .

Message dated 20 October, 1965, from the Prime Minister of Rhodesia, the Hon. Ian Smith, M.P., to the Prime Minister, the Right Hon. Harold Wilson, O.B.E., M.P.

I note that you say that you are still open to any ideas and to any further way of seeing whether agreement can be reached between us. Well, here is my response to this appeal: it is that it would be reasonable and just for the British Government to grant Rhodesia its independence on the 1961 Rhodesian Constitution. This Constitution covers your five principles, if only you will admit it; they are enshrined there for all to see. . . . Rhodesia is being condemned not for what we have done, but for what others say we might do in the future. Therefore, at this grave hour, I repeat to you the suggestion I made to you at the London talks that the statesmanlike thing for you to do is to grant us our independence and to put us on trust to observe and to abide by the principles of the 1961 Constitution. . . .

Message dated 21 October, 1965, from the Prime Minister, the Right Hon. Harold Wilson, O.B.E., M.P., to the Prime Minister of Rhodesia, the Hon. Ian Smith, M.P.

I accept that successive Governments, both in Britain and in Rhodesia, have made a genuine effort to seek agreement on conditions on which Rhodesia could advance to independence. For our part we have always made clear that we were not seeking to impose precise conditions and were ready for a genuine negotiation. At the same time there are certain basic matters of conscience, of honour and of duty to which all parties in this country have consistently adhered. For the reasons both I and my predecessors have explained to you, I cannot accept that the grant of independence simply on the basis of the 1961 Constitution would satisfy the five principles you and I have accepted. There was never any undertaking explicit or implicit, that Rhodesia would be granted independence on the basis of the 1961 Constitution without further change. This was made clear to you by the previous Administration in the September 1964 talks, and in Sir Alec Douglas-Home's letter of 16 September, 1964. Moreover it was acknowledged in your own legislature by the Rhodesian Prime Minister who was responsible for the 1961 Constitution. Further, both we and our predecessors have made it clear to you that progress under the 1961 Constitution has not yet resulted in sufficiently representative institutions to satisfy the British Parliament that the grant of independence would be justified. . . .

You say that Rhodesia is being condemned not for what you have done, but for what others say you might do in the future. You will forgive me if I say that the detention or restriction over a long period of Nationalist leaders, the recent restriction of a former Prime Minister [Garfield Todd], the banning of a prominent newspaper [African Daily News], have suggested to the outside world the pattern of what might happen in the future.

THE BRITISH WARNING

To deter the Rhodesians from an illegal declaration of independence, which became an immediate possibility after the Labour Party—pledged to implement African majority rule—came to power in October 1964, the following statement was issued.

DOCUMENT 38. LABOUR GOVERNMENT STATEMENT ON THE CONSEQUENCES OF AN ILLEGAL DECLARATION OF INDEPENDENCE, 27 OCTOBER 1964

A mere declaration of independence would have no constitutional effect. The only way Southern Rhodesia could become a sovereign independent state is by an Act of the British Parliament; a declaration of independence would be an open act of defiance and rebellion and it would be treasonable to take steps to give effect to it.

In the final communiqué of the meeting of Commonwealth

Prime Ministers in July it was made clear that no Commonwealth Government would be able to recognise a unilateral declaration. There would then be no prospect of Southern Rhodesia becoming a member of the Commonwealth, with all the economic consequences that would then ensue.

The British Government would be bound to sever relations with those responsible for such a declaration. It would not be possible for Southern Rhodesia to establish a new and special relationship with the Crown or with Britain. The British Government would not be prepared to advise Her Majesty to accede to any request that she should become a separate sovereign of a territory which has rebelled. The ultimate result would inevitably be that Southern Rhodesians would cease to be British subjects.

The reactions of foreign governments would likewise be sharp and immediate. With one or two exceptions, they are likely to refuse to recognise Southern Rhodesia's independence or to enter into relations with her. Many of them might recognise a government in exile if, as seems probable, one were established.

The economic effects would be disastrous to the prosperity and prospects of the people of Southern Rhodesia. All financial and trade relations between Britain and Southern Rhodesia would be jeopardised. Any further aid or any further access to the London money market would be out of the question. Indeed, most serious consequences would be involved for anyone in the United Kingdom who afforded aid, financial or otherwise, to the illegal government. Southern Rhodesia's external trade would be disrupted.

An illegal declaration of independence would bring to an end relationships between Southern Rhodesia and Britain, would cut her off from the rest of the Commonwealth, from most foreign governments, and from international organisations, would inflict disastrous economic damage upon her, and would leave her isolated and virtually friendless in a largely hostile continent.

THE UNILATERAL DECLARATION OF INDEPENDENCE

The Rhodesian illegal declaration of independence, modelled, ironically, on the American Declaration of 1776, concluded with 'God save the Queen'.

DOCUMENT 39. TEXT OF THE DECLARATION OF INDEPENDENCE, 11 NOVEMBER, 1965. RHODESIAN GOVERNMENT STATEMENT

Whereas in the course of human affairs history has shown that it may become necessary for a people to resolve the political affiliations which have connected them with another people and to assume among other nations the separate and equal status to which they are entitled,

And whereas in such event a respect for the opinions of mankind requires them to declare to other nations the causes which impel them to assume full responsibility for their own affairs,

Now therefore, we the Government of Rhodesia, do hereby declare:

That it is an indisputable and accepted historic fact that since 1923 the Government of Rhodesia have exercised the powers of self-government and have been responsible for the progress, development, and welfare of their people; that the people of Rhodesia, having demonstrated their loyalty to the Crown and to their kith and kin in the United Kingdom and elsewhere throughout two world wars; and having been prepared to shed their blood and give of the substance in what they believed to be a mutual interest of freedom-loving people; now see all that they have cherished about to be shattered on the rocks of expediency.

That the people of Rhodesia have witnessed a process which is destructive of those very precepts upon which civilisation in a primitive country has been built, they have seen the principles of Western democracy and responsible government and moral standards crumble elsewhere, nevertheless they have remained steadfast.

That the people of Rhodesia fully support the request of their Government for sovereign independence, and have witnessed the consistent refusal of the Government of the United Kingdom to accede to their entreaties.

That the Government of the United Kingdom have thus demonstrated that they are not prepared to grant sovereign independence to Rhodesia on terms acceptable to the people of Rhodesia, thereby persisting in maintaining an unwarrantable jurisdiction over Rhodesia, obstructing laws and treaties with other States in the conduct of affairs with other nations and refusal of assent to necessary laws for the public good, all this to the detriment of the future peace, prosperity and good government of Rhodesia.

That the Government of Rhodesia have for a long period patiently and in good faith negotiated with the Government of the United Kingdom for the removal of the remaining limitations placed upon them and for the grant of sovereign independence.

That in the belief that procrastination and delay strike at and injure the very life of the nation, the Government of Rhodesia consider it essential that Rhodesia should obtain without delay sovereign independence, the justice of which is beyond question.

Now therefore, we, the Government of Rhodesia, in humble submission to Almighty God, who controls the destiny of nations, conscious that the people of Rhodesia have always shown unswerving loyalty and devotion to Her Majesty the Queen and earnestly praying that we the people of Rhodesia will not be hindered in our determination to continue exercising our undoubted right to demonstrate the same loyalty and devotion in seeking to promote the common good so that the dignity and freedom of all men may be assured.

Do by the proclamation adopt, enact and give to the people of Rhodesia the Constitution annexed hereto.

God save the Queen.

THE LABOUR GOVERNMENT'S FAILURE: THE
Tiger CONFRONTATION

Having failed to prevent the UDI, the British Government began a long series of negotiations with the illegal rebel régime which began in April 1966 and continued intermittently until an agreement was reached by the Conservative Government (Sir Alec Douglas-Home) and Mr Smith in November 1971, but rejected by 'the Rhodesian people as a whole' in the test of opinion in 1972.

The Labour Prime Minister, Mr Wilson, had two abortive meetings with Mr Smith after the UDI—one on board HMS *Tiger* in December 1966 and the other on board HMS *Fearless* in October 1968. The differences between the two sides were virtually the same on both occasions, although the issue of the rebels returning to 'legality' was rejected by the Rhodesians in 1966 and quietly buried by the British side in subsequent negotiations.

In the following account of the negotiations, the Labour Government were most anxious to 'prove' that their proposals for a settlement conformed to the 'Five Principles' (to which a sixth had been added on minority rights). Not only the British Parliament and people had to be convinced that there had been no 'sell-out' to a white minority régime; the Commonwealth and the United Nations were also concerned that any settlement would need to take account of the legitimate aspirations of the African majority.

As the record of the conversations between the two sides shows, the negotiations broke down mainly over the Rhodesian refusal to 'return to legality' by renouncing their illegally acquired independence and to meet the conditions laid down for a free and fair test of Rhodesian opinion on the proposed settlement, in accordance with the fifth principle. However, at the final meeting between the two sides, Mr Smith was doubtful whether he could accept the proposals at all, let alone recommend them to his Cabinet, and denied that he had come to the meeting empowered by his Cabinet to conclude any agreement at all.

DOCUMENT 40. *Rhodesia: Documents relating to proposals for a settlement, 1966* (CMND 3171, DECEMBER 1966), THE *Tiger* PROPOSALS

The Six Principles

The approach of successive British Governments towards the problem of granting independence to Rhodesia has throughout been governed by certain basic requirements. These have been formulated as five principles, to which the present Government subsequently added a sixth. . . . It would be necessary to ensure that, regardless of race, there was no oppression of majority by minority or of minority by majority.

The meeting between the Prime Minister and Mr Smith

39. The meeting took place in HMS *Tiger* off Gibraltar between 2 and 4 December, 1966. There were present the Prime Minis-

ter, the Commonwealth Secretary and the Attorney-General: the Governor and the Chief Justice of Rhodesia: and Mr Smith and Mr Howman. Advisers were also present on both sides.

40. The discussions centred on the issues of a return to legality, the form of an independence Constitution based on the principles and the testing of opinion under the fifth principle.

41. On the first day the discussions appeared to give rise to sufficient prospect of bridging the differences of view for the meeting to turn its attention on the second day to the possibility of producing a working document covering all three major areas of the problem. . . .

42. It appeared to the British Ministers that the document in its final form furnished the basis for an acceptable settlement. It set out proposals for an independence Constitution which satisfied the six principles. It provided for unimpeded progress to majority rule (i.e., the first principle), while finding the means of introducing European reserved seats, to give effect to the sixth principle. It met the second principle, by establishing an effective blocking mechanism in a Senate and Lower House voting together, and by providing a right of appeal against the amendment of specially entrenched clauses of the Constitution to a Constitutional Commission in Rhodesia and from that Commission to the Judicial Committee of the Privy Council. It met the third principle (i.e., an immediate improvement of the political status of the Africans) by an extension of the 'B' Roll franchise to cover all Africans over 30 years of age; by increasing the 'B' Roll seats in the Lower House from 15 to 17, and by a total of 14 African seats in the Senate of which eight would be elected. The fourth principle was met by a proposal for a Royal Commission and a Standing Commission thereafter to study and make recommendations on the problems of racial discrimination and land apportionment. Finally, in order to conform with the requirements set out in the Commonwealth Prime Ministers' Communiqué arrangements were suggested for a return to legality by means of the appointment by the Governor of a broad-based administration. Provided that the test of opinion of the people of Rhodesia as required by the fifth principle took place after the restoration of constitutional government and in conditions of political freedom the British Government were prepared to

agree that the interim government, which would contain five independent members of whom two would be Africans, should be headed by Mr Smith.

43. The British Ministers were therefore ready to reach a final decision before the end of the meeting if (as it at first appeared) Mr Smith was prepared to do likewise. But, when the document in its final form was presented to the meeting, he took the line that he had no authority either to accept or reject it on behalf of the illegal régime. He declined even to go so far as to agree to commend it to his colleagues, and insisted that he must return to Salisbury before taking up a final position. Accordingly, under the terms of the statement . . . which was signed by the Prime Minister and Mr Smith in the presence of the Governor, it was agreed that both sides would decide by 12 noon (Salisbury time) 5 December whether the document was accepted in its entirety. The British Government published their acceptance of the document on the evening of 4 December. The illegal régime in Salisbury rejected the document on the evening of 5 December.

Record of a Meeting Held in the Wardroom of HMS Tiger on Friday, 2nd December, 1966: Return to Legality and the Fifth Principle

The Prime Minister asked Mr Smith for his views on the return to legality and the fifth principle. He recalled that the British Statement of Terms of 15th October recognised the differing views. But the British Government's position remained that it should be possible to reach agreement on a return to legality within the next 24 hours as well as on the constitutional matters which they had just discussed.

Mr Smith said that he found it difficult to understand and accept the logic in the British Government's claim that only under a constitutional government could a fair test of public opinion in Rhodesia take place. He could agree to lifting the censorship and to releasing political detainees who were not guilty of serious crimes, but he saw no reason why the test of opinion must be conducted under a constitutional government. Opinion could be tested that very day under the present régime. It was timing rather than principle that was being discussed. Any reasonable person would allow more time for discussion.

The Prime Minister said that the British Government had to have regard to paragraph 10 of the Commonwealth Prime Ministers' communiqué, and would have to apply mandatory sanctions if the United Nations adopted a resolution to that effect. There had been ample time for reflection and discussion since the previous May, let alone since September.

Mr Smith asked whether the British Government had not entered into commitments before the informal talks had started.

The Prime Minister recalled that sufficient indication of the Government's intentions had been given to Sir Cornelius Greenfield [Commonwealth Office emissary to Rhodesia]. Besides, unless there was a legal Rhodesian Government with which to deal, the British Government would be placed in an impossible position in trying to make a fair test of opinion.

Mr Smith repeated that, if the shape of the proposed Constitution were made known to the Rhodesian people, it should be possible to test public opinion under the Governor's auspices without a constitutional interim government having first been formed. No one could be sure that 90 per cent of Rhodesians would accept the proposed Constitution. The Prime Minister was asking the Rhodesian people to give up their *de facto* independence. This they would not lightly do.

The Prime Minister said that the Rhodesian régime possessed independence only in their own minds. What other country regarded them as independent?

Mr Smith replied that it was a lot to ask them to give up independence. The Prime Minister was asking him and his colleagues to climb down. He personally was prepared to accept the proposed Constitution and to give a lead to his colleagues. He accepted that it was necessary to return to legality but he did not see why it was necessary to go through a process which would not help his colleagues.

The Prime Minister accepted Mr Smith's difficulties; but, if he were able to return to Salisbury the following day as Prime Minister designate, having reached agreement subject only to the Rhodesian people's agreeing speedily to accept the new Constitution, would he not be greeted on his return with acclaim?

Mr Smith indicated his dissent. The Rhodesians would say that, every time they had had a new Constitution, it had disappointed them except when they had seized independence. When the Prime Minister asked whether he had conducted a referendum for the changes made in 1965 Mr Smith said that he had held an election instead in order to obtain a mandate for u.d.i.

The Prime Minister reminded Mr Smith that he had not fought the election on the issue of a unilateral declaration of independence.

Mr Smith dissented from this. He added that, if he reached agreement with the Prime Minister, he would have to refer back to his colleagues in Salisbury for approval. It had been impossible for him to give any indication at all before he left what sort of conclusion might be reached at the present meeting.

The Prime Minister said that Mr Smith had just made an exceedingly serious statement. The meeting had been arranged on the basis that each side was endowed with plenipotentiary power to reach a settlement one way or the other. His Cabinet colleagues would not have agreed to the present meeting, had the two sides not been plenipotentiaries. Mr Smith would recall making a statement on his own responsibility that he was prepared to consider a return to the 1961 Constitution as an earnest of his intentions.

Mr Smith then said that it had not been made clear to him that he had been asked to obtain a mandate from his colleagues. He had been asked to agree to come to the meeting before he had had an opportunity of consulting his colleagues. He had asked that the meeting should be delayed in order to complete his consultations and had in fact talked with his colleagues until after midnight before his departure from Salisbury at 5 a.m. on Thursday, 1st December. His agreement to come to the meeting was distinct from his agreeing to any proposals made at the meeting. He had indicated that he would want a day or two to examine with his colleagues the advantages and disadvantages of any proposed Constitution. . . .

Record of a Meeting Held in The Wardroom of H.M.S. Tiger *on Saturday, 3rd December, 1966*

Sir Hugh Beadle [Chief Justice] said that, even if Mr Smith committed himself before leaving the ship to commend the proposals to his colleagues in Salisbury, they might still reject them by midnight on 4th/5th December. But, if so, did it really matter if they rejected them without Mr Smith's having endorsed them? What really mattered was whether there was any chance that Mr Smith's colleagues would accept them on their merits, irrespective of Mr Smith's own attitude.

Mr Smith replied that he could not be very optimistic on this point. The settlement still embodied provisions to which he and his colleagues had consistently objected ever since contact with the British Government had been originally renewed earlier in the year.

The Prime Minister said that the reason why he attached importance to Mr Smith's undertaking to commend the proposals to his colleagues on his return to Salisbury was the fact that he had agreed with Sir Hugh Beadle, in the Prime Minister's hearing, that, if he commended the proposals, his colleagues would probably accept them. That was why he had insisted, and was still insisting, that, before leaving the ship, Mr Smith must either reject the proposals or undertake to try to persuade his colleagues to accept them.

Mr Smith repeated that before he could undertake to try to convince his colleagues he must convince himself; and he was still trying to do so.

The Prime Minister replied that either Mr Smith was convinced or he was not. All that was needed was his undertaking to try to convince his colleagues.

Mr Smith said once again that he himself was not yet convinced. On all the three major outstanding issues he had lost the day. The first was the entrenchment of Clause 37 [on number of seats in legislature].

Sir Hugh Beadle interjected that this was untrue; so far from wholly losing on this point, Mr Smith had gained 15 European reserved seats.

Mr Smith retorted that, if the British Government would go back to the position on Section 37 as it had originally been, he would be content. Second, there was the question of the broad-based interim government.

Sir Hugh Beadle pointed out that, on the basis of the settlement as it now stood, the interim government would last for only four months.

Mr Smith said that, third, there was the British insistence on a return to legality as a prior condition of the test of Rhodesian opinion.

The Prime Minister said that it was untrue that Mr Smith had lost everything and gained nothing. On the question of Section 37 he himself had strained his authority from the British Cabinet both in conceding the European reserved seats and in modifying the stipulation about a British military presence in Rhodesia. But there had to be give and take on both sides. He himself was prepared to regard the settlement as a whole as a reasonable one; and Mr Smith should be prepared to adopt the same attitude.

Sir Hugh Beadle reminded Mr Smith once again that, if the constitutional provisions could be regarded as agreed, all that was at issue was four months of interim government, after which Rhodesia could be back to constitutional government on the basis of the 1961 Constitution.

Mr Smith admitted that this was a sound point, which Sir Hugh Beadle had repeated to him several times on recent occasions. There was something in it.

The Prime Minister pointed out that he had made a considerable concession to Mr Smith on this issue. He was committed by the communiqué issued at the end of the Meeting of Commonwealth Prime Ministers to insist on the establishment of a broad-based government after the end of the illegal independence; and it was a very considerable concession to agree that this need last for only four months.

Mr Howman [Rhodesian Minister] interjected that he and Mr Smith had made it clear throughout that they would have to consult their colleagues before committing themselves, albeit fully understanding that the timetable was very tight and that, if they sent no reply by midnight on 4th/5th December, this would be regarded as a rejection of the proposals. Against this background it was unreasonable to accuse Mr Smith of procrastinating.

The Prime Minister repeated that some members of his Cabinet had been opposed to his meeting Mr Smith at all, on the grounds that Mr Smith would treat the encounter as no more than a propaganda device for leaving with the British Government the onus of responsibility for a final break. But he himself had continued to believe in Mr Smith's good faith. Was he now to be shown to be wrong?

Mr Smith replied that some of his colleagues had voiced exactly the same suspicions about the British Government's motives in promoting the meeting. But this did not trouble him; what mattered was the substance of the issues at stake.

Sir Hugh Beadle said that it was surely valuable to the British Government to have it known that they had made one last attempt to reach agreement at the highest level. By comparison it was unimportant whether their proposals were rejected—if they were rejected—that night or the following night.

The Prime Minister replied that, even so, he could not be left in a position in which he was fully committed to the proposals but Mr Smith would not commit himself even to commend them to his colleagues. If the proposals were to be *ad referendum* to Mr Smith's associates, perhaps they must now be *ad referendum* to the British Cabinet as well—even though this would create a very difficult situation, since the Commonwealth Sanctions Committee was due to meet on Monday in order to take the first steps in bringing mandatory sanctions into effect.

Sir Hugh Beadle said that it was surely right that the proposals should now be regarded as being *ad referendum* both to the British Government and to Mr Smith's colleagues in Salisbury. And each side should decide their attitude by midnight on 4th/5th December.

The Prime Minister suggested that the meeting should now be adjourned for 15 minutes in order to enable both sides to take stock of the position.

*

The settlement proposals worked out at the meeting on board HMS *Tiger* were based on the 'legal' Constitution of 1961. They contained certain alterations of that Constitution, for the stated purpose of implementing the 'Five Principles' and thereby fulfilling the conditions laid down as a basis for the grant of independence.

Mr Leo Baron, formerly a legal adviser to many African trade unions and political leaders, and now a Judge of the High Court in Zambia, provides a critical analysis of the 1961 Constitution and of the proposed *Tiger* modifications.

DOCUMENT 41. 'RHODESIA: THE 1961 CONSTITUTION AND THE *Tiger* PROPOSALS' BY LEO BARON (FROM *The World Today*, VOL. 23, NO. 9, SEPTEMBER 1967)

One could not pretend to any great surprise to find Mr Smith asserting that the 1961 Constitution satisfied Britain's five principles (of course it did not, and Mr Wilson himself has been at pains to point out that there would have to be important amendments). But one did not expect both the Government and the Opposition in Britain to put out the grossly misleading statement that 'it enshrines the principle and intention of unimpeded progress to majority rule'. It enshrines nothing of the kind; on the contrary, it enshrines every impediment necessary to perpetuate white domination. For instance, one particular iniquitous provision is that which permits the raising of what are ostensibly entrenched maximum income qualifications according to the 'ascertained decrease in the purchasing power of money'. Under ordinary conditions of economic growth, price levels and wages will move up together, although not necessarily at quite the same rate, but in countries such as Rhodesia the cost-of-living index is likely to move up more rapidly than the incomes of Africans, so that the effect of this provision would then be actually to reduce the number of Africans able to attain a particular 'real' income qualification.

It is true that the 1961 Constitution was publicized as the document which would mark a new phase in political and social development, would be the first step towards ultimate majority rule, would encourage African development, and would ensure equality before the law, the protection of human rights and liberties, and the elimination of discrimination. All this was said by British and white Rhodesian politicians during the 1960–1 constitutional conference; significantly, they omitted to say it in the Constitution itself. Pious expressions of hope and intention are a very different matter from enshrining or entrenching; and just how seriously the politicians took their own protestations is demonstrated by Sir Edgar Whitehead, then Prime Minister of Rhodesia, who, immediately the conference was over, presented the proposed new Constitution as the charter which would ensure that government would remain in 'responsible' hands for the foreseeable future. This turnabout, seen by African politicians as a betrayal (as of course it was, particularly against the background of the promises made to them during the conference), was a major reason for their rejection of the Constitution; Africans were to be given fifteen seats in the legislature on a B roll, but the qualifications to register on the A roll, which returned fifty members, remained as high as before, and gave no hope of majority rule for generations to come.

The Constitution makes no reference, directly or otherwise, to majority rule. In terms of votes on the A roll (the one that matters) the only things it enshrines are certain maximum income and educational qualifications, which by a strange coincidence have proved to be within the reach of virtually every adult European and beyond the reach of virtually every adult African (probably no more than 6,000 qualify even today). It has long since been demonstrated that it would take upwards of fifty years for Africans to control a majority in Parliament; others, without advancing reasons, suggest that the period *could* be fifteen years. But what Mr Wilson, Mr Heath, and Mr Smith all omit to mention is that such estimates presuppose a substantial economic growth-rate, a substantial expansion in African secondary education, and a benevolent government. In the hands of a hostile administration, armed with all the powers of oppression and discrimination enshrined in the Constitution, there will never be majority rule; and no honest man in Britain would seriously suggest that a white-dominated administration in Rhodesia will be other than hostile to significant African political advance.

The Constitution includes a Declaration of Rights whereunder most of the traditional individual liberties are ostensibly protected (a notable omission is the right to freedom of movement). But these traditional liberties have been rendered largely illusory by a number of careful and far-reaching exceptions and qualifications, the most remarkable of which is the provision which preserves as lawful pre-existing legislation, notwithstanding that it is repugnant to the Declaration of Rights and would be unlawful if the legislature attempted to enact it after the Constitution came into force.

One can only speculate as to what assurances were given to

Britain to persuade her to introduce this saving clause, but she must clearly have been led to believe that the whole of the Statute Book would in time be purged; one draft submitted to the conference by Whitehead indicated that the operation would be completed within five years. The powers to ban political parties and other organizations, to control meetings, to prohibit individuals from attending or addressing meetings, to ban publications, were all in existence prior to the 'appointed day' (1 November 1962, the date on which this part of the Constitution came into force); and it is these powers which are largely responsible for the successful erosion of most of the important rights and freedoms expressed to be protected. It is inconceivable that Britain can have contemplated that these measures would remain permanent features of the law; one does not frame a comprehensive and detailed charter of human rights and proceed in the next breath to destroy it, yet this is precisely what the saving clause has done.

In addition to draconian machinery for oppression, the Constitution enshrines not only pre-existing discriminatory legislation but also the power to enact new legislation of a similar type provided it is no more discriminatory than the existing—a provision which, in view of the state of the law at the time, was quite acceptable in even the most reactionary circles. Advancement for Africans, in terms of both education and employment, could be and was being, prior to UDI, effectively blocked quite legally.

This is the Constitution which Labour had inherited from the Tories. It had failed completely—as Britain was warned in 1961 that it would—in both the political and the legal fields; long before UDI Mr Wilson wanted to change it—and rightly so, because apart from its own inherent inadequacy, indeed immorality, it represented an ever-increasing danger to peace and order in Rhodesia for so long as it remained in force. But since, as will be seen, the necessary amendments are far-reaching and fundamental, one can hardly take seriously the assertion that the Constitution as framed 'enshrines the principle and intention of unimpeded progress to majority rule'. And since, as will also be shown, the *Tiger* proposals were a substantial retrogression from the 1961 Constitution, one cannot take seriously the protestations from both sides of the House at Westminster that *Tiger* would have been an honourable settlement.

1961 plus and Tiger

The 1961 Constitution failed because it was not equipped to succeed. It failed in the political field precisely because it did *not* ensure unimpeded progress towards majority rule; it failed in the legal field precisely because it did *not* protect the rights and liberties of the individual. '1961 plus' must be a document in which these defects have been rectified. The defects are major, but to rectify them is not, in terms of legal techniques, a major operation; nor does the political aspect of the recti-fication require more than to keep the political defect always in sight. This was not done on board HMS *Tiger* last Decem-ber; the working document which Britain was anxious to turn into an agreement contained a constitutional formula which must rank as one of the major betrayals of history, and one infinitely more cynical than the 1961 Constitution which it purported to improve.

But *Tiger* was worse than simply 1961 minus. It satisfied neither the five principles nor the undertakings given to the Commonwealth Prime Ministers a few weeks earlier. It cannot, for instance, be seriously argued that a Royal Commission meets the commitment to submit the constitutional settlement to the people of Rhodesia as a whole 'by appropriate demo-cratic means', or that the general world community would accept such a test of opinion as fair and free.

The failure of *Tiger* to meet the five principles is even more blatant. It widens the B roll franchise to universal suffrage for all Africans over the age of thirty, and increases the B roll seats from 15 to 17—both empty gestures; and far from im-proving the political status of the African population, the number of open A roll seats is reduced from 50 to 33, the other 17 being reserved European seats. To win a bare majority, therefore, Africans must, under *Tiger*, win 17 out of 33 A roll seats as against 18 out of 50 under the 1961 Constitution. Clearly *Tiger* does not improve, but worsens, the political status of the African people; and it is idle to talk proudly of the blocking quarter, when the necessity for this minimal and token increase arises only because of the quite purposeless introduction of a Senate in place of the far stronger protection against the amendment of entrenched clauses which was contained in the 1961 Constitution.

But perhaps the subtlest inroad into the African position is made by the new delimitation proposal:

> The overriding objective of the [Delimitation] Commission is so to divide the constituencies that the proportion of those with a majority of African voters on the A roll . . . is the same as the proportion of African voters . . . on the A roll for the country as a whole.

This at first blush represents a far-sighted protection against cramming African A roll voters into constituencies already safe; and, indeed, the provision could well have the effect of protecting African interests in the early stages when the numbers of African A roll voters are by comparison small. But closer examination reveals that when it really matters—when the marginal position is approached and majority rule is in sight —this delimitation gimmick operates to *reduce* the number of seats likely to be won by the African vote. The Rhodesian cross-voting provisions are such that (assuming for this purpose an unlimited number of available B roll voters, and assuming also completely racial voting) the African vote will be poised to win an A roll seat when the proportion of African to European A roll voters is 3 to 5; in other words, in a constituency containing a total of 2,000 A roll voters, 1,250 of whom are white and 750 black, the B roll vote can count for 25 per cent of 2,000, producing parity. When, therefore, there are 80,000 white and 48,000 black voters on the A roll there is, with the aid of the B roll, theoretical parity, and the practical probabilities are that one side or the other will score a narrow victory. Majority rule could come in such circumstances notwithstanding that Africans might be in a minority on the A roll in every constituency; but in terms of the proposed delimitation provision, Africans must be placed in a majority on the A roll in twelve of the thirty-three constituencies—a complete waste of a third of their A roll voting strength, resulting inevitably in the loss of at least some of the remaining A roll seats they would otherwise have won.

The fourth principle—that there would have to be progress towards ending racial discrimination—is allegedly met in *Tiger* by the setting up of another Royal Commission 'to study and make recommendations...'; and yet another Standing Commission 'will keep the problems of racial discrimination under regular review'. Provisions of this kind, which do not impose any obligation on the Rhodesian Government to accept any of the recommendations, are toothless and worthless.

These, then, are the proposals presented by the British Government as making good the shortcomings of the 1961 Constitution, as satisfying the six principles (they do indeed satisfy the sixth), and as the charter which could lead to majority rule in two or three elections. There is no warrant whatever, no vestige of justification, for such a statement; even Sir Edgar Whitehead, a middle-of-the-roader in his own estimation and as reactionary as any white supremacist in the estimation of many others, called *Tiger* an astonishing document and condemned it as 'greatly postponing the possible date of African majority rule almost certainly beyond the end of the century'. (His reference to postponement was by comparison with his own highly optimistic estimate of 1977 under the 1961 Constitution; his 'beyond the end of the century' is equally optimistic—'for all time' would be more realistic.)

There is a suggestion abroad that Mr Wilson was content to give Mr Smith everything for which he asked as to the actual constitutional proposals, because the more he asked for, and was given, the less chance there was of the proposals passing the test of acceptability to the people of Rhodesia as a whole. In one sense, one could hope that this was indeed Mr Wilson's tactic, since the mind boggles at the thought that a Labour Prime Minister would really have been prepared to perpetrate the outrage which the *Tiger* proposals represent. Certainly no Tory Prime Minister has been prepared to go anything like so far, even in a pre-independence Constitution; and one trusts that the fact that Mr Duncan Sandys sees no necessity to go further gives Mr Wilson little comfort.

But if this was Mr Wilson's tactic, he has caught only himself in the trap. He has created a general assumption that *Tiger* is the automatic starting-point of further talks. The fact that those proposals were put forward at a particular time, and subject to particular essential preconditions, is conveniently overlooked. The fact that undertakings have been given as to Britain's future policy is ignored. Mr Wilson has gone so far as to indicate that he is willing to break the NIBMAR pledge —a pledge given to the Commonwealth and the United Nations. The argument appears to be that because it was unwise to give the pledge in the first place it may be validly broken—surely a new low in political morality.

But above all, it appears to be of no concern whatever to the British Government that *Tiger* represents the blackest page in the whole of British colonial history.

THE CONSERVATIVE GOVERNMENT'S FAILURE: PEARCE REPORTS 'NO'

After the second failure to reach a settlement of the independence issue—at the meeting on board HMS *Fearless* in October 1968—the Rhodesian régime proceeded to implement its own republican constitution (see Constitution of 1969, Part IV, Document 13) and to obtain the endorsement of the European electorate in a referendum on both the Constitution and the republic. Since the contents of that Constitution were in clear violation of every one of the 'Five Principles' which were supposed to be the basis for a settlement with Britain, and since the adoption of republican status in 1970 severed the last remaining formal link with Britain, the possibility of any settlement with the British Government became increasingly remote.

However, after the return to power of the Conservative Party—pledged to seek a settlement with the rebel régime— negotiations were renewed in 1971 and agreement was reached between Sir Alec Douglas-Home and Mr Smith in November of that year. The settlement was based on the 1969 Constitution, with certain amendments to allow for the possibility (exceedingly remote) of African representation increasing to parity and from there to majority rule. But half the Africans would continue to be elected by, and representative of, the tribal chiefs, themselves in the service of the Government.

Before the settlement could be implemented, the proposals had to be seen to be 'acceptable to the people of Rhodesia as a whole', in accordance with the fifth principle. (The other principles were alleged by the Conservative Government to have been met by amendments to the 1969 Constitution providing for 'an immediate increase in African representation' and a 'justiciable' Declaration of Rights.) Since the Rhodesian Government would never have agreed to a general referendum in which all races would participate, provision was made for a Royal Commission, under the chairmanship of Lord Pearce (acceptable to the Rhodesians because of his judicial pronouncement in favour of the 'legality' of the régime), and composed of former members of the British Colonial Service, to test the opinion of the Rhodesian people on the settlement proposals. While the test was being conducted, the Smith régime would remain in power (there would be no 'return to legality') and thus in control of police and security forces and of access to all media of communications. Under the agreement, 'normal political activities' were to be permitted during the test, but what was 'normal' in the Rhodesian context was never defined.

The Pearce Report is a remarkable document. It is the only measure of African opinion ever conducted in Rhodesia, since every general election and referendum in that country have been almost exclusively European expressions. The Report also provided a wealth of information on the political views of the Africans, which had been censored and suppressed over the preceding decade of Rhodesian Front rule. The excerpts selected from the Report summarise the reasons for European acceptance and for African rejection of the Proposals agreed by the British and Rhodesian Governments. (The details of the Proposals emerge from these replies.) From this evidence, the Commission could only conclude that the Proposals were *not* 'acceptable to the people of Rhodesia as a whole'.

DOCUMENT 42. *Report of the Commission on Rhodesian Opinion under the Chairmanship of the Right Hon. the Lord Pearce* (CMND 4964, MAY 1972)

3. The Foreign and Commonwealth Secretary gave us the following terms of reference: 'To satisfy themselves that the proposals for a settlement as set out in Annex B to Command

Paper 4835 have been fully and properly explained to the population of Rhodesia; to ascertain by direct contact with all sections of the population whether the people of Rhodesia as a whole regard these proposals as acceptable as a basis for independence; and to report to the Foreign and Commonwealth Secretary accordingly.'

4. In answer to the first part of our terms of reference we are satisfied that the Proposals have been 'fully and properly explained to the population of Rhodesia'. We believe that the great majority of those from whom we heard had a sufficient understanding of the contents and implications of the Proposals to enable them to pass judgment on them.

5. So far as the second part of our terms of reference is concerned we have no doubt that apart from a small minority the European population was in favour.... But the majority of those Africans whom we consulted privately or publicly was against the Proposals. We believe ... that this represents the opinion of the African population. We have reached the conclusion that the people of Rhodesia as a whole do not regard the Proposals as acceptable as a basis for independence.

Reasons Given for Acceptance or Rejection

Reasons for European Acceptance

298. The European reasons for acceptance can be summed up in the words of one team of Commissioners:

'(a) Necessary for economic reasons—Rhodesia will thrive economically only if there is a settlement.

(b) Majority rule inevitable—many Europeans adopted a fatalistic attitude with the reservation that they did not really welcome majority rule but realised it had to come, so that the more gradual and peaceful the road to it the better.

(c) The only possible way to the future—European domination or African revolution were the unsatisfactory alternatives. The Proposals were regarded as the best and the only compromise possible between two very different sets of aspirations.

(d) Essential for the Africans—many Europeans gave this reason in the sincere belief that Africans would be better off this way than under permanent European control or immediate African control.'

Reasons for European Rejection

300. The small minority from among the European letter-writers and those appearing in person who rejected the Proposals can be divided into two mutually opposed groups: those who felt too much had been given to the Africans and those who thought too little.

301. It was the conviction of the first group that the government of Rhodesia should be retained permanently in civilised and responsible (i.e. European) hands. . . .

304. Rejection on grounds of conscience—not enough for the African. . . . They showed a great distrust for the Government based on its past record. . . . Many of this group criticised the inadequacies of the Terms themselves, particularly the high franchise, the irrelevance of the Lower Roll, indirect elections by Electoral Colleges, and the probable ineffectiveness of both Declaration of Rights and the Commission on Racial Discrimination. . . .

Reasons for African Rejection

310. The reasons given were broadly speaking the same whether given privately, in groups, at mass meetings or in writing. The general impression we received was that Africans, given the opportunity of expressing their views, rejected proposals which they held did not accord them dignity, justice or fair opportunities, and which did not accord them the parity of recognition which was as important to them as parity of representation. Their reasons for rejection fall into two main categories: the wider issues and specific objections.

311. The wider issues. Mistrust of the intentions and motives of the Government transcended all other considerations. Apprehension for the future stemmed from resentment at what they felt to be the humiliations of the past and at the limitations of policies on land, education, and personal advancement. One summed it up in saying 'We do not reject the Proposals, we reject the Government'. This was the dominant motivation of African rejection at all levels and in all areas. Few could bring themselves to believe that the Government had changed its policies or that the European electorate on whom it

depended was prepared to change its attitudes or its way of life. Most refused to see advantages in the Proposals. Those who did doubted whether the Government would ever implement them. These people thought that as soon as Independence was recognised and sanctions revoked, a Government which had torn up previous constitutions could do so again; and even if the Government kept faith, the white electorate would turn them out and replace them by representatives and parties not committed to the present terms. A majority of Africans were convinced that the present governing party was committed to the perpetuation of white supremacy in Rhodesia. . . .

312. A corollary of this deep mistrust was the belief that the guarantees against constitutional change were inadequate. It was argued:

(a) Half the African members in Parliament represent and are elected by the Chiefs, Headmen and Councillors. These members could not be relied upon to understand the implications for the African of major constitutional changes and were also open to pressure and influence by the Government. The internal provisions against adverse changes of the Constitution were therefore too weak.

(b) The absence of external guarantees against further change was argued by those (not many) who saw good points in the Proposals which might otherwise be worth trying as a starting point. But if independence were recognised no country could intervene in Rhodesia's internal affairs. If promises were not kept the African would then have no-one to turn to. They objected to the recognition of independence at this stage on the basis of the Proposals which left effective power in the hands of a small minority.

(c) There should be a trial period to see whether the Proposals were good and would be properly worked out in good faith. A few thought independence should not be granted for a period of 5 years to see whether the Government honoured its undertakings. Many more held that Britain should retain the right to see that the Proposals were carried into effect properly and should not concede recognition of Independence before parity had been reached.

(d) Many said that sanctions should not be lifted until the Government had demonstrated its determination to change course and to implement the Proposals in the spirit as well as the letter; sanctions might affect the African more seriously than Europeans, but this was a price they were ready to pay.

(e) British involvement in the future of the Africans in Rhodesia should continue and ties with Britain should not be broken. Those who argued thus did not wish Britain at present to surrender its claim to be able to influence affairs in Rhodesia.
. . .

313. Many criticised the lack of effective consultation with African leaders. No Africans had been involved in the negotiations: they were therefore not a party to them. If their national leaders had been involved and said they should accept, that would have been different. Some said that for this reason earlier British proposals would also have been unacceptable to Africans. It was also argued that the issue was essentially one between the Europeans and Africans in Rhodesia, or between the Rhodesian Government and the Africans; it was not between the British and Rhodesian Governments; it had to be settled in Rhodesia. . . .

314. Another criticism heard was that the time to majority rule was too indefinite and too long. Most accepted a gradual, if not too gradual, process and recognised that the future of the country lay in co-operation between the two races. But they feared that under the Proposals parity or majority rule would never materialise: 'The road was too steep.' Some thought that a starting point higher than a ratio of 50 European to 16 African seats was necessary. Others wanted a definite date set for parity. A variant of this argument was that a specific time-table should be fixed for the creation of additional African seats in Parliament. All feared that progress to parity would be controlled and slowed down by the encouragement of white immigration, by holding down African wages and by job reservation so that the African Higher Roll voters never caught up with the Europeans. Previous speeches by Mr Ian Smith saying that there would be no African rule in his lifetime were constantly quoted. Immediate majority rule as such did not figure so high in priority. . . .

316. There was criticism that the new constitution was based on the 1969 Constitution which was racialist in concept and illegal. On looking back some thought it had proved a mistake

to have rejected the 1961 Constitution: this had features which should be considered again.

317. There was a fear that acceptance of the Proposals would lose Rhodesian Africans the sympathy of the outside world when Independence would make any intervention by Britain impractical. If the Proposals were not honoured people would say 'It was you who said "Yes". You have brought it on yourselves'. They were forced to reject something which fell so far short of their aspirations that it would be tantamount to suicide to say 'Yes'. . . .

318. What they now wanted, the Africans said, was a national convention, or a constitutional conference, or a meeting together of leaders of Rhodesian Africans and Europeans under some independent chairman when these issues could be discussed and progress made towards their resolution. . . .

Specific Objections to the Proposals

319. The Franchise was criticised on the following grounds:

(a) The African Higher Roll was too high and progress to parity consequently too slow. A graduate teacher might take 20 years to qualify and most teachers would never qualify; ministers of religion certainly could not. Qualifications based on income and wealth were wrong in principle as they would disqualify from voting or from standing for Parliament, many highly educated, many respected and many wiser but older men. It was also wrong to place so much reliance on wealth as a principle in determining responsibility to vote, since the wealthy would disregard the interests of the poor.

(b) The franchise divided Africans among themselves on the basis of wealth. It divided the communities on the basis of race. A constitution should unite rather than divide.

(c) Equality of qualifications with the European Roll was unjustifiable when Africans, by law or by practice, were debarred from equal rates of pay when doing the same or similar jobs, particularly for instance in the teaching profession.

(d) The immovable property qualification was impossible for all but a very few. An African could only own land and any building on it in the African Purchase Areas where 3 per cent of the population lived or in similarly limited areas of most townships. There was no private ownership in the Tribal Trust Lands and few home ownership schemes in townships—except perhaps in Bulawayo.

(e) There should be a Common Roll or cross voting so that Africans could vote for Europeans they respect and Europeans would have to seek African votes. Under the Proposals the Prime Minister would never have to seek an African vote.

(f) Voters on the African Higher Roll who had earned the increased representation in Parliament would have no control over half of those elected. Chiefs and tribal authorities should not be used as a means of controlling political representation.

(g) The African Lower Roll was meaningless. However many might qualify on the Lower Roll, they could only vote for the present eight seats and they could exercise little or no influence in Parliament.

(h) An influx of European immigrants would step up the numbers of Africans needed to qualify as voters on the Higher Roll for additional African seats, would reduce the opportunities for obtaining jobs at rates of pay which would enable them to qualify, and would delay general rises of African rates of pay. . . .

320. Declaration of Rights. This was felt to be irrelevant to the immediate problems and inadequate to remedy wrongs because:

(a) it would be ineffective and weak. It did not cover existing laws which gave the Government all the powers they needed. Moreover it could be largely nullified through a declaration of emergency which, on present form, the Government would not hesitate to use;

(b) since there was said to be no legal aid for such cases, it would be too expensive for Africans to bring cases before the Court. At best it would be most difficult;

(c) the Courts were under the influence of the Government and the impartiality of the judges was questioned.

321. Detention. Some called for the release of the remaining detainees. Their continued detention was regarded as a great injustice. There was little faith in the proposed Special Review of those still detained. It was pointed out that the British representative would not be able to play any effective role in

this because he was only an observer. Many noted that the tribunal which would conduct this review was the same tribunal which had already recommended continued detention of those concerned.

322. Racial Discrimination and Land. The powers of the Commission on Racial Discrimination were thought to be inadequate because they were not mandatory on the Government; the Government would be able to find plenty of reasons for not accepting recommendations they did not like. . . . Discrimination hurt most in human relations—in job reservation and opportunities for employment and promotion, in wage differentials for the same job, in comparative educational opportunities and particularly the grading system in African schools and the lack of openings in polytechnics or higher technical education. . . .

323. The prospects of any change in the Land Tenure Act through the operations of the Commission seemed slight. Insufficient assurances fell far short of expectations particularly in Manicaland. The five million acres available when needed was poor land far distant from their existing lands. Development aid would be of little real help until the Land Tenure Act was repealed. The effects of the Act on the work of the Churches was a recurring complaint. Europeans, and especially farmers, would never agree to an equitable redistribution of land.

324. Development Aid. This was widely regarded as sugaring the pill or too little and too late. We were told that Africans would not sell their country for this or that it was a bribe to buy African support. Although intended to assist Africans it was feared that most would be spent on salaries for Europeans or used to European advantage. . . .

Assessment of Evidence

TABLE I *Numbers of People Met by Commissioners*

	Number of Europeans	Number of Africans	African population (over 18) for the area covered by each team	Percentage of African population seen by Commissioners
Total	6,130	114,600	1,986,000	5·78

TABLE II *Views of Europeans Recorded by Commissioners*

	Acceptances	Rejections	Undecided or Abstained
Total	5,634	390	94

TABLE III *Analysis of African Oral Opinions*

	Public Meetings (and groups of more than 20)		
	Acceptances	Rejections	Undecided or abstained
Total	670 (less than 1 per cent)	97,800	1,830

	Groups (under 20) and individuals			
	Acceptances	Rejections	Undecided or Abstained	Total Seen
Total	2,264 (about 15 per cent)	9,509	2,461	114,534

DOCUMENT 43. THE PEARCE COMMISSION REPORT: BROADCAST STATEMENT BY THE PRIME MINISTER, the HON. I. D. SMITH, 23 MAY 1972

The report of the Pearce Commission shows that the overwhelming majority of Europeans, Asians and Coloureds in Rhodesia supported the settlement. So did a considerable number of Africans who realized the benefits that would flow from the agreement. Regrettably, however, Lord Pearce and his colleagues formed the opinion that a majority of Africans were opposed to the settlement and from this they have concluded that the people of Rhodesia as a whole do not accept the proposals.

The report is a comprehensive document, covering over 200 pages, and it takes time to study it carefully and thoroughly. I would not have credited that any report could contain so many misinterpretations and misconstructions of the true position. ... I submit that there is only one conclusion: the Pearce Commission had the wool pulled over its eyes.

When one reads this report, in spite of its naivety and inept-ness, the only responsible conclusion that one can come to is that the answer should have been 'Yes'. However, in view of the fact that the Commissioners were unable to assess African opinion, and that they were able to make contact with less than 6 per cent of the African adult population, the only other logical answer, apart from an affirmative, is that it was im-possible to assess the opinion of the African people, and, there-fore, the two Governments concerned should face up to their responsibility.

Tragically, after all we have been through, culminating in an agreement, signed by the two governments, the whole thing has landed up on the rocks, through the bungling of the test on which the United Kingdom Government insisted, against our advice. To make things worse, they spurned the help of all our experts when it came to planning and preparing the exercise.

We have had many different inquiries and reports during our history; I believe this one will go down as the most irres-ponsible of them all.

As far as I and my colleagues in Government are concerned, we did our best to ensure the success of the operation—*we dedicated ourselves to obtaining a 'Yes' answer* [editor's italics]. . . .

I believe that when you read this report you will share my disbelief that a British Commission could reach a conclusion which is so unrealistic, contrary to the evidence in their own report, and so palpably against the interests of all Rhodesians and particularly of the Africans. . . .

So in the end, this is a disappointment for us. However, many worse things have happened to Rhodesia, and I have a feeling that much good, at present unseen, will flow from this experience which we have been through. For some time now it has been your Government's assessment, that whatever the outcome of the Pearce Commission, Rhodesia's progress and success are assured.

PART IX

The World Outside

THE BRITISH CASE

The Labour Government's policy following the Rhodesian Unilateral Declaration of Independence: the British Prime Minister, Mr Harold Wilson, in his address to the United Nations, rejects the use of force, denies the practicability of immediate majority rule and appeals for support for economic sanctions.

DOCUMENT 44. UNITED NATIONS GENERAL ASSEMBLY, *Official Records* (20TH SESSION, 1397th MEETING, 16 DECEMBER 1965)

47. I hope this Assembly will accept that no one could have done more than we did to warn the then Government of Rhodesia of the incalculable risks they were taking if they plunged into the illegal action which they formally, finally and irresponsibly announced on 11 November. I hope the Assembly will agree that we did everything in our power to agree on a just and honourable settlement. We failed, and we failed because of the racialist obsessions of the people with whom we were dealing. For not only did they defy the British Government, the legally constituted authority for their country; not only did they show their contempt for world opinion; but worst of all, they have, while paying lip-service to 'civilized standards', outraged the moral law which is working its purpose out as year succeeds year in world history—the right of all men to live their lives in the dignity of social and political freedom. In a broadcast to the British nation before the tragic decision of 11 November, some weeks before, I said that in dealing with Mr

Smith, as I then was, I was talking the accents of different worlds and, indeed, of different centuries.

48. Britain carries the responsibility. Sometimes I could wish it were otherwise. No Government, I believe, in our life has had to face a problem so complex, so multidimensional. In theory, and under constitutional law, this is a bilateral matter between the British Parliament, who alone has the responsibility of decision in Rhodesia, and the people of Rhodesia. But those in any country who believe that this can be contained within the confines of Britain and Rhodesia, those who do not recognize the fact that this is a world problem both in what it symbolizes and in what its effect can be, such people are victims of self-delusion.

49. It was the recognition of this fact which led the British Government, within minutes of the illegal declaration of Mr Smith and his colleagues, to instruct the Foreign Secretary to proceed at once here to the United Nations and take the initiative in raising the matter in the Security Council. We accept the responsibility for dealing with this matter because it is our responsibility. But having embarked on a series of measures of unprecedented severity, at considerable cost and still greater risk to ourselves, in order to secure the return of the Rhodesian people to their true allegiance and to constitutional courses of action, we have the right to ask every Member of this Assembly to give us their fullest support. Above all, we have the right to demand that the financial and economic measures we have instituted are not frustrated by the nationals of other countries seeking to earn a sordid profit by traffic with those who have defied the opinions of mankind.

50. I know there are many nations represented here, many of our closest friends in the Commonwealth, who have criticized us bitterly for not invoking the use of military force to suppress this rebellion; and it is a sad thought that in this Organization, created to maintain and establish the peaceful settlement of disputes, there is a deep disagreement between us on the question of what is held to be our failure to settle this matter by war-like means. Their passions run deep, and every one of us understands this. But I say to them that what they propose is not the way to settle this problem.

51. We shall not let up until Rhodesia has returned to consti-

tutional rule. We believe that, given time and given patience, the British Government and the British Parliament will effectively assert their authority in consultation with those who can claim to speak more representatively on behalf of the Rhodesian people as a whole.

52. Equally I repeat—and this has been the view expressed by successive Governments in my country—that the future of Rhodesia, as we have ensured with so many formerly subject nations that have achieved independence in these past few years, the future of Rhodesia must be on the basis of multiracial harmony leading to democratic majority rule.

53. Our disagreement is not about principles but about the methods for realizing those principles. The methods we use to achieve a settlement must be based on the realities of the Rhodesian situation, realities which every one of us here must be prepared to face. And there are two facts I must underline. First, Rhodesia is in legal terms a colony, yes, but as our representatives here in the United Nations have had to make clear on many occasions, Rhodesia has had a unique degree of internal self-government for over forty years, unknown in any other part of the former British Empire. In all our long, proud record of ending British colonial rule, I do not believe there is any example, apart from Rhodesia, where, at the stage of qualified self-government, the local régime exercised control over powerful armed forces. One may regret this fact, as one may regret that over these last forty years previous British Parliaments failed to uphold and assert their right to insist on the maintenance of human rights, and the protection of the African people in Rhodesia. But however we may regret failures of the past, we have to deal now with the consequences of those failures for 1965.

54. My second point is this. It has been a cardinal aim of British policy to secure a more rapid advance of self-government for African peoples and to train those peoples for self-government. I believe—and I have said this many times to Mr. Smith—that it is a tragic commentary upon the European record in Rhodesia that there is not in Rhodesia, as elsewhere, an African nationalist movement capable of the responsibility of self-government at this moment. For one thing, it is tragically divided. For another, it has been denied the opportunity of

practical political experience and, in particular, of multiracial co-operation. It is for these reasons that I have had to make it clear that, so far as we are concerned, a return to constitutional rule would not and could not mean an immediate advance to majority rule. Time will be needed, and time, as I have said in London and in Salisbury, will be measured not by clock or calendar but by achievement in working within a multiracial Rhodesian Government, during a period in which the British Parliament remains in a position to ensure the protection of human rights, to guarantee the advance, the unimpeded advancement of the majority and to safeguard the rights of minorities. This has been done with success elsewhere in Africa, and it can be done in Rhodesia.

55. We are facing a dangerous situation. The wind of change in Africa is blowing at gale force. The tragedy is that there are deluded men who have seized the helm and who, with all the apparatus of a police state, have in turn deceived a lot of their fellow citizens into believing that the relative stillness which is found at the centre of a cyclone can be a basis for quiet and stability. . . .

58. This is a moral issue. More than two years ago, when Leader of the Opposition, speaking at my Party Conference, I said this Rhodesian issue was one in which there could be no neutrals. There is no neutrality here in this Assembly. . . .

But the British Government is not going to be deflected from the course that we are convinced is right, and in which I believe the whole British people is behind us. But I do have the right to appeal to this Assembly to recognize that words and resolutions and criticism and passions, while they have their place, are not a substitute for action.

THE COST TO BRITAIN

An appraisal of the cost of sanctions to the British economy.

DOCUMENT 45. 'A HARD LOOK AT SANCTIONS' BY J. D. F. JONES, (FOREIGN EDITOR, THE *Financial Times*, LONDON, 23 JUNE 1969)

Counting the Cost

To be realistic, there is no possibility of any official acknowledgment that sanctions are a waste of energy; a host of political factors, domestic and international, will ensure that the British Government makes strenuous noises about its intention to carry on with fresh vigour. But the debate will grow, and the subject, of course, is not so much whether we continue with sanctions but when and whether Britain is prepared to accept Rhodesian independence as a fact.

Any government which faces up to this important political decision will have to start by counting the cost of sanctions to Britain. The trouble is that it is next to impossible to produce a meaningful figure, because the cost of sanctions to the balance of payments—which is the immediate area where it is said that we 'cannot afford' sanctions—depends on so much guesswork, arising out of the civil servants' attempts to compare, say, the loss of British trade earnings in Rhodesia with the consequent improvement in other countries.

Mr Wilson has said that the balance of payments cost is roughly £40m. a year, and Whitehall reckons that this is the sort of annual level that would extend into the future. This figure ought not, perhaps, to be taken too seriously. It excludes, for example, that part of the emergency aid to Zambia which did not become a charge on the balance of payments; it excludes any estimate of the extra cost to this country of copper imports, where the rising trend since 1965 (cash wirebars went above £650 last week) has been partly, not wholly, caused by Central Africa's transport problems. However, it apparently does include such things as the extra cost of tobacco imports, the meeting of Britain's guarantees on the World Bank loans to Rhodesia (up to £3m. a year), and a whole range of charges directly arising out of UDI.

£2–3m. Aid to Zambia

The cost to the Exchequer, in terms of total payments, can be calculated more easily and is officially put at £36·5m. between November, 1965, and March, 1969. This figure includes such things as the expense of the British naval patrol outside Beira (which is still being carried out by a couple of frigates, though costing only an extra £1·5m. since the Navy would, presumably, have to keep itself busy somewhere). Contingency aid to Zambia, particularly for the road improvement schemes and the former oil airlift, has now dropped back to £2–£3m. a year. Then there are minor and declining items such as support of Rhodesian civil servants who refuse to accept UDI.

With the exception of the Rhodesian debt obligations, most of the costs can be expected to run down gradually, so that the £40m. balance of payments figure may be an overestimate. But, of course, it is the uncertainty about the value of the lost exports that makes all these calculations so unhelpful.

With this sort of figure in mind, and remembering that an immediate 'scrap sanctions' decision is out of the question, we have to decide whether the price is acceptable. What, indeed, are we trying to do? The purpose of sanctions was originally said to be to persuade enough White Rhodesians to change their minds and return to legality. No-one, not even in the fustier recesses of Whitehall, today believes that this is going to happen—at least in the foreseeable future. The most the Government is now expecting is to make the Rhodesians thoroughly fed up; in this there has certainly been some success, mainly at the higher-income levels and among those few Whites who can appreciate the stultifying impact of sanctions and pariahdom on the country's development.

The damage may be considerable but no one can pretend that the Rhodesian economy is going to be destroyed. In effect, Rhodesia is being punished by Britain and the world for constitutional and ideological misconduct.

The extent of the punishment already meted out should never be underestimated, despite the brave words from Salisbury. The point about a sanctions campaign, very crudely, is to block a country's export outlets so as to deprive it of the foreign exchange earnings which it requires to pay for essential imports; at a certain point, and in theory, that country will then collapse. Rhodesia was originally thought to be vulnerable to such a campaign because of its reliance on a small number of identifiable exports and its heavy dependence on sophisticated imports.

The Rhodesian answer has been to move exports through the blockade, and to hold down the import bills with enough success to keep the economy going at the cost of minor inconveniences for the Rhodesian population and—very important—a complete halt to the sort of development progress the country needs so badly. Sanctions have driven Rhodesia's export earnings back from £164m. to under £100m.; while Salisbury has used import quotas and ingenious import substitution so as to hold imports back to about the same level. In other words, sanctions have succeeded, but not enough.

Everyone has heard about the various ways the Rhodesians have hung on—the heavy dependence on co-operation from South Africa and Portugal, the evasion of the oil blockade, the neighbouring African states' inability to sever their commercial links, the forging of trading documents, the smuggling and the readiness of so many foreign businessmen to break into a new market so long as they can get away with it.

This is ancient history. The important question is whether sanctions will maintain their present degree of effectiveness— or, of course, whether they can be improved. The present situation is moderately encouraging for the Rhodesians. The agricultural sector—always excepting the wretched tobacco farmers—has recovered well from last year's drought and frost and there are high hopes of the new mineral developments, where nickel, in particular, should soon be giving a boost to the export receipts. There is no sign that Pretoria or Lisbon will translate their undoubted irritation with Mr Smith's referendum into any slackening of their present assistance, and the Zambians are still having to take far more goods from Rhodesia than they would like.

This economic war is naturally surrounded in secrecy, but there is enough evidence of success to give the Rhodesians a short-run encouragement. They are probably moving more of their tobacco, for example—as much as 100m. lbs of the 132m. lbs crop, though this compares with the 280m. lb pre-UDI sales and the stockpile is still vast, representing at least £35m. Some of the newer agricultural crops, such as cotton, are doing well and maize has had a very good year. The sugar has been selling again, thanks to the Portuguese. It is clear that Rhodesia's gold production—which used to be worth about £7m.—is now being sold in Switzerland by various means. Car assembly is going ahead merrily in the former BMC and Ford plants, with Japanese and French models smoothly available.

On the other hand, it is wise to keep a sense of proportion. The Rhodesians may be getting a lot of exports through the blockade, but they are certainly not getting the right prices. The middle men must take their cut. Evasion is always expensive. There are plenty of businessmen in the world who will try to ignore the UN sanctions, but only if it is made worth their while. Or again, the minerals have been the big success of the operation, but the stockpiles are still large, the value of production has risen only very marginally and it will be years before the present prospecting fever can be transformed into a producing industry. Here, as in so much else, the nightmare for many thoughtful Rhodesians is the almost total failure since UDI to put in the massive development capital that is needed and which would normally have been available from outside.

The present position has been well summed up in a calculation offered by Britain to the UN recently. It admits that certain countries are either unwilling or unable to apply the UN sanctions. After the total Rhodesian exports to these countries have been deducted, there remained last year £44m. of Rhodesian exports to non-African countries which are nominally observing sanctions—of which only £7m. appeared on those countries' official statistics, the £37m. balance presumably passing under false documents.

This £44m. figure is the size of the problem. (It is interesting to see that it approximates to the Rhodesian trade surplus in the year before UDI.) The UN has a choice of tactics—either it can aim to force down the trade level with Africa (as it tried to do in the first two years), or it can face the fact that South Africa will not and Zambia cannot change, and therefore concentrate on chipping away at the £44m. evasions. Or rather—to be more realistic—it will have its work cut out to keep the £44m. from soaring by tens of millions of pounds.

It is often said that sanctions are bound to weaken as the years go by, presumably because the Rhodesians will become more skilful and world opinion less committed or alert. Possibly, though, this is not quite as true as it appears at first sight, for two reasons. The first is that for the first time the British Government has found, in the UN Security Council Committee set up last year, an international authority prepared to try to implement the sanctions resolutions. The second report of this Committee has just been published and makes fascinating reading in its description of the diplomatic machinery now being employed against Rhodesia's exports. In the past Britain could only make private representations to a government when it discovered an evasion attempt, and for some time there was no mistaking the exasperation in Whitehall with the casual way the many governments responded to British requests.

Tougher for Evaders

To-day, when Britain's diplomatic or intelligence services report that a deal is under way, the information is passed to New York, where the Committee may ask the Secretary General to refer to the Government of the businessman involved. If a government fails to do anything, the matter is public knowledge —and the word will no doubt be passed around fast enough, particularly to the developing countries that feel most strongly about Rhodesia.

I am not suggesting that this has brought immediately evident and dramatic results. Evasion continues. The Portuguese, for instance, are content to ignore the British analysis of the strange inconsistencies in Mozambique's trade statistics. But people who are in a position to know do believe that this public pressure on governments has a definite deterrent effect—and can continue to do so. It is suggested that there is already evidence of a tightening in customs inspection, that fake documents are less easily accepted, and that it is far more difficult for a country to allow its businessmen to get away with secret deals. This deserves to be noticed as one factor favouring the continued relevance of sanctions.

The second reason for caution is the smallness of Rhodesia. The truth—though Mr Smith would be horrified to hear it— is that Rhodesia is a hunk of African bush which does not matter very much to anyone. Now of course, this works two ways—it can be argued that the insignificance of Rhodesian trade makes it impossible to police properly. But even in Britain because of the long connection, there may still be a tendency to overestimate the importance of the Rhodesian market and economy.

If it were South Africa, it would be a different matter. But the Rhodesian market is worth a comparatively small £100m. or so, and no country except Zambia, certainly not Britain, has suffered particularly as a result of the sanctions campaign. Any government calculating whether to maintain sanctions has to weigh up the importance of Rhodesia set against the consequences of relaxation in other countries. Japan, for example, would clearly be most unhappy if the Black African States where it is making such trading progress were to get the impression that Japanese businessmen were flaunting sanctions.

Commonwealth Threatened

For Britain, it is a particularly important point and will have to figure in the debate about post-referendum policy. After UDI, Britain forfeited £35m. in exports to Rhodesia. Yet British trade with Zambia, for example, has soared to £35m. and British exports to the African Commonwealth countries totalled no less than £230m. last year, a figure which casts a rather different light on the loss in Rhodesia.

No one knows how much of this trade might be lost, if, say, Britain recognised Ian Smith and called off sanctions after all. Britain has been unpopular enough in these states for refusing to use military force against UDI and has been grudgingly forgiven. Nor can anyone be sure that these governments would look to other pressures, such as the reserves they presently hold in London—say £300m.—if Britain did something they considered utter betrayal. What is certain is that, disillusioned and bitter though many Commonwealth and African leaders have become over these past three years, they would not stand for a British decision to allow Mr Smith his victory.

It is a factor that must bulk quite as large as the Exchequer cost or the loss of the tobacco crop in making a decision about where we go from here. A British sell-out would, I should think, be impossible to conceal from the world, and would surely mark the end of the Commonwealth as we know it now, not to speak of our relations with the rest of the developing world. The end of the Commonwealth and a guess at £40m. on the balance of payments—they are part of the same equation.

THE COMMONWEALTH VIEW

Rhodesia's illegal declaration of independence was an issue which divided the Commonwealth into two distinct and irreconcilable groups. The most crucial meeting of the Prime Ministers, so far as the question of Rhodesia was concerned, and the one which nearly culminated in the breakdown of the Commonwealth as an institution was held in London in September 1966. The meeting at Lagos in January of that year was also significant in that it was the first to be devoted to a single issue, the first to be convened on the initiative of the African leaders, through the institution of the Commonwealth Secretariat, and the first to be held in an African Commonwealth country.

The outcome of the Lagos conference, which had as its purpose the consideration of measures to end the illegal régime, was largely determined by the British Prime Minister's statement that the cumulative effect of economic sanctions might well bring the rebellion to an end within a matter of 'weeks rather than months'. Those who had misgivings in this regard were reassured that the conference would reconvene in about six months time to review the effects of the application of economic sanctions.

When the Commonwealth Prime Ministers met again in September, nearly a year had elapsed since the UDI and no end to the rebel régime was yet in sight, in spite of the application of economic sanctions. Furthermore, the British Government were in the midst of negotiations with the rebel régime (in preparation for the *Tiger* talks) which they had previously denied any intention of ever doing so long as that régime refused to 'return to legality'.

As the final communiqué shows, the conference was bitterly divided over the means to bring about the end of the rebellion. The division was revealed by recording the views of both camps in what was supposed to be an 'agreed communiqué'. The division was roughly along racial lines, with Britain supported mainly by the old white 'Dominions' of Australia and New Zealand, and on most occasions by Malta and Dr Banda's Malawi. Thus, the policies favoured by 'most Heads of Government', including the use of force, were those of the Afro-Asian-Caribbean bloc, while those of 'others' were held by Britain and its supporters.

The final British concession, which preserved the Commonwealth intact, was the three-month limit for negotiations with the rebel régime, after which, in the event of their failure, Britain would seek United Nations support for mandatory sanctions and revoke any independence proposals that did not ensure African majority rule. (A commentary on these conferences and that held in 1969 appears in the document following the communiqués.)

Two further conferences were held after the Conservative Party returned to power—in Singapore in January 1971 and in Ottawa in August 1973. Although the Rhodesian issue was raised on both occasions, no change in British policy resulted from the exchanges and the pressure from the Afro-Asian-Caribbean bloc was considerably lessened, either from resignation that it would be to no avail or from conviction that change could only be affected through other channels.

DOCUMENT 46. EXTRACTS FROM THE *Final Communiqués* OF THE COMMONWEALTH PRIME MINISTERS CONFERENCES: LAGOS, 12 JANUARY 1966 (CMND 2890); LONDON, 15 SEPTEMBER 1966 (CMND 3115)

The Prime Ministers reviewed and noted the measures taken by Commonwealth and other countries against the illegal régime. Some expressed concern that the steps taken so far had not resulted in its removal. They called on all countries which had not already done so to act in accordance with the recommendations of the Security Council Resolution of 20th November, 1965, making at the same time necessary arrangements to provide for the repercussions of such further measures on the economy of Zambia.

The Prime Ministers discussed the question of the use of military force in Rhodesia and it was accepted that its use could not be precluded if this proved necessary to restore law and order.

In this connection the Prime Ministers noted the statement by the British Prime Minister that on the expert advice available to him the cumulative effects of the economic and financial sanctions might well bring the rebellion to an end within a matter of weeks rather than months. While some Prime Ministers had misgivings in this regard, all expressed the hope that these measures would result in the overthrow of the illegal

THE WORLD OUTSIDE

régime in Southern Rhodesia within the period mentioned by the British Prime Minister. . . .

2. As at Lagos, in January of this year, the members of the Conference reaffirmed that the authority and responsibility for guiding Rhodesia to independence rested with Britain but they acknowledged that the problem was of wider concern to Africa, the Commonwealth and the world.

3. They reaffirmed the view expressed in the communiqué issued at the end of the Lagos Conference as follows:

> The Prime Ministers declared that any political system based on racial discrimination was intolerable. It diminished the freedom alike of those who imposed it and of those who suffered it. They considered that the imposition of discriminatory conditions of political, social, economic and educational nature upon the majority by any minority for the benefit of a privileged few was an outrageous violation of the fundamental principles of human rights. The goal of future progress in Rhodesia should be the establishment of a just society based on equality of opportunity to which all sections of the community could contribute their full potential and from which all could enjoy the benefits due to them without discrimination or unjust impediment. To this end several principles were affirmed. The first was the determination of all present that the rebellion must be brought to an end. All those detained for purely political reasons should be released. Political activities should be constitutional and free from intimidation from any quarter. Repressive and discriminatory laws should be repealed.

4. They further reaffirmed the statement made in their London Communiqué of 1965 and repeated in Lagos that 'the principle of one man, one vote was regarded as the very basis of democracy and this should be applied in Rhodesia'.

5. They remain unanimous on the objective that the rebellion in Rhodesia must be brought to an end speedily. In order to achieve this objective, most of the Heads of Government expressed their firm opinion that force was the only sure means of bringing down the illegal régime in Rhodesia. Others, however, shared the British Government's objections to the use of

force to impose a constitutional settlement, while agreeing that it was not ruled out where necessary to restore law and order.

6. Most Heads of Government urged that Britain should make a categorical declaration that independence would not be granted before majority rule is established on the basis of universal adult suffrage and that this declaration should not be conditional on whether the illegal régime agreed to surrender or not. They further urged that Britain should refuse to resume discussions or to negotiate with the illegal régime.

7. The British Prime Minister stated that the British Government would not recommend to the British Parliament any constitutional settlement which did not conform with the six principles; that they attached particular importance to the fifth principle, namely that any settlement must be, and be seen to be, acceptable to the people of Rhodesia as a whole; that they regarded it as implicit in this fifth principle that the test of acceptability must enable the people of Rhodesia as a whole to indicate whether or not they were prepared to accept any settlement which provided for the grant of independence before majority rule was achieved; and that there would be no independence before majority rule if the people of Rhodesia as a whole were shown to be opposed to it.

8. The Conference noted the following decisions of the British Government:

(a) After the illegal régime is ended a legal government will be appointed by the Governor and will constitute a broadly based representative administration. During this interim period the armed forces and police will be responsible to the Governor. Those individuals who are detained or restricted on political grounds will be released and normal political activities will be permitted provided that they are conducted peacefully and democratically without intimidation from any quarter;

(b) The British Government will negotiate, with this interim administration, a constitutional settlement directed to achieving the objective of majority rule, on the basis of the six principles;

(c) This constitutional settlement will be submitted for acceptance to the people of Rhodesia as a whole by appropriate democratic means;

(d) The British Parliament and Government must be satisfied that this test of opinion is fair and free and would be acceptable to the general world community;

(e) The British Government will not consent to independence before majority rule unless the people of Rhodesia as a whole are shown to be in favour of it.

9. Most Heads of Government made it clear that in their view political leaders and others detained should be immediately and unconditionally released before an interim representative Government was formed, in which they should be adequately represented. They further expressed the view that any ascertainment of the wishes of the people of Rhodesia as a whole should be by a Referendum based on Universal Adult Suffrage, i.e., one man, one vote.

10. The Heads of Government also noted that the British Government proposed immediately to communicate its intentions as indicated above through the Governor to all sections of opinion in Rhodesia and to inform the illegal régime there that if they are not prepared to take the initial and indispensable steps whereby the rebellion is brought to an end and executive authority is vested in the Governor, the following related consequences will ensue:

(a) The British Government will withdraw all previous proposals for a constitutional settlement which have been made; in particular they will not thereafter be prepared to submit to the British Parliament any settlement which involves independence before majority rule.

(b) Given the full support of Commonwealth representatives at the United Nations, the British Government will be prepared to join in sponsoring in the Security Council of the United Nations before the end of this year a resolution providing for effective and selective mandatory economic sanctions against Rhodesia. . . .

15. The Heads of Government have had one overriding purpose in their consideration of the Rhodesian situation; a consideration which has now extended over four meetings of Commonwealth Prime Ministers. That purpose is to end the perpetuation of power in that country in the hands of a minority with only ineffective and inadequate guarantees of the political rights of the majority. Such a situation must be replaced by an arrangement based on a multi-racial society in which human

and political rights will be vested in all the people without discrimination and in accordance with the true principles of democracy.

THE COMMONWEALTH VIEW

A former lecturer at the University of Rhodesia examines the significance of the Rhodesian issue for the future role of the Commonwealth.

DOCUMENT 47. 'THE IMPACT OF THE RHODESIAN CRISIS ON THE COMMONWEALTH' BY JAMES BARBER (FROM *Journal of Commonwealth Political Studies*, VOL. VII, NO. 2, JULY 1969)

Open Division Within the Commonwealth

A loose, consensus-minded Commonwealth was well suited to Britain's ambitions to use the organisation as a projector for her world role. Instinctively British Governments have sought as wide a consensus as possible, and this has been true even over Rhodesia. Although insisting that Rhodesia is a colonial question, for which they must bear final responsibility, successive British Governments have agreed to discuss the problem at Commonwealth meetings. They agreed because they hoped to achieve support for their policies, and because they feared that a refusal to discuss the problem would itself create a serious division. Furthermore, the British saw that a united Commonwealth could be a source of pressure on the Rhodesian Government. On several occasions before UDI the British Government suggested to the disbelieving Rhodesians that a Commonwealth delegation might be able to mediate in the constitutional dispute. And both before and since UDI the British have told the Rhodesians that they do not have a free hand in reaching a settlement; that Commonwealth as well as British opinion had to be satisfied. An example of this came as early as December 1963, when Mr Duncan Sandys wrote to Mr Winston Field that Britain could not afford to wreck the Commonwealth over Rhodesia. A much later example came when Mr Wilson met Mr Smith aboard *Tiger*. Mr Wilson is reported to have said 'It has only been with the greatest difficulty that the British Government had resisted at the September Commonwealth

Prime Ministers' Meeting demands for immediate action against the Rhodesian régime and had achieved a further three months' respite in which to attempt a negotiated settlement; they could not hope to obtain any further extension of time'.

Until the Rhodesian crisis a major internal conflict was avoided.

As first the prospect and then the certainty of a deep division became apparent doubts grew about the Commonwealth's ability to survive. The Commonwealth had identified Rhodesia as a problem of special importance to itself well before UDI. This was because Rhodesia had claims to future membership (indeed Rhodesian Prime Ministers had previously attended Commonwealth Conferences) and, even more significantly, because it presented a major problem of race relations within the Commonwealth itself. As early as 1964 Mr Lester Pearson revealed his fears when he said: 'If we can solve the Rhodesian problem, the Commonwealth will grow greater still in world importance. If we cannot, the the future of the Commonwealth is dim indeed'.

The danger of Commonwealth disintegration grew with UDI and reached a climax during 1966 when it became clear that Mr Wilson's policy was not going to bring a quick end to the rebellion. A unique situation arose in which a Commonwealth member, Tanzania, broke off diplomatic relations with Britain, although she remained in the Commonwealth. The two Commonwealth Conferences of 1966 saw other unique features stemming directly from the Rhodesian crisis.

The Lagos Conference in January 1966 was the first Prime Ministers' Conference to be held outside London, and it was also the first organised by the newly formed Commonwealth Secretariat. Both these points indicated Britain's declining role, but it was possible to draw a further inference. This was that Mr Wilson was being summoned to Africa to answer charges against his handling of an issue on which all black Africans felt incensed. There was no other item on the agenda—just Rhodesia. Mr Wilson was to be grilled. Certainly this is how Sir Robert Menzies saw it. In explaining why Australia refused to send a representative to the Conference, he said: 'My Government has consistently opposed the giving of any Commonwealth orders to Britain as to how she should exercise that authority and discharge that responsibility [i.e. for Rhodesia]. To have her, in effect, attacked and threatened at a special conference would be a grave departure from proper practice in a Commonwealth gathering'. Australia's refusal to send a representative (an observer was sent) was symptomatic of the division which was now openly exposed. Australia's refusal was based upon opposition to the Commonwealth taking upon itself the right to dictate to Britain. At the other end of the scale, Tanzania refused to attend because she said that Britain was not prepared to accept majority Commonwealth opinion. Even with these notable absentees the Lagos conference failed to reach agreement about the means to bring down Mr Smith, and so the communiqué simply recorded a deep division.

The division at Lagos was formalised at the London Conference in September. For the first time a distinct caucus emerged within the Commonwealth. This has as its core most of the African members, who were also able to attract to their point of view a majority of the other members. The caucus members, who aimed at pressuring Britain into a commitment to no independence before majority rule in Rhodesia, and to using force to fulfil the commitment, met separately to discuss their tactics and lines of argument, and while they did this they were prepared to keep the other members waiting for hours, if need be. The other members had no choice but to wait, for to go on without a substantial number of their colleagues would have finished the Commonwealth there and then. This was a situation outside any previous Commonwealth experience.

Although the caucus was in part distinguished by its insistence that Britain should use military force in Rhodesia, the members claimed that this militancy was based upon an ideal of racial equality, I shall therefore call them the 'militant-idealists'. Against their demands the British stressed the difficulties and dangers of using force, and in any case claimed that sanctions would in time achieve the desired end. The main British emphasis was upon what *could* be done while the 'militant-idealists' stressed what *should* be done. A few Commonwealth members, Australia, Malawi, Malta, and New Zealand—supported Britain, and although they were never organised into a precise group I shall identify them as the 'pragmatists'. There were some members, like Canada and

Malaysia, who attempted to mediate between the two groups, but the position became so polarised that near the end of the conference every member became identified with one or other of the groups. . . .

At the 1966 Conferences, Britain was vulnerable for several reasons. First, in her continued commitment to the Commonwealth she aimed at reaching some agreement with her colleagues even if on a limited scale, and so she was open to pressure. Secondly, Mr Wilson in his handling of the crisis had himself increased the tension and drama, and then had become the victim of his over-confident predictions. It was Mr Wilson who, at the United Nations in December 1965, quoted Abraham Lincoln to say that while angels could not save him if he were wrong, 'if the end brings me out all right, what is said against me now won't amount to anything'. And then, of course, at Lagos he made his famous 'weeks and not months' prediction. Finally, during 1966 the Rhodesian crisis was still a fresh, live, emotional issue. It was difficult in such a climate to defend a 'pragmatic' policy against the strong moral, idealist tone of the 'militant-idealists'.

With Mr Wilson on the defensive, the pressure from the 'militant-idealists' may well have influenced British policy. It may have persuaded Britain to follow a tougher sanctions policy, to take the Rhodesian question to the United Nations and temporarily to toughen the terms which were offered to Mr Smith, for example by promising a period of direct British administration. Another achievement of the group may be the establishment of the Commonwealth sanctions committee, serviced not by the British but by the Commonwealth Secretariat. Certainly President Obote claimed that it was Commonwealth pressure which had forced Britain to go to the United Nations and to ask for such severe sanctions. Although these successes may be attributed to the 'militant-idealists', and although they had succeeded in placing Britain in the dock at the Conferences, these successes fell far short of their aims. From the beginning there was a serious weakness in their position. Neither individually nor as a group did they feel they had sufficient strength to act directly against Rhodesia. The limit of their self-conceived strength was to organise international pressure—through the United Nations, the Organisation of African Unity, and through the Commonwealth—to make Britain act. The weakness of the position is obvious. While they have been able to humiliate Britain and thereby seriously dent 'the myth of sophistication', their pressure has only been one of a range of pressures shaping British policy. In the event it has not been the critical one.

Although the 'militant-idealists' had failed to dictate British policy, the clash over Rhodesia still left a divided Commonwealth. In the long period between Conferences, September 1966 to January 1969, the uncertainty about the Commonwealth's future persisted. As the leaders assembled for the 1969 Conference the Commonwealth's ability to survive the Rhodesian crisis was again brought into question. In fact, the problem of survival never arose, for the 'militant-idealist' group had disintegrated. There were no separate caucus meetings, no attempts to organise tactics, no common caucus policy. The old group was in such disarray that President Kaunda was the only leader still publicly calling for the use of force. Even President Nyerere, whose country had previously broken off diplomatic relations with Britain, now stressed the common objective of majority rule, rather than the division over how to achieve it. At the end of the Conference, the danger of disintegration had disappeared, at least for the present. The leaders went away praising the Commonwealth's strengths and usefulness, not bemoaning its inadequacies. Rhodesia had been an important item on the agenda but it had not dominated all else and, while there had been criticism of British policy, it was relatively mild.

How can such a change be explained? There are several possibilities. One line of argument could be to emphasise that the 'militant-idealists' never aimed at anything more than exerting pressure and that by 1969, while it was clear that their pressure had achieved some of its objectives, such as forcing Britain to take the issue to the United Nations, it was equally clear that no amount of additional pressure would induce Britain to use military force. Furthermore, so this argument could be developed, it was also clear by 1969 that Britain was much less vulnerable to Commonwealth pressures, because she had at last abandoned the pretence of searching for consensus on issues which were discussed at the Conferences. This, it may be suggested, was an inevitable development, but it was in fact Rhodesia which provided the final breaking point. Mr Wilson went to the 1969 Conference knowing that he could not convert his Commonwealth opponents and yet unwilling to compromise his own stand. He listened to the opinions of others, he accepted that a majority opposed the *Fearless* terms, yet at the end of the day he confirmed that British policy was unchanged, that Mr Smith still had an option on the *Fearless* terms. Consensus politics had been abandoned, and were seen to have been abandoned.

Another possible development from the emphasis upon 'pressure' would be to claim that the 'militant-idealists' had overplayed their hand in 1966. The rantings of Sir Albert Margai, the cutting insults of Mr Kapwepwe, the caucus's obsession with Rhodesia, and their behaviour towards the other members, had become counter-productive. Not only Britain but other non-African leaders were determined that they would never again subordinate their own views and interests as they had over Rhodesia. According to this argument, the 'militant-idealists' would themselves have realised the futility of another all-out onslaught. Added to this might be a growing realisation of the benefits of the Commonwealth and the fear that those benefits could be lost if they continued to pursue an intransigent policy on Rhodesia, a policy which, in any case, they now realised could not bring success.

Another explanation of the change could be that time had mellowed the first, fierce reactions—that men had learned to live with Mr Smith and his illegal independence as they had learned to live with Franco's Spain, a Europe divided between East and West, and a timeless war in Vietnam. With the initial heat out of the Rhodesian situation, the Commonwealth, so this explanation runs, was able to take a less emotional and longer term view of the crisis, and in doing this the 'pragmatists' and the 'militant-idealists' came closer together.

These arguments are persuasive and clearly may help to explain the change, but I do not believe that they offer the full explanation. Even accepting these arguments, there would still have been a bitter and perhaps fatal conflict in the Commonwealth if the 'militant-idealists' had not collapsed from weakness in themselves. Since the Rhodesian UDI many African

Commonwealth states have revealed serious and sometimes tragic internal weaknesses. . . .

In dealing with the Rhodesian crisis, the 1969 Conference revealed characteristics which could be important for the Commonwealth's future. Although it demonstrated that the Commonwealth was able to absorb an open division on a major issue, it was only able to do this by revealing that it was subject to the same limitations as other international organisations. These limitations are tied to the claim of sovereignty by each member. Before the Rhodesian crisis Britain, in her own case, had often been prepared to mask this fact because of the advantage to her of appearing to follow consensus policies on Commonwealth issues. This has broken down entirely over Rhodesia. Military action against Rhodesia was not taken because Britain, the only country capable of taking this action, refused to subordinate her policy to the majority will of the Commonwealth.

THE ORGANISATION OF AFRICAN UNITY

The OAU, like the Commonwealth and the United Nations, has repeatedly expressed its deep concern for the situation in Rhodesia arising out of the minority régime's illegal declaration of independence. This concern has been recorded in a number of resolutions, adopted by the conferences of the Council of Ministers and Heads of State of the independent African countries comprising its membership. The liberation of southern Africa has been one of the main objectives of the Organisation since its foundation in May 1963. For this purpose it has established an African Liberation Committee, based in Dar-es-Salaam (Tanzania), responsible for the direction and finance of African liberation movements recognised by the Organisation.

The resolution adopted by the conference at Rabat (Morocco) in 1972, like those of the previous years, and also like those of the United Nations, called upon Britain, as the 'legal' administering Power, to withhold independence from the illegal minority régime and to intervene to ensure that power was effectively transferred to the people of Zimbabwe (Rhodesia) on the basis of one man, one vote. Since these demands were dependent for their fulfilment upon the military

258

intervention of Britain, they were not likely to be implemented by a Government which had repeatedly renounced the use of force. The OAU resolution of 1972, more realistically perhaps, like the memorandum submitted to the conference by the Tanzania President, also contains a strong case for the implementation of the mandatory sanctions programme prescribed by the United Nations Security Council (see next document).

DOCUMENT 48A. RESOLUTION ON ZIMBABWE ADOPTED BY THE ORGANISATION OF AFRICAN UNITY, COUNCIL OF MINISTERS, NINETEENTH ORDINARY SESSION, RABAT (MOROCCO), 5–12 JUNE 1972 (FROM GENERAL SECRETARIAT OF THE ORGANISATION OF AFRICAN UNITY, ADDIS ABABA, 1972)

Reaffirming that any attempt to negotiate the future of Zimbabwe with the illegal régime on the basis of independence before majority rule would be in contravention of the inalienable rights of the people of that territory and contrary to the provisions of the UN Charter and of the General Assembly Resolution 1514 (XV); Recognizing the importance of the continued imposition of political, diplomatic, economic and social sanctions against the illegal Smith régime until that illegal minority racist régime is brought to an end;
1. Pledges to increase its assistance to the people of Zimbabwe in their armed struggle for self-determination and independence;
2. Reaffirms support for the principle that there should be no independence before majority rule in Zimbabwe;
3. Calls upon the Government of the United Kingdom not to transfer or accord, under any circumstances, to the illegal régime any of the powers or attributes of sovereignty, and urges it to promote the country's attainment of independence by a democratic system of government in accordance with the aspirations of the majority of the population;
4. Urges the United Kingdom Government, as administering authority, to convene as soon as possible a national constitutional conference in which the genuine political representatives of the people of Zimbabwe would be able to work out a settlement relating to the future of the territory for subsequent endorsement by the people under free and democratic processes;

259

5. Calls upon the United Kingdom Government to create the conditions necessary to permit the free expression of the right to self-determination, including;

(a) the release of all political prisoners, detainees and restrictees;

(b) the repeal of all repressive discriminatory legislation;

(c) the removal of all restrictions on political activity and the establishment of full democratic freedom and equality of political rights;

6. Further calls on the United Kingdom Government to ensure that in any exercise to ascertain the wishes of the people of Zimbabwe as to their political future, the procedure to be followed will be in accordance with the principle of universal adult suffrage and by secret referendum on the basis of one man, one vote without regard to race, colour or to educational, property or income considerations;

7. Condemns the United Kingdom Government for its failure to take effective measures to bring to an end the illegal régime in Zimbabwe;

8. Decides to give full support and co-operation to the United Nations in all measures designed to enforce strictly the mandatory sanctions imposed by the Security Council in accordance with the obligations assumed by member-States under Article 25 of the Charter of the United Nations;

9. Expresses full agreement with the recommendations and the suggestions contained in the Special Report of the Committee established in pursuance of Security Council Resolution 253 (1968) for improving the effectiveness of the machinery of sanctions;

10. Further expresses full agreement with the four proposals submitted by the delegations of Guinea, Somalia and Sudan, in their capacity as members of the Security Council. . . .

11. Condemns the United States Government for its continued importation of chrome ore from Zimbabwe in open contravention of Security Council resolutions 253 (1968), 277 (1970) and 314 (1972) and contrary to the specific obligations assumed by the United States under Article 25 of the United Nations Charter;

12. Expresses grave concern about the detrimental consequential development which acts of this nature could have on the

effectiveness and, in the wider sense, on the authority of the Security Council;

13. Calls upon the Government of the United States to desist from further violations of sanctions, and to observe faithfully and without exception the provisions of Security Council resolutions on this question.

DOCUMENT 48B. MEMORANDUM TO THE OAU HEADS OF STATE MEETING AT RABAT FROM PRESIDENT NYERERE OF TANZANIA, 3 JUNE 1972 (EXTRACTS FROM *Africa Contemporary Record*, 1972/3)

The British Government has informed Commonwealth Governments that it accepts the conclusion of the Pearce Commission that the settlement Proposals are not acceptable to the people of Rhodesia as a whole; the British Government also said that it will shape its future policy in the light of this conclusion. But obviously this does not solve the Rhodesian issue. It merely means that the Smith régime continues in power in Rhodesia; that it continues to be regarded as illegal, to be without international recognition, and that sanctions against it continue.

But it would not be true to say that the situation has therefore returned to what it was previously. The power situation is the same; but the effect of the Commissioners' visit to Rhodesia, the African reaction to that visit, and the Report itself, can never be undone. It is the implications of these things which have to be considered in answering the question 'What now?'

If no further external action is taken, the immediate result of the African 'no' is likely to be an intensification of oppression within Rhodesia, further development of the close link-up which now exists between South Africa and the Rhodesian authorities, and even more rapid steps towards apartheid in the colony itself. All these trends were present before the so-called agreement between Ian Smith and Sir Alec Douglas-Home. They would not have been precluded by the settlement if this had been accepted by the Africans; indeed they would have taken place in a more favourable international climate. But the real point is that the Pearce Commission Report gives a new opportunity for international action against the régime, as it shows the real meaning of the régime. It therefore gives a new, though faint, possibility of avoiding widespread violence in Rhodesia.

The purpose of sanctions, of refusing international recognition to the Smith régime, and of other forms of pressure, is to prepare the ground for a real settlement in Rhodesia—that is, one which leads, by peaceful means or with the minimum of violence, towards independence on the basis of majority rule. The immediate objective is therefore negotiations between representatives of the African majority of Rhodesia; of the White minority which is now in power; and of either the British Government which is legally responsible for the situation in that colony, or some other body such as the United Nations. The purpose of such negotiations must be, and must be understood to be, the next step towards majority rule. The question of independence for Rhodesia comes only after that majority rule has been obtained.

The prime responsibility for the future freedom of Rhodesia lies with the people of Rhodesia. But the peoples and Governments of free African States have an inescapable duty to assist them. There are six things which African States must do as a minimum:

(a) They must themselves participate in, and actively enforce, the United Nations Mandatory Sanctions, and give maximum assistance to those neighbours of Rhodesia who have paid, and are still paying, most heavily for the sanctions policy.

(b) They must exert the maximum possible pressure to ensure that Governments of other countries enforce sanctions; and each African State should concentrate its efforts on that foreign power with which it has special links.

(c) They must discriminate against those firms and businesses which are breaking sanctions or are otherwise assisting the economy of Rhodesia, so that such organisations are forced to make a choice in their trading and other activities.

(d) They must work in the United Nations to make international enforcement procedures more effective, particularly in relation to giving publicity about sanction-breaking, and must work for an agreement to seize without compensation goods exported from Rhodesia, even if these are travelling under false documents.

(e) They must seek to get sanctions extended into the communications field and other areas still exempted.

(f) They must step up their support for the Liberation Movements of Southern Africa, including those of Rhodesia.

Certainly the prospects for the immediate future in Rhodesia are not good; but in the long run there is reason for optimism. For the Africans of Rhodesia are now more politically conscious than ever before, and have made clear their determination and ability to endure suffering and still seize every opportunity to make their voice heard. The people of Rhodesia, under the leadership of the ANC, or whatever replaces this if the ANC is banned, deserve Africa's support. They must receive it.

*

The limitations and the achievements of the OAU in dealing with the Rhodesian issue are analysed by Aniruhda Gupta of the Indian School of International Studies.

DOCUMENT 49. 'THE RHODESIAN CRISIS AND THE ORGANISATION OF AFRICAN UNITY', BY ANIRUDHA GUPTA (FROM *International Studies*, VOL. 9, NO. 1, JULY 1967)

In Rhodesia the Organisation of African Unity (OAU) faces its most critical test. Its vacillating stand on that issue and disunity in the ranks of its members have brought it increasingly under criticism. In the Western Press generally there is criticism of the 'immature' conduct of the OAU as demonstrated by its hasty decision to break off relations with Britain and by the use of 'intemperate' language by its members in the United Nations and other international forums. Even in Africa there seems to be widespread disillusionment. . . .

Analysts have made several attempts to find a rationale for the African behaviour. They have pointed out the extreme economic and military vulnerability of African states which has made it difficult for them to intervene actively in Rhodesia. The difference in the approaches of the 'radical' and 'moderate' groups of states is pointed out to be another contributory factor for the OAU's weakness. Some think that the comparative immaturity of Africans in diplomacy is the cause of their impatient and rather 'immature' behaviour, and others explain that African political postures 'express a hope rather than a reality, a momentary assertion of an idealism rather than a firm commitment'. Perhaps all these provide plausible explanations, but it would be worth while to suggest another line of investigation: the series of *coups d'état* which started off in different parts of Africa, beginning with General Mobutu's seizure of power in the Congo a fortnight after the Unilateral Declaration of Independence (UDI), posed a bigger threat to independent Africa than the Rhodesian crisis. . . . The immediate result of these developments was that African Governments became more involved in their domestic problems than in Rhodesia, and this, in effect, weakened their pan-African commitments. . . .

Limits and Scope of the OAU

Though the 'emancipation' of all dependent territories was listed as an aim of the OAU, it does not seem that any serious thought was given to the realization of this aim. In point of fact, this issue seriously divided the OAU members. Thus the Liberation Committee set up in Dar-es-Salaam suffered from the beginning from lack of co-operation. In the second conference of the heads of states in Cairo (21–23 July 1964), the Committee's functions featured prominently when Nyerere clashed with Nkrumah and accused him roundly of not helping the liberation movements. The dwindling finances of the Committee hampered its activities, and when, in the Addis Ababa conference (November 1966), a move was made to raise funds for it, even some members demanded the scrapping of the Committee itself. In protest, Nyerere walked out of the conference, saying that 'African countries will have to make up their minds whether they will give priority to Africa or to their associations with their former rulers'. This lack of unanimity among members about the Liberation Committee's work had a direct bearing on the nationalist movement in Rhodesia. The year in which the OAU was founded, the nationalist movement in Rhodesia got divided into two rival groups, Zimbabwe African People's Union (ZAPU) and Zimbabwe African National Union (ZANU), and even though the ZAPU received support from the majority in the OAU, some members gave moral and financial support to the ZANU also. Apart from worsening the relations between the two groups, this accounted for the failure of the OAU to give concrete support to the Rhodesian nationalists.

On the Rhodesian issue itself, the OAU adopted an ambivalent attitude. In the first Addis Ababa summit conference, member nations pledged their 'effective and political support' to the nationalists in case the European minority seized power in Rhodesia. It would appear, however, that no concrete programme was devised to give substance to the pledge. Indeed, if one reviews the conduct of the OAU in regard to Rhodesia until the time of the UDI, one gains the impression that the OAU was concerned more with *preventing* the Rhodesian crisis from exploding than with working out a plan of action in the event of an explosion. It is for this reason that the OAU concentrated its activities on two items, i.e. (1) calling upon Britain to prevent the UDI, and (2) raising the Rhodesian question in the United Nations and in Commonwealth meetings to focus world attention on the happenings in Rhodesia. Quite naturally, this course of action frequently brought African states into clash with the United Kingdom even though they generally conceded that the latter was ultimately responsible for Rhodesian affairs. This dichotomy in their attitude prevented them from taking a long-term view of the crisis. Instead, their occasional outburst of annoyance notwithstanding, they continued to believe that Britain would somehow control the Whites in Rhodesia. The only time when they seem to have awoken to the full significance of the UDI danger was when, in the Accra summit conference of October 1965, they passed a resolution calling upon Britain to abrogate the 1961 Constitution and hold a constitutional conference of representatives of the whole people of Rhodesia. The importance of the conference lay in the fact that, for the first time, members of the OAU agreed that they would use all possible means, *including force*, against an illegally constituted régime in Rhodesia. They also prepared a plan of action in case Britain granted negotiated independence to a minority régime in Rhodesia. The plan was (1) to refuse recognition to such a government; (2) to recognize a government-in-exile; (3) to hold an emergency meeting of the OAU council of ministers with a view to involving the United

Nations more directly in Rhodesia; (4) to reconsider relations with Britain; and (5) to treat the White minority government in Rhodesia on the same footing as South Africa. The programme, however, did not signify that the OAU was considering any move to wrest the initiative from British hands. On the contrary, despite the Accra resolution, which many statesmen later tried to forget, the hope persisted that Britain would succeed in solving the crisis. When, therefore, on 11 November 1965, the UDI came, the Africans were completely taken by surprise. The general mood in Africa was that Britain had finally let them down. This explains, also, why Africans expressed their anger more loudly against Britain than against Smith's rebellious régime.

Significance of the UDI

Had not the Africans kept their faith in Britain so long, they would not have found themselves so unprepared at the time of the UDI. Their unpreparedness forced them to adopt several contradictory and vacillating attitudes. In this context, the OAU's hasty decision to break off relations with Britain and its failure to implement the decision fully can be well understood. In fact, some members later argued that in view of the lack of unanimity among African states, it would not be advisable to take the decision seriously.

The contradiction in the African attitude became more marked when on the one hand they accepted British initiative on Rhodesia and on the other insisted that the policy of sanctions had proved ineffective. The situation gets more complicated when one notes the divergence of views between the British and African Governments on the objective of sanctions. Whereas the British attitude to sanctions is not yet clear, it can be argued that it is not Britain's objective to bring immediate majority rule in Rhodesia, but to provide only a basis for constitutional talks to bring the crisis to a peaceful settlement. The African Governments, on the other hand, maintain that the basic issue in Rhodesia is that of securing majority rule as demanded by them in the various resolutions of the OAU. Yet it does not seem that they have themselves become aware of the total import of this divergence of views between them and Britain.

Again, as the sanction measures proceeded, the OAU failed to evolve a comprehensive strategy in support of countries like Malawi and Zambia, which were as likely to feel the pinch of the economic warfare against Rhodesia as the latter itself. It was not until March 1966 that the OAU considered it necessary to establish a Zambia Solidarity Committee comprising Tanzania, Kenya, Ethiopia, the Sudan, and the UAR, with a view to providing help to Zambia. The functions of the Committee are not very clear, and this uncertainty about how far Zambia can depend on the support of the OAU has made it adopt a cautious attitude towards both the OAU and the sanctions. [But the closure of the border between Zambia and Rhodesia by the Rhodesian Front Government in 1973 has altered this situation.]

Finally, the Defence Committee, which the OAU hastily set up in November 1965 to study and report on the Rhodesian situation, failed to show any concrete result owing mainly to the lack of understanding about its scope and purpose.

By pointing out these shortcomings it is not suggested that African states and the OAU have failed completely in Rhodesia. That would be oversimplifying the issue. In order to assess the African role one should find out the factors which govern and restrict African actions in this regard. It is worth while to note that most African states achieved their independence from colonial rule by making use of two familiar tactics, i.e. (1) building political agitation at home to back the nationalist demand, and (2) using various international forums to bring pressure on the imperial Governments through external agencies. Besides, most African states obtained their independence from colonial rule more or less by constitutional means. It is mainly this framework of past experience that governs and restricts today African actions in regard to Rhodesia. Despite their impatience, they are more than anxious to settle the crisis by constitutional means. This fact explains why in spite of the attempts made by certain members of the OAU, the majority have shown reluctance to use force in Rhodesia. Thus, in January 1966, when Nkrumah's Government circulated a statement saying that the United Kingdom had lost control in Rhodesia and that the OAU was the proper organization to deal with the situation, very few African Governments took serious note of it. They still continued to believe that the tactics which they had once used against colonial Powers would prove effective in Rhodesia also. What they failed to take into account was the fact that in Rhodesia they were not dealing with an imperial Government, but an armed and defiant racial minority, which had staked everything in order to retain political power. Perhaps Africans themselves recognize today that violence is the only means to suppress the Rhodesian rebellion, but they are unwilling to use it. . . .

OAU's Measure of Success

In assessing the role of the OAU in respect of the Rhodesian crisis, its objectives and limitations have to be kept in view. In the first place, the OAU was founded to provide a recognized code of behavior to regulate inter-state relations of the newly independent nations. As a result, both African unity and the liberation of dependent territories became only secondary goals. This is why despite the possibility of the UDI the OAU failed to evolve any clear-cut programme. Secondly, Africans believed far too long that Britain would be able to avoid the crisis, which explains their inability to cope with the situation when the UDI took place. Thirdly, they applied in Rhodesia the same tactics which had brought them ready dividends in an earlier era. So long as these tactics help African Governments to gain some 'concessions' from Britain or to preserve their pan-African image, their joint diplomacy may continue to play a certain role. In this respect, the OAU has, indeed, been able to build a consensus in Africa on the Rhodesian peril. Without the summit conferences and the meetings of the OAU council of ministers, it would perhaps have been difficult for African Governments to co-ordinate their policies in regard to Rhodesia. It is true that the OAU has passed several resolutions which have proved to be either contradictory or ineffective, but at present it is the only organization that can channelize the energies of different states towards a single goal. It is again at various OAU meetings that member states have been able to chart a course of action which, despite its numerous short-comings, has finally induced Britain to invoke Chapter Seven of the UN Charter for mandatory sanctions against Rhodesia.

The success of the sanctions depends mainly on the role of the Governments of South Africa and Portugal in the current dispute; but it also depends on how far the OAU succeeds in boosting the morale of weaker and smaller members during the protracted economic warfare. In the coming days all Africa to the north of the Zambesi will face greater difficulties and tensions resulting from the doings of the Salisbury régime. It is, perhaps, as well that they should tackle such problems jointly, under the aegis of the OAU, rather than individually.

UNITED NATIONS EFFORTS

A background to the UN sanctions measures, evidence of sanctions evasion and recommendations for combating it are contained in the following report, which was submitted to the Secretariat of the UN in 1972.

DOCUMENT 50. *Rhodesia: Token Sanctions or Total Economic Warfare* BY GUY ARNOLD AND ALAN BALDWIN (THE AFRICA BUREAU, SEPTEMBER 1972)

The imposition of economic sanctions against Rhodesia took place in three phases following UDI in November 1965. The first phase covered the period from UDI to the first talks between the British Prime Minister, Harold Wilson, and Ian Smith on board HMS *Tiger* in December 1966. It consisted of unilateral action by Britain in stopping most trade, blocking funds and forbidding currency transfers; and most members of the UN co-operated in refusing recognition of the régime, banning arms and certain other supplies and preventing oil reaching Beira (Mozambique).

Following the rejection of the British *Tiger* proposals by Salisbury, Britain agreed to UN mandatory sanctions to cover the major imports into Rhodesia and her main exports including asbestos, chrome, tobacco, sugar and meat. Since that time members of the UN have been bound according to the terms of the Charter to uphold sanctions.

The third phase dates from May 1968 (following the illegal execution of three Rhodesians despite a reprieve by the Queen in March) when the UN passed Resolution 253, broadening the scope of mandatory sanctions and establishing the Sanctions

Committee of the Security Council to administer the implementation of the Resolution. Thereafter the only exceptions to the trade embargo were to be educational materials, medical supplies and news materials, money for certain pensions and other materials if considered necessary for humanitarian purposes—in certain circumstances these could include food.

There has been a good deal of confusion over the years as to what sanctions were meant to achieve. Once Britain had ruled out the use of force to crush the Rhodesian rebellion sanctions, for some, were seen as the non-violent alternative that would, in the words of the British Prime Minister, act in a matter of weeks rather than months to force the illegal régime to surrender the independence it had taken and return to legality. For others, especially African countries, they were regarded with deep suspicion as an excuse or pretence in lieu of stronger action; and for others again they were a gesture against racism but were not expected to work.

After four and a half years of full-scale Mandatory Sanctions following resolution 253 in May 1968 two things are clear. First, that sanctions have not worked in the sense of forcing the illegal régime to abandon its illegality and return to the *status quo ante* the rebellion. The Smith régime is still very much in control in Salisbury and there is every indication that it will continue in control indefinitely if sanctions are only maintained at their present level. Second, it is also clear that sanctions have achieved certain important results. Apart from their effects upon the Rhodesian economy they can be said to have achieved a number of more limited aims as follows:

(a) They have denied outright victory to the Smith régime.

(b) They have kept Rhodesia in a state of complete diplomatic isolation.

(c) They have forced the régime to go on struggling for economic survival at ever rising costs to itself.

(d) They have encouraged and strengthened internal opposition to the régime by demonstrating continuing world interest in its cause.

(e) They have maintained international concern over the Rhodesian issue.

(f) They have sustained the world view of the unacceptability of the régime.

At their present level of functioning, therefore, sanctions may be said to have achieved a stalemate: the world at large can express its disapproval of the illegal régime in Rhodesia without either exerting itself too much or taking action that will seriously cost it anything; and the Smith régime can continue in uneasy control of Rhodesia, sitting on a racial powder keg, and having to spend more and more of its energies and resources in devising new ways to evade sanctions and, in consequence of them, standing still economically.

To break this deadlock much tougher action is required on a whole series of fronts by the United Nations.

The failings of sanctions arise from several causes: the long period of time that elapsed between UDI and the imposition of full-scale Mandatory Sanctions in May 1968 which enabled the régime to make adjustments and arrangements for their evasions; the total refusal of South Africa and Portugal to apply sanctions both by trading 'as normal' with Rhodesia and also by acting as go-betweens to market her goods and import on her behalf; the lack of a general political will on the part of most members of the United Nations to make sanctions work effectively.

Sanctions have failed to prevent Rhodesia exporting many of its products; it now (1972) exports almost as much by value as in 1965 by finding outlets for its minerals in Europe, America and Japan through South Africa and Mozambique. It also manages to import many products such as cars, machinery and certain large-scale capital goods through South Africa. Sanctions have given a boost to secondary industry in Rhodesia by leaving it free to manufacture import substitutes without competition from outside. By preventing the international mining corporations from repatriating their profits sanctions have further provided that potential capital for development remained in the country.

Against the above must be set the positive economic effects of sanctions. The tobacco industry has been decimated and large state subsidies have been required to maintain those farmers who have not moved into other crops. The Beira patrol has prevented oil reaching Rhodesia by the cheapest route and although supplies have been re-routed through South Africa this has substantially increased the costs which have been spread across the Rhodesian economy. The most telling long-term effect of sanctions has been to cut Rhodesia off from the world's money markets and create a chronic shortage of foreign exchange. This manifests itself in three ways: first, the régime has had great difficulties in obtaining replacement stock for the railway which, in consequence, has become progressively less efficient and more costly to run with a reduced carrying capacity; second, some sectors of industry have been held back due to the difficulty in obtaining machinery; third, the régime has been brought (1972) to attempt urgent measures to develop export-oriented industries and export markets in order to earn foreign exchange.

A vicious circle exists for the régime which only the evasion or dismantling of sanctions can break; the one reason why Smith was prepared to talk with the British Foreign Secretary in November 1971 was the hope that sanctions could be brought to an end as the result of any agreement between Britain and Salisbury.

Much of the effect of sanctions lies in the less tangible area of politics and psychology, however. It is argued that sanctions have drawn the white minority closer together politically. They have also forced the régime to enter negotiations with Britain on three occasions. The white population feel themselves to be isolated and to some extent outcasts. Despite this, many Rhodesians can still travel abroad on foreign passports while the rest can travel to Malawi and South Africa. They still receive news material and television programmes from outside; individual sportsmen and teams, entertainers, and political sympathisers and many others visit Rhodesia; white immigration is increasing again to pre-UDI levels although emigration is high. . . .

Finally, it is important to realise that the white minority is so privileged and cushioned by the present structure of Rhodesian society that only total economic collapse will make them voluntarily surrender the position they now enjoy.

Sanctions Evasion

The overwhelming majority of sanctions breaking is achieved by trading through South Africa and Mozambique. Evasions may be with the knowledge of the other trading country and company or not. Papers may be those of a genuine trading company in South Africa or of a letterhead company which simply provides a South African front for a Rhodesian firm. There have also sprung up since 1965 a number of trading companies in Beira and Lourenço Marques whose *raison d'être* is to falsify papers covering Rhodesian goods or to re-route imports into Rhodesia.

Although information may be available to the United Nations that a cargo is of Rhodesian origin this cannot be proved merely from an examination of the papers. Thus, an importing country can insist that goods are of South African origin. Japan has imported Rhodesian chrome consistently since 1965 with such papers. Similarily, sanctions can be evaded with goods being imported by Rhodesia. The French, Italians and others have constantly claimed that car kits from Renault, Alfa Romeo, Datsun, etc. have been going to South Africa or Mozambique. It has been a relatively simple operation thereafter, since these companies have assembly plants in Southern Africa, for the cars subsequently to find their way into Rhodesia.

Several countries have been in open breach of the comprehensive sanctions imposed by the United Nations in 1968. West Germany, whilst agreeing to abide by the United Nations resolution although not a member, has allowed trade under 'long term' contracts even though many such contracts were signed at the time of the imposition of sanctions. Switzerland, also a non-member, whilst accepting sanctions in principle, decided merely to restrict trade with Rhodesia to the level of the three years preceding UDI. Although her actual trade with Rhodesia is small, Swiss banks have performed an important function for the rebels in arranging foreign exchange transfers: many white Rhodesians use and maintain bank accounts in Switzerland. Australia has exported wheat to Rhodesia, justifying this under the humanitarian clause in Resolution 253, even though the argument was rejected by the United Nations since Rhodesia produces a surplus of maize and the wheat imports allowed farmers to diversify into other crops. Japan has consistently turned a blind eye to the many cases of suspected violations of sanctions which the United Nations has requested the Japanese Government to investigate.

Botswana, Malawi and Zambia have maintained some trade with Rhodesia though the geographical position of these countries and their strong economic connections with Rhodesia through the former Central African Federation and up to UDI caused the United Nations to make exemptions in their cases. Zambia and Botswana have made strenuous efforts to eliminate their trade with Rhodesia and the former now imports only coke and a few consumer goods. Other Zambian links with Rhodesia—passenger rail traffic, the joint Kariba power supplies, coal, migrant workers—have been severed. Malawi, while still trading with and providing some valuable outlets for Rhodesia such as air traffic, holidays and 'international sport', has also cut down on the re-exporting of Rhodesian goods which it did for some years after UDI. Other African countries with no previous strong ties with Rhodesia have subsequently traded with her: Gabon has imported Rhodesian meat for several years and Zaire has imported Rhodesian shirts and cigarettes.

Much evasion of sanctions, however, is achieved through the sophisticated operations of international commerce, very often taking great care not to contravene the strict letter of the law.

*

The following Security Council Resolution (333, 1973) was adopted by twelve votes to nil, with Britain, the USA and France abstaining, after Britain had vetoed (with the USA) an alternative resolution calling for the limitation of imports from South Africa and the Portuguese territories to 1965 (pre-UDI) levels; for denying landing rights to the airlines of countries granting such rights to Rhodesia; and for extending the British blockade of Beira to the Mozambique port of Lourenço Marques. This was the ninth British veto of a Security Council resolution on Rhodesia; the others having been cast mainly to oppose the use of force and the extension of sanctions to South Africa and Portugal.

DOCUMENT 51. UNITED NATIONS SECURITY COUNCIL, *Official Records* (27TH YEAR, 1716TH MEETING, 22 MAY 1973)

The Security Council,

Recalling its resolutions 320 (1972) and 328 (1973),

Noting that measures so far instituted by the Security Council and the General Assembly have not brought to an end the illegal régime in Southern Rhodesia,

Reiterating its grave concern that some States, contrary to Security Council resolutions 232 (1966), 253 (1968) and 277 (1970) and to their obligations under Article 25 of the Charter of the United Nations, have failed to prevent trade with the illegal régime of Southern Rhodesia,

Condemning the persistent refusal of South Africa and Portugal to co-operate with the United Nations in the effective observance and implementation of sanctions against Southern Rhodesia (Zimbabwe) in clear violation of the United Nations Charter,

Having considered the second special report of the Committee established in pursuance of resolution 253 (1968) [Security Council Sanctions Committee],

Taking note of the letter dated 27 April from the Chairman of the Special Committee on the Situation with regard to the Implementation of the Declaration on the Granting of Independence to Colonial Countries and Peoples,

1. *Approves* the recommendations and suggestions contained in paragraphs 10 to 22 of the second special report of the Committee established in pursuance of resolution 253 (1968);

2. *Requests* the Committee, as well as all Governments, and the Secretary-General as appropriate, to take urgent action to implement the recommendations and suggestions referred to above;

3. *Requests* States with legislation permitting importation of minerals and other products from Southern Rhodesia to repeal it immediately;

4. *Calls upon* States to enact and enforce immediately legislation providing for imposition of severe penalties on persons natural or juridical that evade or commit breach of sanctions by:

(a) Importing any goods from Southern Rhodesia;

(b) Exporting any goods to Southern Rhodesia;

(c) Providing any facilities for transport of goods to and from Southern Rhodesia;

(d) Conducting or facilitating any transaction or trade that may enable Southern Rhodesia to obtain from or send to any country any goods or services;

(e) Continuing to deal with clients in South Africa, Angola, Mozambique, Guinea (Bissau) and Namibia after it has become known that the clients are re-exporting the goods or components thereof to Southern Rhodesia, or that goods received from such clients are of Southern Rhodesian origin;

5. *Requests* States, in the event of their trading with South Africa and Portugal, to provide that purchase contracts with those countries should clearly stipulate in a manner legally enforceable, prohibition of dealing in goods of Southern Rhodesian origin; likewise, sales contracts with these countries should include a prohibition of resale or re-export of goods to Southern Rhodesia;

6. *Calls upon* States to pass legislation forbidding insurance companies under their jurisdiction from covering air flights into and out of Southern Rhodesia and individuals or air cargo carried on them;

7. *Calls upon* States to undertake appropriate legislative measures to ensure that all valid marine insurance contracts contain specific provisions that no goods of Southern Rhodesian origin or destined to Southern Rhodesia shall be covered by such contracts;

8. *Calls upon* States to inform the Committee of the Security Council on their present sources of supply and quantities of chrome, asbestos, nickel, pig iron, tobacco, meat and sugar, together with the quantities of these goods they obtained from Southern Rhodesia before the application of sanctions.

PART X

The Liberation Movement:
'Terrorists' or 'Freedom Fighters'?

THE RHODESIAN RÉGIME'S DEFENCE

The Rhodesian Front Government's public pronouncements on the menace of 'terrorist' invasions have necessarily been contradictory. On the one hand they have used the alleged threat to justify their increased expenditure on the security and defence forces and their continuous resort to states of 'emergency' to legalise repressive measures against internal as well as external opposition (see Document 54 on the extension of the state of emergency). It has also served as a useful propaganda device to ensure the unity and support of the European population, which might otherwise become increasingly critical, or even hostile, as the intensification of economic sanctions resulted in the deterioration of the economic structure on which the society is based. If all economic misfortunes and material inconveniences, as well as the fears of isolation from the world community, can be attributed to the menace 'from the north', the otherwise divisive forces operating within the white *laager* can be diverted towards the enemy from outside.

On the other hand, the rebel régime has also felt it necessary to minimise the threat of external invasion in order to reassure its white supporters that their privileged status was being contained. Without such a guarantee white immigration would gradually fall off, as it began to do towards the end of 1973 and white emigration would constantly increase; both being affected by the prospect of military call-up to bolster the relatively small European forces defending an extensive border area. Evidence that the régime is concerned to conceal

277

the nature and extent of the threat was provided by the arrest of a journalist reporting on the scale of guerrilla warfare (see Document 56 by Peter Niesewand). It is also evident from a survey of the reports of the police and defence forces. That the situation is being contained is never left in doubt by official sources, and even references to casualties among Rhodesian forces, admitted in earlier years, have been conveniently omitted.

The following document is one of the first public statements recognising the existence of a 'terrorist' invasion. Ironically, Mr Smith directs his protests about alleged invasions from the independent State of Zambia to the British Government, which ceased to be responsible for the former protectorate of Northern Rhodesia since its independence in 1964. Also ironically, since no country in the world has recognised the illegal régime, Mr Smith continues to operate under the delusion that Rhodesia, in a state of rebellion against the Crown, remains a Commonwealth country deserving to be 'friendly and cooperative'.

DOCUMENT 52. RHODESIAN FRONT GOVERNMENT PROTEST ON 'TERRORIST' INVASIONS (FROM PRIME MINISTER'S DEPARTMENT, *Note to the United Kingdom Government from the Rhodesian Government*, 28 AUGUST 1967, C.S.R. 45–1967)

The Rhodesian Government wishes to draw urgently to the attention of the British Government the following situation in Rhodesia.

2. Leaders of the two banned Rhodesian African Nationalist Organizations, the Zimbabwe African People's Union (ZAPU) and the Zimbabwe African National Union (ZANU) are now firmly established in Zambia and it is from Lusaka that these people plan subversive operations directed against the Government of Rhodesia, including the infiltration of armed terrorists and offensive materials into this country.

3. At one time the President of Zambia, through his security forces, tried to control the movement of terrorists and offensive materials through his country. From about the middle of 1966, however, when Rhodesian terrorist activities commenced to increase, all vestige of control appears to have vanished and the Zambian Government has since progressed from a policy of ignoring or condoning such activities to one of offering direct encouragement.

4. Rhodesian terrorists receive training in a number of communist countries, including Russia, Red China, Cuba and Algeria, and also at three or more camps in Tanzania. Irrespective of their place of training, terrorists invariably move from Tanzania to Zambia where they are billeted in specially constructed holding camps, established in the vicinity of Lusaka and within easy striking distance of Rhodesia.

5. In Zambia there are also a number of centres used by subversive organisations for the storage of arms, ammunition and other offensive materials used in the equipping of terrorist groups. At their respective holding camps ZAPU and ZANU Party officials indoctrinate the terrorists in Communist and Party Ideology, particularly in the context of the part they are to play in creating a sense of fear and uncertainty in Rhodesia.

6. Groups for terrorist incursions into Rhodesia are issued with arms and equipment and conveyed, quite openly, in ZAPU or ZANU vehicles along one or other of the Zambian road complexes to the Rhodesian border, where they are finally instructed on methods of infiltration and briefed on their targets in Rhodesia. During the hours of darkness they are expected to infiltrate across the Zambezi River into this country.

7. Not only does the Zambian Government condone the activities of Rhodesian terrorists in that country, but it is known that on occasions Zambian Government officials actually assist these people in passing through the border between Zambia and Tanzania.

8. The main supplier of arms and other offensive materials used by Rhodesian terrorists is the African Liberation Committee (A.L.C.) of the Organization of African Unity (O.A.U.) in Dar-es-Salaam. Here the material is received from a number of Communist countries and is stored by the Tanzanian Government which is responsible for the control and subsequent issue of this material to various Nationalist movements.

9. Although there is no proof of direct co-operation between the Governments of Tanzania and Zambia in respect of the movement of offensive material, it is known that the former Government has already suggested to the latter that it adopts some method of control. It is extremely unlikely that the Zambian Government is ignorant of the movement and storage of terrorist arms in Zambia.

10. Since terrorist activity against Rhodesia was intensified about the middle of last year, an ever-increasing number of armed men, of both ZAPU and ZANU factions, have been infiltrated into this country from Zambia. Initially, only small groups of terrorists entered across the Zambezi River from Zambia. In recent months larger bands—comprising up to thirty or more terrorists—have crossed into Rhodesia. Little credence can therefore be given to any denial by the Zambian Government that it is unaware of the movement of such large numbers of men and quantities of material.

11. The current security operation being waged against the large band of mixed South African African National Congress (SAANC) and ZAPU terrorists in Western Matabeleland shows without any doubt that the Zambian authorities are not only prepared to condone terrorist activities directed against Rhodesia, but are also willing to allow their country to be used as a rallying point for terrorists bent on a campaign of violence against South Africa.

12. The recent threat issued by the Organization of African Unity to Rhodesian nationalists that they can expect no further financial support unless they can produce proof of militant action against Rhodesia has had a two-fold effect. It has influenced both ZAPU and ZANU to intensify the infiltration of terrorists from Zambia across the Zambezi River, and has stimulated ZAPU to abduct over two hundred Rhodesian Africans, in legitimate employment in Zambia, for terrorist training in Tanzania. Thus the Zambian Government has become further implicated by permitting these activities with little or no intervention.

13. On the 19th August in Lusaka, James Robert Chikerema, Vice President of ZAPU, and Oliver Tambo, Deputy President of the SAANC, issued a joint Press release extolling the activities of their combined terrorist groups presently operating in Western Matabeleland.

14. The aim of these terrorists bands is to carry out indiscriminate killing, burning and looting in rural and urban areas. The Rhodesian Government will adopt the most vigorous measures to protect the people and their property and to seek out and destroy these terrorist bands and individual gunmen.

15. The British Government cannot escape its share of respon-

sibility for these developments. There has been a complete absence of any protest by the British Government to the Zambian Government about the passage of arms and offensive material, the reception and harbouring of communist trained terrorists and the use of Zambia as a base for offensive operations against Rhodesia.

16. Here is a case where a Government of one Commonwealth country is lending itself to a policy of violence against another Commonwealth country [*sic*] which has committed no aggression and desires to be friendly and co-operative. The Rhodesian Government considers that Britain continues to have obligations in Zambia to influence that Government towards a policy of moderation and the discouragement of violence against Rhodesia. The Rhodesian Government accordingly lodges a strong protest against the British Government's lack of action in this respect and against its connivance of the hostile attitude of the Zambian Government towards peace and good government in Rhodesia.

DOCUMENT 53A. THE BRITISH SOUTH AFRICAN POLICE (FROM *Annual Report for 1968* C.S.R. 23–1969)

In recent times Rhodesia's Police have been faced with a different type of criminal, the armed gangs of thugs who infiltrate our borders with complete disregard for the laws of the country, and intent on murder and creating chaos for political ends. These people are sometimes known as 'freedom fighters' or other such righteous sounding name, but to the Police they are criminals and as such they must be dealt with according to the law. Those who surrender are arrested, the others who resist are not so fortunate.

This threat to the security of the country dictated an addition to normal Police training, in the form of military type training to counter the well armed insurgents and also to enable members of the Force to operate efficiently and confidently in the border and remote areas of Rhodesia. All members of the Force responded magnificently to this added facet of training and Police Anti-Terrorist Units now patrol far and wide seeking out terrorist type criminals.

The year under review has again seen armed aggression

against this country and its people mounted from territories to the north—an armed aggression which has been met with signal success by the combined security forces achieving the almost total elimination of terrorists from within our territory. This is most gratifying and reflects well on the smooth functioning of our security organisation and inter-services liaison. It is most fitting that I pay tribute to the Rhodesia Army and the Royal Rhodesian Air Force for the highly efficient part they have played in these operations and the co-operation extended to Police. The strengths and limitations of all three Services are known and appreciated at all levels and the combination of all three working in complete harmony creates a formidable security force.

Despite the results obtained, experience has shown that there are those who, still undeterred, will venture into further foolhardy incursions. Accordingly, it can be expected that this threat will remain and all our efforts are geared to maintaining, and improving where possible, our state of preparedness to deal promptly and efficiently with any violations of our territorial sovereignty.

The internal maintenance of law and order has continued to show the favourable trend reported last year. In 1966 security offences totalled 724, in 1967 this dropped to 310; in 1968, I am happy to report, the number dropped yet further, to 101.

DOCUMENT 53B. *Annual Reports of the Secretary for Defence, 1967–1971* (C.S.R. 25–1968, 21–1969, CMD R.R. 15–1971, 16–1972)

The year 1967 saw an expected increase in counter-insurgency operations. Thanks to the planning so ably carried out by the Security Forces, and, in particular, the Joint Planning Staff, the threat was contained most effectively, although regrettably *not without some casualties among our forces* [editor's italics]. . . .

As had been expected, there was a further increase in terrorist infiltration during the year 1968, which, of necessity, meant an appropriate increase in the number of counter-insurgency operations mounted by the Security Forces. The careful planning and efficiency of the Security Forces contributed significantly to the success of these operations, though *not without casualities to the forces* [editor's italics]. . . .

As in past years, the regular members of the Army have again this year spent many months away from home stations on border patrol duties and operating against terrorist gangs which had infiltrated into Rhodesia. . . .

Following the lull in terrorist activity during the preceding year, the early months of 1970 saw a marked increase in incursions into Rhodesia from Zambia-based terrorists. Continuous patrolling of sensitive areas was maintained throughout the year by the Army and its sister Services in the Security Forces, and a number of operations against terrorist gangs was successfully concluded. . . .

The year 1971 has been comparatively free of terrorist activity; only one operation being mounted against a gang of terrorists which intruded into Rhodesia from Moçambique. Continuous patrolling was maintained both in border zones and in depth, in conjunction with other elements of the Security Forces. . . .

During the period under review there were no known incursions by Rhodesian terrorists, although Zambia continues to harbour a number of these.

A FRELIMO gang, however, crossed into Rhodesia from Moçambique on 29th August. This gang was soon contacted by the Security Forces and several casualties were inflicted on it.

DOCUMENT 54. THE STATE OF EMERGENCY: THE MINISTER OF LAW AND ORDER MOVES THE EXTENSION (FROM RHODESIA *Parliamentary Debates*, VOL. 81, 16 JUNE 1972, COLS 668–75)

Mr. Lardner-Burke:

So far as the external threat is concerned, the possibility of infiltration by groups of armed terrorists from across our borders has in no way diminished. Indeed, we know that trained terrorists in considerable numbers are waiting in Zambia. Others are undergoing training elsewhere. The fact that no large infiltrations have occurred in recent years does not mean that they are unlikely to occur in the future. This apparent inactivity can, I am glad to say, be attributed to the heavy losses inflicted by our security forces on the terrorists in earlier actions. It is, no doubt, also due to the internal and tribal differences and arguments which constantly divide the terrorists among themselves. There is evidence to suggest that these organizations have examined the tactics which they have employed in order to find a more efficient means of destroying law and order within Rhodesia.

Instead of large bands being sent across the Zambezi it has become the practice to infiltrate intelligence agents and specially selected men with specific instructions. During the period the Pearce Commission was in this country, three such terrorists entered Rhodesia but fortunately were apprehended before they were able to do any damage. The pattern now appears to be directed towards stimulating internal subversion with the aid of those dissidents already within the country.

During the past year an additional threat to our borders has emerged as a result of increased terrorist activity in the Tete district of Moçambique. Hon. members will be aware that Frelimo, the organization dedicated to the overthrow by violence of the Portuguese administration, had extended its terrorist activites to the Tete district immediately on our northeastern border. There have been a number of sabotage incidents on the main road between Rhodesia and Malawi in which Rhodesians and their vehicles have been harmed.

The presence of hostile forces adjacent to our border is a potential threat to the security of this country. This threat is underlined by the statement made by a Frelimo leader in Cairo recently when he stated that Frelimo would be able to assist the Rhodesian terrorist organizations.

The Organization for African Unity appears to have taken on a new lease of life and even though its members may quarrel amongst themselves they are united in their hostile attitude to civilized countries of Southern Africa. Communist aid in the form of arms and money continues to flow via the O.A.U. to the terrorist movements. The World Council of Churches and certain left-wing organizations in the west and in Scandinavia continue to give moral and financial support.

As hon. members know, as recently as the 5th of this month, it became necessary to issue emergency regulations to prevent foreign aid from such sources being sent to organizations and persons in Rhodesia. . . .

Indeed, in some cases the so-called do-gooders have made known their aim to help terrorist organizations. One can only conclude that they desire a breakdown of civilized government in this part of the world.

Also, it is obviously undesirable that a political party in Rhodesia should be dependent on overseas financial resources. If it has little or no financial backing in Rhodesia, it should not be able to look elsewhere to keep alive. To extend the scope of this prohibition to all political parties would not, however, be appropriate under the emergency regulations which must be related to the emergency—not all political organizations interfere with law and order and public security.

Reverting to my main theme, that is to say the need for renewing the emergency, I am sorry to report that the dangers facing us are not diminishing, and I would agree with a statement made recently by the South African Commissioner of Police in his Annual Report for 1970/71, that, despite the apparent and superficial peacefulness that is at present being experienced, the terrorist threat is increasing. Within Rhodesia the recent disorders have demonstrated the truth of my earlier warnings that, in the field of security, we must not be complacent. It is essential to be ready to deal with any eventuality when it arises.

THE AFRICAN LIBERATION STRUGGLE

The African leaders of the liberation movement present their version of the origins of the movement, the justification for the policy of direct confrontation and the objectives of their struggle.

DOCUMENT 55. THE ZIMBABWE AFRICAN PEOPLE'S UNION (ZAPU) AND THE ZIMBABWE AFRICAN NATIONAL UNION (ZANU), STATEMENTS TO THE UN/OAU CONFERENCE ON SOUTHERN AFRICA, OSLO, 9–14 APRIL 1973 (FROM *Southern Africa, The UN/OAU Conference: Part 1: Programme of Action and Conference Proceedings. Part 2: Papers and Documents*, EDITED BY OLAV STOKKE AND CARL WIDSTRAND, SCANDINAVIAN INSTITUTE OF AFRICAN STUDIES, OSLO, 1973)

(A) ZAPU: Zimbabwe: The Enemy We Confront and the Assistance We Need

It is under the stress of this oppression that the people of Zimbabwe have taken up arms as the only solution to their problem.

The question of dealing with the settlers through force of arms is not new to the Rhodesian problem. It was discovered by our forefathers in the last decade of the last century that trying to reason with the British Government or the settlers was entertaining ones self to a system of tricks in which one always came out the loser. Hence they took up arms and established the point. From 1911 to 1961 various organisations in Zimbabwe—the Native Association, the Voters League, the Industrial and Commercial Workers Union, the African National Congress, the Supreme Council, the National Democratic Party all tried the peaceful approach to bring about majority rule and therefore freedom and independence, without success. This is why we have now taken to the supreme instrument of appeal—the armed liberation struggle.

Both the United Nations and the Organization of African Unity have recognised the legitimacy of our liberation struggle. Both have, by several resolutions, pledged moral and material assistance to our struggle. The OAU has of course by all neccesity, taken all out responsibility for the African liberation struggle.

The primary burden, indeed the full square of it, is ours, the oppressed people in the struggling territories. All approaches to our liberation struggle should take cognizance of our full awareness to this responsibility.

Rhodesia is today very much in the news, no longer because of the erstwhile boastings of Ian Smith but because the guerrilla offensive is closing in on the régime from nearly every corner and centre of the country.

From July last year to January this year a new systematic strategy of a series of land mine offensives forced panic into the régime and made it to precipitate Rhodesia–Zambia border fiasco. Elsewhere in the north eastern area of the country fraternal forces have struck panic on the settler farming population of the area. The régime can no longer lie to its followers as casualties fill their hospitals.

The prospects of a consolidated armed revolutionary stuggle to maintain a solid offensive towards the elimination of the Rhodesian settler fascists, are very bright. We believe this should create the most conducive circumstances for the effective participation of the international community in our liberation struggle. It is a crucial phase of our history of struggle. Here we refer to the Political Council of Zimbabwe recently formed by our External missions and the Joint Military Command we have reviewed and rededicated ourselves to.

Whilst our offensive is taking its strides the enemy is indulging in cruelties exceeding all international norms of war. Freedom fighters who should be treated as prisoners of war are treated as criminals, scores of whom have been kept in death cells for more than five years. African civilians are murdered, their properties confiscated as reprisals for guerrilla confrontations. The international community has an obligation to demand investigation and seek assertion of its norms on this issue against criminal racist and fascist régimes of southern Africa. . . .

Peace does not mean quiet imposed by the dominance of an oppressive force. Peace explicitly means the direct elimination of oppressive force. Since there is no such thing as peaceful oppression there can be no such thing as peaceful elimination of oppression. Colonialism and *apartheid* in southern Africa are, in every essence, the most violent forms of oppression. They have, logically, bred violent resistance from their victims— hence the armed revolutionary struggle in southern Africa.

The United Kingdom, Ian Smith, Vorster and Caetano are not exploiting and oppressing the peoples of southern Africa by mistake or misunderstanding. They are doing so by conscious systematic and deliberate plan. Peaceful decolonisation in southern Africa is therefore irrelevant.

Programmes of action, non-violent in themselves, but auxiliary to the armed liberation struggle, are of course of paramount importance, for example

(i) Diplomatic support for the struggle in the international sphere.

(ii) Financial, material and moral support to the liberation movements.

(iii) Educational and technical assistance to liberation movements.

Whilst we share common general beliefs on the decolonisation programme it is our observation that the weakest link which accounts for poor solidarity is lack of direct regular contact and co-ordination between supporting countries, international organisations and the respective liberation movements.

Regular mutual exchange of information and ideas should lead to mutual understanding which should lead to mutual confidence, mutual confidence should lead to greater co-operation and therefore to more effective solidarity of action to expedite the liberation cause.

Regarding requirements for our liberation struggle in Zimbabwe it is only appropriate for us firstly to express our profound gratitude to the international community for all the diplomatic, material and moral assistance given in our support hitherto.

In considering the needs of the Zimbabwe struggle the following realities should be universally accepted, acknowledged and taken as the working basis for support to our struggle.

(a) That the people of Zimbabwe have suffered and continue to suffer violent oppression.

(b) That the oppression suffered by the people of Zimbabwe is being carried out by the United Kingdom using its settler racists and fascists as direct agents.

(c) That economically and in other forms of war logistics the United Kingdom in Rhodesia is reinforced, for its oppression of the people of Zimbabwe, by its NATO allies particularly the United States, West-Germany and France and South Africa and Japan.

(d) That the current armed liberation struggle launched by the people of Zimbabwe in resistance to this oppression is the only just and inevitable means of liberating themselves.

Our immediate needs are as follows:

(i) Sufficient, substantial, direct financial assistance to service all our liberation activities such as fuel for transport, repairs and replacement of parts. Grant of financial assistance should take into account that the Rhodesian fascist régime apart from military hardware spends $50 million annually to service its forces of oppression.

(ii) Sufficient transport in the form of jeeps, heavy-ton carriers (lorries) and fast manœuvrable cars suitable for mobility and speed in this type of struggle considering the sophisticated transportation and communication system of the enemy.

(iii) Relevant hardware and technical equipment with the imparting of the necessary of skills.

(iv) Information dissemination equipment—typewriters (portable and large carriage) duplicators (small and large) plus relevant equipment and spares; printing machines (manageable)—photostat machines (large and small) and the relevant equipment.

(v) Material needs, shelters, blankets, large quantities of all types of clothing—male and female—to meet the needs of freedom fighters as well as for welfare purposes.

(vi) Medicines for casualty and tropical disease purposes plus hospital equipment and assistance for professional medical training.

(vii) Education and technical training for mechanical, civil, agricultural, chemical and electrical engineering, book-keeping and accountancy.

In the field of diplomatic assistance our needs are as follows:

(i) The present trend of accepting liberation movements as observers in international forums should be permanently legitimised and universalised so that for example the liberation movement in Zimbabwe should be recognised as the sole authentic and representative spokesman of the Zimbabwe people as a whole in all international activities.

(ii) Consequently the present international firm stand of isolating the Rhodesian fascist régime from all international activities should be steadfastly maintained and extended to refusing to recognise United Kingdom pretensions to either speak on behalf of the Zimbabwe people or to be the impartial arbitrator in the situation. The United Kingdom is the culprit in the situation.

(iii) Countries giving diplomatic support to the United Kingdom, like the United States of America, should be condemned and dissuaded from giving this support.

(iv) Governments or organizations which are genuine supporters of the liberation struggle in Zimbabwe and southern Africa as a whole should give influence where possible to potential supporters to be more active and effective with relevant means in their possession.

International mass mobilisation. Governments and non-governmental organizations should liaise with the Zimbabwe liberation movement for information on the progress of the struggle and then use all propaganda media available to keep their respective populations up-to-date and properly directed on the progress and needs of the struggle. This should include direct regular contact with the liberation movement.

Economic action. Ways of making the sanctions programme against the Rhodesian régime scrupulously effective should be sought and implemented. The scarecrow argument that the Zimbabwean people are the more likely to suffer from such action should never be given any credence as it is most untrue.

All the above mentioned requirements are of both short-term and long-term requirement because their sustenance and progressive expansion should relate to the liberation struggle as it extends in time and needs.

(B) ZANU: Zimbabwe: From Confrontation to Armed Liberation Struggle

The armed confrontation in Zimbabwe is an inevitable development in the African people's struggle for freedom from colonialist settlement, oppression and exploitation, which began with the arrival of the white settlers and agents of British imperialism.

In 1963 when ZANU was born, our founder and president Ndabaningi Sithole, declared in his famous clarion call: 'We are our own liberators.' And at once he prescribed the method: 'By direct confrontation.' That direct confrontation has developed into the armed struggle of today.

The nature of the confrontation must be clearly understood. The African people of Zimbabwe have been exploited, degraded, humiliated for years. Their struggle, however, is not for the alleviation of these wrongs. It is for the inalienable right of man to self rule. We do not seek to be ruled well by whites, we seek to rule ourselves; colonialism and imperialism are evil, because by taking away from peoples their right to self-rule they dehumanise people.

For that reason colonialism and imperialism are universally condemned by all civilised and progressive people of the world. Racism and *apartheid* are simply by-products of imperialism and colonialism.

Our struggle against the settlers of Rhodesia (Zimbabwe) and their backers abroad is part of the common struggle of all progressive forces in the world against the evils of colonialism, imperialism, and *apartheid*. For that reason, even while we ourselves struggle in our own country, we join in solidarity with all other peoples and organisations everywhere struggling to rid themselves of the same evils for the struggle against imperialism and colonialism is indivisible. In their fight for survival, colonialism and imperialism resort to the most diabolic and vicious methods of repression and suppression. That is how the Rhodesian régime has become fascist and as the challenge of the régime by the people's confrontation increases, so does the régime degenerate further into fascism. Today the Rhodesian régime maintains itself by methods which approximate the Hitlerite Reich in their ruthlessness and cruelty.

A régime is fascist if it denies to any human beings the possibility of human progress; negates the sanctity and dignity of human life; refuses to accept that government can only be based on popular support, or the responsibility of the rulers to the ruled; denigrates freedom of thought or the right of criticism, and repudiates the necessity of universal education, impartial justice or the rule of law; or if it puts emotion above reason; elevates racism or élitism to a dogma, relegating those who are outside the racial or class élite to little short of slaves. . . .

The African people of Zimbabwe, have over a long period of time appealed to the settlers and the British government, which claims responsibility over Rhodesia, to rectify the wrongs. They have offered to discuss and seek agreement on ways of bringing an end to this situation. With monotonous regularity, their appeals and offers were derisively spurned upon, by both the settlers and the British government. In the exploitation and oppression of our people it is now clear that the British and their settler kith and kin are co-conspirators. That is the logical conclusion and experience from events since UDI. . . .

We make no apologies for either initiating or continuing the policy of direct confrontation. All civilised legal systems recognise the right to use violence and even to kill in self defence. This is a necessary corollary of the respect for human life which all civilised countries regard as an important cornerstone of public policy. We have been under the constant attack of aggressive racist settler oppression for 80 years. We have a right violently to defend ourselves against a régime that not only has but would in perpetuity, enslave, dehumanise, and make things of us. We are entitled to ask all progressive and civilised people and countries to support us in defending ourselves. . . .

The African people of Zimbabwe decided in 1963 to take matters into their own hands, guided by the famous words of Ndabaningi Sithole—'We are our own liberators.' There have been ups and downs and set-backs along the way to liberation, but on the whole progress has been made. Three years ago we decided on a new strategy; at the end of that period towards the end of 1972, in quick succession, Altena farm, belonging to a settler farmer Marc de Borchgrave, and used by the rebel régime's forces as an anti-freedom fighter operation centre was attacked, and two whites were injured. Shortly afterwards Whistlefield farm also used as an army command post was also attacked by ZANU forces, with the loss of 25 white soldiers, and two trucks carrying the forces of repression were blown up by ZANLA laid mines killing or wounding many white soldiers. On December 30 another truck carrying 15 white soldiers was blown up by a mine; and on the 6th of January, 1973, a police station, the local army officers mess were attacked by ZANU forces at Mt Darwin. Two days later 2 police reservists working under cover as land inspectors were killed by ZANU forces and a third was taken captive. The régime in utter desperation turned against and closed the border with neighbouring Zambia. That the decision was ill-considered and taken in panic is clear from the fact that at first the closure was total then it excluded copper in transit to the seaports, and finally it was withdrawn altogether.

The fateful closure of the border with Zambia, far from reducing the activities of ZANU in fact provoked more and more attacks on the supporters of rebel injustice and oppression. On 25 January another police reservist, Ida Kleynhans, was killed and her boisterous husband, another police reservist, was seriously wounded, during an attack on a farmstead used by the Smith forces of repression. In early February a supply camp at Sipolilo was destroyed and on 4th February one Leslie Jellicoe, a Briton, was killed in yet another attack.

The area of these activities in north-eastern Zimbabwe, has become unsafe for white soldiers, and other supporters of the Ian Smith régime. The roads have been mined, so they have had to resort to Alleutian Helicopters supplied by France. Helicopters have been shot down so they have now turned to indiscriminate bombing of the area, using British made jet bombers. And all to no avail, for the dreaded Freedom Fighters are nowhere to be seen, because they are in fact with the workers, the peasants and the general African masses. In characteristic fascist fashion Ian Smith has now turned his wrath against all black people in the areas, and ordered communal punishment against all and sundry. Under this diabolical decree cattle and other property are forceably taken from the poor peasants, as punishment for failing to report the presence of so-called guerrillas or giving to them succour and support. Schools, shops, markets, and other commercial and business activities have been closed throughout the northeastern area of the country. No one except soldiers and police is allowed in the area. To all intents and purposes all the Africans there are in prison. Under this blanket cover of secrecy every conceivable vice and brutality is perpetrated.

Today ZANU operations cover an area of 50,000 sq. miles in the E.N.E., North and Northwestern parts of the country. The area has an African population of between 1·5 and 2 million. White farmers in the area are living in a state of fear. Many have moved their families out in fear and make their farmsteads available for use by so-called security forces. Some women and children who have remained on the farmsteads sharing with the soldiers have been killed or injured in confrontations between ZANLA (The Zimbabwe African National Liberation Army, the military wing of ZANU) and the defenders of settlerist colonialist oppression of our people.

Practically the whole of the army, police and air forces are on permanent duty. Units of reservists and territorials have been called out.

The rise of the African people of Zimbabwe in resistance to oppression is not Smith's only problem. His futile closure of the border with Zambia has led president Kenneth Kaunda to permanently abandon the southern routes for export of copper and imports of goods. This is a great loss to a régime struggling hard to beat international sanctions, of much needed foreign exchange. Even nature seems to have turned against the régime, for Rhodesia is facing the severest drought in living memory. At the United Nations moves are afoot to strengthen existing, and probably extending sanctions; we hope they succeed. . . .

The struggle has been heating up, and will continue to do so. More and more Africans everywhere in Zimbabwe will embrace armed struggle. So it must proceed inexorably to its end of inevitable victory for justice against injustice and fascism, human dignity against humiliation and degradation, freedom against oppression, and progress against exploitation and racial greed. Smith's diabolical measures will not turn the African people from the path of liberatory revolution to which ZANU has committed them. Quite the contrary these measures are the fire that will steel them, and remove from them any unrevolutionary dross they may still have.

Not content with closing the border with Zambia, the régime has engaged in ceaseless efforts to undermine, subvert and openly violate the integrity of Zambia. More than 10 Zambians have been killed in these nefarious activities. From them it is clear that Smith's closure of the border did not stem any serious belief that Freedom Fighters crossed into Rhodesia at Chirundu, Livingstone or Kariba, the points where the closure was applied; or indeed from Zambia in general. The closure stemmed from his fascist racism. He could not tolerate the juxtaposition of progressive Zambia with his fascist Rhodesia. The comparison was too odious. About the confrontation in Zimbabwe he knew that his own and the acts of his predecessors in office had turned nearly every African Zimbabwean into a Freedom Fighter at heart. . . .

In our view, resistance, violent resistance to the rebel settler régime is justified. We sincerely believe that that régime will not respond to persuasion, reasoning or discussion. We are therefore bound to insist as priority number one that:

(a) Assistance to us be geared towards helping us in our programme of direct confrontation, so that we can spread and widen our areas of operation in Zimbabwe. It is our belief that only by continuing the direct confrontation is there any hope of any change in Rhodesia. This help involves of course: (i) Arms; and (ii) Logistic support, e.g. transport and accessories, uniforms, tents, blankets, boots and shoes, food and medicines. These are not only for militants but also for many civilians who have been victimised by the reckless conduct of the régime.

(b) The struggle for liberation is itself accompanied by many social and human problems. Some are a direct result of participation in the struggle, others are the direct result of the régime's policies of suppression, oppression and brutality. ZANU realised this as far back as 1967, and created the Zimbabwe African Welfare Trust Fund, a special organisation working independently of the party, to cover humanitarian needs including: (i) The education; and (ii) The maintenance of the dependants of those who have been arrested, detained or restricted by the régime, and those who have died in the struggle or are on a full time basis engaged in the struggle, whether inside or outside Zimbabwe.

We believe that the Fund could receive support to be extended to cover, not only the classes described above, but to include all who need education but are denied the opportunity because it is settler policy to deny Africans education.

We need to provide primary education to the millions of children who are denied education by the régime through all sorts of ruses. We need to teach adults who have never had any opportunity to study at least to read and write, to teach simple health care, etc. in rural areas.

We are now, through the fact of having operational areas or zones, in a position to offer on the spot education to some of the masses in combat zones. In order to give this education we need books, writing materials, etc. Our publicity department can provide the manuscripts from which such books, reflecting the African personality, in history, geography, culture and civics, can be printed. The settler propaganda distorts history, culture and even such subjects as mathematics to suit its purposes.

Even at secondary school level our ZANLA forces could help organise suitable courses to meet the needs of the people on the spot. By helping promote education on the spot we could be giving not only secondary education but laying the basis for a recognised secondary education system for the Zimbabwe of tomorrow. We must also mention the need for higher technical and university education for the Zimbabwe of tomorrow.

(c) On the diplomatic front, we cannot press too strongly the necessity to make existing sanctions work, and even to extend them. This is the international community's way of demonstrating its disapproval of the régime and indirectly of supporting armed struggle.

REVELATIONS FROM THE PRESS

Peter Niesewand, the author of the following report on Rhodesia's security crisis, was detained just after sending the story out of Rhodesia for publication, on the ground that he was 'likely to commit or incite the commission of acts which would disturb or interfere with the maintenance of law and order'. After winning his appeal against conviction on 1 May, he was released from detention on condition that he depart from the country directly from Salisbury airport; in fact, his departure was to London. Mr Niesewand is a Rhodesia citizen, of South African birth, who served as a correspondent in Rhodesia for several news agencies and for the BBC.

DOCUMENT 56. 'RHODESIA: WHAT SMITH REALLY FACES' BY PETER NIESEWAND (FROM *Africa Report*, VOL. 18, NO. 2, MARCH–APRIL 1973.

The north-eastern district of Rhodesia is a hot, rugged area. The Matusadonha Mountains, with their caves and many hiding places, run along the Zambezi escarpment, and adjoin Tribal Trust Land. The border with Mozambique is ill-defined, and Africans in the area have family links across in the Portuguese territory. Inside Mozambique, the bush thickens out. Flying across hundreds of miles of this territory, you think: an army could hide there.

In fact, an army is hiding there, and there seems little the Portuguese forces can—or will—do about it. According to reliable sources, FRELIMO (the Mozambique Liberation Front) maintains an extremely sophisticated headquarters in the belt of land between the Zambezi River as it flows through Mozambique, and the border with Rhodesia. The sources say that at least two Chinese instructors are working at this guerrilla H.Q., training not only FRELIMO men, but Rhodesian insurgents as well.

With FRELIMO in fairly secure control of this area, it has extended its umbrella to protect and assist the two banned Rhodesian nationalist organizations, ZANU (the Zimbabwe African National Union) and ZAPU (the Zimbabwe African People's Union).

It is not generally known in Rhodesia that Mozambique—the friendly territory on the eastern flank—has now superseded Zambia as the main base for guerrilla operations.

This is an extremely sensitive political matter. Ian Smith's decision to reopen the Rhodesian border with Zambia looked to many whites here like a major climb-down. Mr Smith announced that the 'agreement' with President Kenneth Kaunda would affect only guerrillas crossing directly from Zambia into Rhodesia, across the Zambezi River. It would have no bearing on the situation in the north-east, as the guerrillas there crossed from Mozambique. Yet it is in the north-east that Rhodesia's major security problem occurs.

To many white Rhodesians, Mr Smith's announcement seemed like a cynical exercise in semantics. His protestation that Zambia could not be held responsible for infiltrations from Mozambique sounded hollow, when measured against the general belief that the guerrillas were all based in Lusaka, and merely used Mozambique as a spring-board.

Surely, white Rhodesians said, the object of closing the Zambian border was to force President Kaunda to clamp down on terrorist bases in his country. If he did that, there would no longer be a security problem.

Had Mr Smith felt able to disclose that the Portuguese territory had become self-sufficient as a rebel base, and that the insurgents operating in the north-east had never touched Zambia at all, he would not have lost as much political credibility internally. But on the other hand, he would have angered the Portuguese authorities, who are extremely touchy about their conduct of the Mozambique war, and who vehemently deny that FRELIMO is in firm control of any territory at all. Yet this is the position—and Mr Smith chose to protect the Portuguese sensibilities, rather than his own political back.

There is a good reason for this. The Rhodesians are extremely worried about the security situation in Mozambique, and have a very low opinion of the Portuguese fighting man. But they realize the Portuguese react adversely to criticism, especially when loss of face is involved. It is in Rhodesia's security interests to maintain good working relations with her eastern neighbors, despite evidence of military inefficiency and timidity. In particular, the Rhodesians need Portuguese permission for sporadic operations across the border in Mozambique—and the fear is that this will be refused if the Portuguese are angered.

Present Rhodesian contingency plans include extending their frontier of constant anti-guerrilla patrols deep into Mozambique territory, to guard the vital road and rail links to the sea, and particularly to Beira. There are fears that within a short time, guerrillas will stage ambushes on this route. If this occurs in any serious form, the Rhodesians will request Portuguese permission to move into Mozambique territory—as the South Africans have done in Rhodesia—to help safeguard their own interests. Meanwhile, Mr Smith is obliged to play the Portuguese game, and pretend publicly that the FRELIMO bases near the border just do not exist, despite information that the guerrillas are so well equipped and entrenched that they even have cinema shows.

The security situation in southern Africa is changing dramatically, and despite officially-expressed optimism, the future is bleak. However privately critical the Rhodesians may be of the Portuguese performance in Mozambique, they are also closely examining their own contribution towards the security breakdown in the north-east. There is evidence that the ruling quarter-million white Rhodesians have persistently broken a cardinal rule, and have believed their own propaganda. While to do this may be merely foolish for the ordinary white voter, it is much more serious when indulged in by any senior member of the ruling Establishment.

The Pearce Commission provided the first indication that all was not as secure as the government believed. Neither the British nor the Rhodesian administrations, nor indeed the ordinary white Rhodesian, thought for a moment that the five million black majority would give anything but a resounding 'Yes' to the 1971 Anglo-Rhodesian settlement proposals. The powerful Ministry of Internal Affairs had assured the Government that this was so, and Mr Smith in turn had told white Rhodesians that their country had 'the happiest Africans in the world'. So when Lord Pearce recorded an unqualified 'No' from black Rhodesians the whites were shown the racial gap for the first time. It was a nasty shock to the ruling minority. But the complacency lingered on—especially in the Internal Affairs Ministry, even though it, unlike most white Rhodesians, has direct contact with the African majority.

This complacency had its sequel in the deteriorating security situation. The signs were there for the District Commissioners to see, but they were ignored. The sudden disappearance of men from certain villages in the north-east; the drying up of sources of information.

Ian Smith explained later that the D.C.s had a vast area to cover, and that it was impossible for them to do an adequate job until their numbers were reinforced. But this does not explain the numerous occasions when the evidence of impending trouble was presented to a D.C., and he paid not attention.

Towards the middle of last year, the guerrillas began moving in—crossing the border from Mozambique and making contact with local people. The Rhodesian authorities have said the guerrillas subverted the local people by intimidation at gunpoint, and by recruiting some local mediums—called 'witch-doctors' by Mr Smith—through whom the ancestral spirits speak. Smith claimed these local mediums were bribed onto the side of the insurgents, and persuaded to encourage Africans to support the guerrilla cause.

There is no doubt truth in both these claims. A certain amount of intimidation has been carried out by guerrillas—recently, two Africans were found by security forces, severely beaten. One had been tied to a tree and whipped. They both blamed guerrillas for the attacks.

But this does not explain the total lack of intelligence information from local Africans to the white authorities over a period of six months. Even if the majority could have been intimidated at gunpoint, or threatened with beatings, surely one man out of the thousands affected would—at some time during the period—have come in contact with a white official into whose ear he could have whispered about the trouble facing his tribe? Yet no one did.

The Rhodesian security forces themselves had information that something was going to happen—but they had no idea what it would be until the guerrillas announced their presence with a raid on a white farmhouse in the tobacco-growing district of Centenary on December 21. Even then, it took nearly a month for the full extent of the security deterioration to sink in. The white authorities were forced to recognize that they had lost the goodwill of the people in the north-east, and that unless they could regain it, they risked losing the war.

Reliable sources say the guerrillas have operated in an extremely sophisticated manner. Their campaign began with some recruiting trips into north-eastern Rhodesia from Mozambique. They found people whose resentment of the white authorities was growing, and who complained that the District Commissioners and the white land officers, with whom they had contact, were rude and arrogant. They objected to the land conservation policies which they had to carry out.

Farmers anywhere tend to be among the more conservative elements of any society, and especially in the case of peasants, resist new techniques. There can also be no doubt about the necessity of measures such as contour ridging and cattle dipping, particularly in the African areas where the land is deteriorating. But even among those African farmers who see the benefits of these new methods, there is anger at the manner in which the white authorities have ordered their implementation.

In addition, the Europeans have insisted that Africans reduce their cattle holdings because of the condition of the land. But cattle form an important part of African spiritual and cultural life: they represent wealth and pride. To force a farmer to destock is a serious move—particularly since a new method exists which, if properly adopted, would allow a tribe to actually increase its cattle holdings, while improving the quality of the land. But like peasant farmers, the Rhodesian authorities too are resistant to change, and so maintain the old policy of destocking without regard to African sensibilities.

Black resentment of whites extends further than this: each ethnic group has members who have gone into towns and cities, and have tales to tell of discrimination and unfair treatment. In many cases, the extended family has contributed towards putting a child through school—at a cost insignificant to a white Rhodesian, but representing a huge sum to a man living in a subsistence economy. In most cases, at the end of his school career, the young man simply swells the ranks of the black unemployed. He wants a white-collar job: he is offered work picking cotton, or as a 'garden boy' in a white suburb, and ends up not significantly better off than the subsistence farmer. At one Salisbury advertising agency, the African who makes the tea and sweeps the floors has university entrance qualifications. But he's lucky to have a job at all.

Meanwhile, Portuguese and Italian immigrants flood in, not speaking English, not particularly well educated, taking jobs that Africans would like. So are African hopes dashed, and so the racial gap increases.

This situation is a potential seedbed for revolution, and the guerrillas have recognized it. They have recruited hundreds of people in the north-east for guerrilla training, or to act as porters for arms and ammunition.

Starting in the middle of 1972, they sent young men to their base camps in Mozambique for intensive guerrilla training, while other local people helped carry weapons and explosives back into Rhodesia to be buried in fairly small caches. At the end of their training, the new guerrillas were sent back into Rhodesia. Unlike previous infiltrators, they were not crossing into an alien area, where the risk of betrayal was high. These were men coming home, and they had scores to settle.

The first attack, on December 21, was launched against Altena Farm, the home of 37-year-old tobacco farmer, Marc de Borchgrave. The farmhouse was riddled with machine-gun fire, and hand grenades were thrown through the windows. The attack was led by a former employee, reported to have a grudge against Mr de Borchgrave. By chance, no one was killed. In the Mount Darwin area, two white land inspectors—who implement unpopular conservation policies—were machine-gunned to death.

It is not known exactly how many men are currently involved in the infiltration campaign, but one reliable report says more than 100 are still undergoing training in Mozambique, and the first wave of guerrillas numbered about 80. Since then, at least one other wave of guerrilla reinforcements has come in.

Sources say that most of the raids in the north-east of Rhodesia are organized by ZANU, although on a military level there is fairly close liaison between ZANU and their political rivals, ZAPU. The sources say that ZAPU forces are mostly engaged in direct crossings into Rhodesia from Zambia, to prepare landmine ambushes. The ZAPU guerrillas cross the Zambezi under cover of darkness, and plant mines on remote dirt roads where security forces are known to patrol. The infiltrators then return to Zambia and are usually safe when the explosions occur. The Communist-manufactured mines weigh 12 lbs. apiece, so each man can carry and plant three of them.

Hit-and-run raids such as these are relatively easy and safe for guerrillas. However, it takes sophisticated planning and a shrewd knowledge of guerrilla warfare to wage the campaign in the north-east. The infiltrators—well-armed and well-trained—have avoided the mistakes of their predecessors. They are not in uniform, and they are not seeking confrontations with the security forces. Some have been employed by white farmers, and are living and working in the areas during the day.

It is usually at night that the laborer becomes a guerrilla. Targets are chosen for their psychological value, rather than for their military significance. A tactic being used by guerrillas after an assault is to 'bombshell'—split up and head off in a dozen different directions. Rhodesian tracker units must then decide whether they themselves should split up to follow each individual guerrilla, whose tracks very often lead to a tarred road and disappear.

The Rhodesian security forces report that they are beginning to win back co-operation from the local people, but it is difficult to know just how this is being done. There are indications, however, that the Rhodesians are using strong-arm tactics. The system of collective punishments introduced under the nationwide state-of-emergency regulations, allows white Provincial Commissioners to impose unlimited fines on communities where they suspect individuals are aiding subversion. It is not necessary to prove guilt, or hear representations from affected parties. The first a community may know of the matter is when soldiers come to collect the fine. If they cannot find sufficient money, the authorities can seize property, including cattle, without ascertaining ownership.

In addition, in areas such as the Chiweshe Tribal Trust

Land, which adjoins the white farming district of Centenary, suspicion by the authorities that guerrillas were active led to the suspension of normal life. Schools, shops, grinding-mills for maize, and even churches were ordered to close their doors 'for security reasons'. Africans were searched and questioned, and strangers were ordered to leave the area. According to reports reaching Salisbury, captured guerrillas—and Africans accused of aiding subversion—have been paraded before villagers as a warning that they should side with the authorities.

Whether these tactics will work is a matter of conjecture, but even if they do, they can only provide a short-term answer. Guerrilla war is an extension of politics. By definition, it cannot be won or lost. It must either become a conventional war, or revert to politics for its conclusion.

A conventional war seems unlikely: the focus must shift then to Salisbury. If Rhodesia in fact had the happiest Africans in the world, as Mr Smith maintained, there would be no need for a guerrilla action. A quick settlement between the races is improbable. Observers therefore expect the guerrilla war to continue sporadically for some years yet, while the political battle is waged in the Rhodesian capital.

Select Bibliography

While there is an enormous amount of documentary material—both British and Rhodesian—on the subject, there is much less in the way of reliable and comprehensive secondary sources on modern Rhodesia, although the periodical selection is extensive and much of it useful. The books listed below provide a survey of the main domestic and international issues confronting Rhodesia since the 1950s; and in most there are also summaries of the historical background to those issues. Excluded from the list are the early historical accounts, the personal apologias and the polemical tracts. On the subject of Rhodesia, there are no 'neutral' authors. Those books by Rhodesians, African as well as European, obviously reflect their own interests and commitments, but those included have been selected for their competent approach to the subject and, in some cases, for their readability.

ARRIGHI, GIOVANNI, *The Political Economy of Rhodesia*, The Hague, Mouton, 1967.

BARBER, JAMES, *Rhodesia: The Road to Rebellion*, London, Oxford University Press, 1967.

BOWMAN, LARRY, *Politics in Rhodesia: White Power in an African State*, Cambridge, Massachusetts, Harvard University Press, 1973.

BULL, THEODORE, ed., *Rhodesian Perspective*, London, Michael Joseph, 1967.

CLEMENTS, FRANK, *Rhodesia: The Course to Collision*, London, Pall Mall Press, 1969.

CREIGHTON, T. R. M., *The Anatomy of Partnership*, London, Faber & Faber, 1960.

DAY, JOHN, *International Nationalism: The Extra-Territorial Relations of Southern Rhodesian Nationalists*, London, Routledge & Kegan Paul, 1967.

GOOD, ROBERT, *UDI: The International Politics of the Rhodesian Rebellion*, London, Faber & Faber, 1973.

GRAY, RICHARD, *Two Nations: Aspects of the Development of Race*

Relations in the Rhodesias and Nyasaland, London, Oxford University Press, 1960.

KAPUNGU, LEONARD, *The United Nations and Economic Sanctions against Rhodesia*, Lexington, Massachusetts, Lexington Books, 1973.

LEYS, COLIN, *European Politics in Southern Rhodesia*, London, Oxford University Press, 1959.

MASON, PHILIP, *The Birth of a Dilemma*, London, Oxford University Press, 1958.

M'LAMBO, ESHMAEL, *Rhodesia: Struggle for a Birthright*, London, George Hurst, 1972.

MURRAY, D. J., *The Governmental System in Southern Rhodesia*, London, Oxford University Press, 1970.

NIESEWAND, PETER, *In Camera: Secret Justice in Rhodesia*, London, Weidenfeld & Nicolson, 1973.

PALLEY, CLAIRE, *The Constitutional History and Law of Southern Rhodesia*, London, Oxford University Press, 1966.

RANGER, TERENCE, *Crisis in Southern Rhodesia*, London, Fabian Commonwealth Bureau, 1960.

SHAMUYARIRA, NATHAN, *Crisis in Rhodesia*, London, Deutsch, 1965.

SITHOLE, NDABANINGI, *African Nationalism*, London, Oxford University Press, 2nd ed., 1968.

TODD, JUDITH, *The Right to Say No*, London, Sidgwick & Jackson, 1972.

TREGOLD, ROBERT, *The Rhodesia That Was My Life*, London, Allen & Unwin, 1968.

WILMER, S. W., ed., *Zimbabwe Now*, London, Rex Collings, 1972.

Index

African Affairs Bill, 197
African Affairs Board, 25
African *Daily News*, 208
African Education Act, 182
African Juveniles Employment Act, 119
African Labour Regulations Act, 119
African Marriages Act, 119
African National Congress, 32, 50-1, 53-5, 86, 97, 286
African National Council, 59-61, 104, 122, 196, 263
African Railway Workers' Union, 51
African (Registration and Identification) Act, 99, 196
African Teachers' Association, 51
African Trades Union Congress, 153
African Wills Act, 119
Afrikaner, xviii
Algeria, 278
Angola, 276
Apartheid, xviii, 35, 112, 287, 290-1
Arnold, Guy, 269-74
Asian community, 62, 64, 119, 146, 161, 186, 235
Associated Chambers of Commerce, 189
Australia, 247, 254

Baldwin, Alan, 269-74
Banana, Canaan, 59, 196-7
Banda, Hastings, 32, 247
Barber, James, 252-8
Baron, Leo, 63, 219-26
Beadle, Chief Justice, 213, 216-19

Bledisloe Commission, 19-22, 26, 32
Borchgrave, Marc de, 292, 301
Botswana, 274
Bottomley, Arthur, 200, 205-6
British South Africa Company, xvi, xviii, 1-7, 14-19
Brown, K. E. E., 128-34
Builders and Artisans Workers' Union, 51
Burombo, B. B., 53
Butler, R. A., 200
Buxton Committee, 2-9

Caetano, Dr, 287
Canada, 254
Capricorn Africa Society, 52
Cave Commission, 15-16, 18
Central African Airways, 202
Central African Party, 52, 62, 64
Central Statistical Office, 154, 172-3
Centre Party, 42, 196
Chigogo, Mr, 81
Chikerema, Robert, 52-4, 58, 280
China, xxiii, 279, 296
Chinamano, Josiah, 51
Chiota, Oldman, 54
Chipunza, Chad, 52
Chirimbani, John, 51
Chisiza, Dunduza, 52
Chitepo, Herbert, 58
Church, 184-90
Churchill, Winston, 2
Clements, Frank, xv, 40-1
Clutton-Brock, Guy, 135-41, 185
Colby, G. F. T., 28
Cold Comfort Farm, 135, 185

INDEX

United Nations—*contd.*
173–4, 180–4; General Assembly, 237–40, 259, 275; Secretariat, 194–9, 245, 269, 275; Security Council, xxi, 238, 244, 248, 251, 260–1, 270, 274–6; Trusteeship Committee, 43–7
Unlawful Organisation Act, 86, 93, 169
USA, 260–1, 271, 274, 288–9

Vagrancy Act, 86, 198
van Heerden, Philip, 142–8
Vietnam, 257
Vorster, Dr, 287
Voters League, 286

Walker, Patrick Gordon, 24
Waring, Walter, 9
Welensky, Sir Roy, 23, 25 31–2, 40
West Germany, 273, 288
Whitehead, Sir Edgar, 42–7, 54–7, 86–7, 89, 97, 203, 220, 225

Wilson, Harold, 200–1, 203–5, 207–208, 211–19, 221–2, 225–6, 237–241, 252–3, 255, 257, 269–70
World Bank, 241
World Council of Churches, 284

Zaire (Congo), 45, 264, 274
Zambia (Northern Rhodesia), xv, xvi, xxi, xxiii, 19, 21–5, 27–30, 32–7, 41, 92, 202, 241, 244–6, 248, 267, 274, 278–81, 283, 286, 293–4, 297, 302
Zimbabwe African National Union (ZANU), 50, 59, 69, 185, 264–5, 278–80, 285, 290–7, 301–2; Liberation Army (ZANLA), 292–5
Zimbabwe African People's Union (ZAPU), 50, 57, 59, 178–80, 185, 264, 278–80, 285–90, 297, 302
Zimbabwe National Party, 55
Zimbabwe Traditional and Cultural Club, 58
Zvobgo Edison, 51